How to Analyze Data

Carol Taylor Fitz-Gibbon
Lynn Lyons Morris

Center for the Study of Evaluation
University of California, Los Angeles

SAGE PUBLICATIONS
The International Professional Publishers
Newbury Park   London   New Delhi

The second edition of the *Program Evaluation Kit* was developed at the Center for the Study of Evaluation, Graduate School of Education, University of California, Los Angeles.

The development of this second edition of the CSE *Program Evaluation Kit* was supported in part by a grant from the National Institute of Education, currently known as the Office of Educational Research and Improvement. However, the opinions expressed herein do not necessarily reflect the position or policy of that agency and no official endorsement should be inferred.

The second edition of the *Program Evaluation Kit* is published and distributed by Sage Publications, Inc., Newbury Park, California, under an exclusive agreement with The Regents of the University of California.

SAGE Publications, Inc.
2455 Teller Road
Newbury Park, California 91320

SAGE Publications Ltd.
6 Bonhill Street
London EC2A 4PU
United Kingdom

SAGE Publications India Pvt. Ltd.
M-32 Market
Greater Kailash I
New Delhi 110 048 India

Printed in the United States of America

Library of Congress Cataloging-in-Publication Data

Fitz-Gibbon, Carol Taylor.
   How to analyze data.

   (Program evaluation kit ; 8)
   Bibliography: p.
   Includes index.
   1. Evaluation research (Social action programs)
I. Morris, Lynn Lyons. II. Title. III. Series:
Program evaluation kit (2nd ed.) ; 8.
H62.F446 1987   361.6′1   87-17321
ISBN 0-8039-3133-6 (pbk.)

95 96 97 98 99 20 19 18 17 16 15 14 13

CONTENTS

List of Worksheets

Acknowledgments

The preparation of this second edition of the Center for the Study of Evaluation *Program Evaluation Kit* has been a challenging task, made possible only through the combined efforts of a number of individuals.

First and foremost, Drs. Lynn Lyons Morris and Carol Taylor Fitz-Gibbon, the authors and editor of the original Kit. Together, they authored all eight of the original volumes, an enormous undertaking that required incredible knowledge, dedication, persistence, and painstaking effort. Lynn also worked relentlessly as editor of the entire set. Having struggled through only a revision, I stand in great awe of Lynn's and Carol's enormous accomplishment. This second edition retains much of their work and obviously would not have been possible without them.

Thanks also are due to Gene V Glass, Ernie House, Michael Q. Patton, Carol Weiss, and Robert Boruch, who reviewed our plans and offered specific assistance in targeting needed revisions. The work would not have proceeded without Marvin C. Alkin, who planted the seeds for the second edition and collaborated very closely during the initial planning phases.

I would like to acknowledge especially the contribution and help of Michael Q. Patton. True to form, Michael was an excellent, utilization-focused formative evaluator for the final draft manuscript, carefully responding to our work and offering innumberable specific suggestions for its improvement. We have incorporated into the *Handbook* his framework for differentiating among kinds of evaluation studies (formative, summative, implementation, outcomes).

Many staff members at the Center for the Study of Evaluation contributed to the production of the Kit. The entire effort was supervised by Aeri Lee, able office manager at the Center. Katherine Fry, word processing expert, was able to accomplish incredible graphic feats for the *Handbook* and tirelessly labored on manuscript production and data transfer. Ruth Paysen, who was a major contributor to the production of the original Kit, also was a painstaking and dedicated proofreader for the second edition. Margie Franco, Tori Gouveia, and Katherine Lu also participated in the production effort.

Marie Freeman and Pamela Aschbacher, also from the Center, contributed their ideas, editorial skills, and endless examples. Carli Rogers, of UCLA Contracts and Grants, was both caring and careful in her negotiations for us. I also want to note Kathleen Brennan's outstanding work as production editor for the Kit.

At Sage Publications, thanks to Sarah McCune for her encouragement and to Mitch Allen for his nudging and patience.

And at the Center for the Study of Evaluation, the project surely would not have been possible without Eva L. Baker, Director. Eva is a continuing source of encouragement, ideas, support, fun, and friendship.

—Joan L. Herman
Center for the Study of Evaluation
University of California, Los Angeles

Chapter 1
Introduction

The Uses of Statistics

A glance at your dictionary will show you that statistics is an area of mathematics seeking to make order out of collections of diverse facts or data. This is another way of saying that statistics helps you to crunch large amounts of information into usable numbers. A major reason for the development and regular use of statistics is a need to cope with the limited capacity of human working memory. Any human being, asked to think about large quantities of information all at once, quickly loses track. Summarization and abbreviation are always necessary.

Thus, despite rumors to the contrary, you should be assured that using statistics is a way to make some tasks in life easier. Using statistics makes numbers more manageable and casts light on data. However, just as you cannot climb out of a hole on a beam of light, so you cannot save a poorly designed study by the use of statistics. The *design* of your study is critical, and this book should always be read along with *How to Design a Program Evaluation* (Volume 3 of the *Program Evaluation Kit*).

Another ongoing objective of statistics is to find those numbers that *most accurately* communicate the nature of attitudes, achievements, processes, and events that need to be described. Statistics aims to condense opinions, performances, and comparisons among them into summary numbers that can be understood in a single glance—or maybe two. These numbers can then be talked about, remembered, and used as bases for making decisions, forming opinions, or developing theories.

The word "statistics" is used in at least three different ways. "Statistics" may refer to raw data, such as statistics on the incidence of various diseases, or statistics on examination results. But it may also refer to numbers computed to summarize raw data. Thus an average is a statistic. "Statistics" is also an academic subject, a specialization in the field of mathematics. Statistical techniques have been developed to help in the investigation of events in which there is a strong element of probability rather than a completely determined outcome. Because plants, animals, and humans are inherently variable—no two are alike—the study of events associated with plants, animals, and humans usually requires statistical techniques. Individually we are unpredictable but collectively we may discern trends and can assess probabilities.

There are three basic ways in which statistical techniques can be applied: to describe data, to generate hypotheses, and to test hypotheses.

To describe data

Suppose, for example, that you have collected a large set of scores on some test or examination and someone asks you to describe the scores. You will need some way to summarize the scores, to describe them economically and yet accurately. Statistics used to describe data are called, not surprisingly, DESCRIPTIVE STATISTICS.

To generate hypotheses

You may have a large amount of information, such as responses from many different kinds of persons to some questionnaire. You might use statistics to see if there are any patterns in the data, to generate hypotheses about whether ability is related to attitude among males in a different way than among females, for example. Searching through your data for relationships is sometimes disparagingly called a "fishing expedition" but can also be called "exploratory data analysis" (Tukey, 1977), and it is often worthwhile as long as you continue to recognize when you are generating, rather than testing, hypotheses.

To test hypotheses

The same procedures used to search a set of data for relationships can also be used to test hypotheses, to see if there is strong evidence that a relationship is more than just a chance pattern in this particular data. The need for this hypothesis testing arises from the fact that we almost always work with limited data and hope to be able to generalize from our own small samples to larger samples. We hope to draw *inferences* from small samples and the statistics we use to do this are often called INFERENTIAL STATISTICS. Using inferential statistics, or "significance testing," simply allows us to rule out, more or less, one source of anxiety about our sample of data: the anxiety that a relationship in our sample might not have been there had we happened to look at other samples. (This idea is clarified in the preamble to several worksheets.) Statistics gives us some reassurance, but not proof or certainty—that is too much to ask in science! Science is about trying to improve our attempts to describe and to predict and to understand: It is not about being absolutely right. We just try to explain a bit more—realizing we might never explain everything. In statistics, in particular, we want to be able to say how likely or unlikely things are. Statistics provides a way of quantifying confidence, of saying how much confidence we place on certain statements. Modest aims, but important.

By helping the evaluator to describe data, search for

relationships, and test hypotheses, statistics proves to be a valuable and enjoyable pursuit.

The Book's Contents and Format

An effort has been made to include here only the most basic and commonly used techniques. The methods outlined in this book are not only suited to answering essential questions to be asked during an evaluation, but knowing about them will provide you with a strong basis for understanding statistics in general. If you have a chance in the course of your experience as an evaluator, you might want to acquaint yourself with more complicated or more recently developed statistics for special circumstances.

The contents of this book are based on the experience of evaluators at the Center for the Study of Evaluation, University of California, Los Angeles, on advice from experts in the field of measurement and statistics, and on the comments of people in school settings who used a field test edition. The first author's experience in teaching research methods to graduate students at a university in England has also been particularly helpful. Adults often have fears of mathematical topics and overcoming these fears has been a very interesting challenge.

The book takes advantage of a development that has made statistics even more enjoyable than previously: the advent of handheld calculators, microcomputers, and mainframe computer packages. These machines and software all provide ways to remove the computational drudgery from statistical analysis, and the increasing availability of graphics packages will further enhance your power to deal with numbers effectively. Because the analysis of most large sets of data will be accomplished on computers, the aim of the book, and of the worksheets in particular, is to *illustrate* various statistical procedures, using small numbers in small quantities so that you can see what is being done. You can also use the small examples to check that any packages or programs you use on computers are giving the answers you expect.

Because the worksheets are not meant to be used for analyzing large bodies of real data, it has been possible to make them simple, using formulas that are meaningful rather than computationally convenient. Furthermore, the layout has been designed with spreadsheets in mind as evaluators will increasingly use microcomputer software, such as spreadsheets, in the management of data.

Although the book will take you a long way in data analysis, it assumes that some readers will be starting from scratch, unfamiliar with constructing graphs and not able to substitute in a formula with any confidence. Working through the worksheets will build up skills and confidence and introduce notation that will assist those pursuing further studies or looking up other reference books.

On the whole we have kept references to a minimum, partly to increase readability and partly because you will learn more by doing than by reading: How to do it is more important than where to read about it. Only in the last chapter, on the relatively new technique of meta analysis, has it seemed necessary to reference more heavily.

May we make a suggestion about how to read this book? Read it with a pencil, paper, and a calculator at hand. Reading about numbers is not like reading a novel: You need to *work through* a book about numbers, not just read it. So be ready to work things out for yourself.

Before outlining the contents of subsequent chapters, there are some terms that are used in the text that it might be helpful to discuss here.

Some Terminology

Throughout the book technical terms have been CAPITALIZED. If you encounter such a word and have doubts about its meaning, you might try looking it up in the index and reading other parts of the book where the term is used. Many technical terms are everyday words that are used with a fairly precise meaning, and some of these are discussed below.

QUALITATIVE and QUANTITATIVE. This distinction is often made with regard to the kind of information collected in an evaluation. Qualitative data would be in the form of words, such as descriptions of events, transcripts of interviews, and written documents. Words have to be read for their meaning; and the illumination of meaning, the interpretation of events, could be described as the main aim of qualitative data analysis.

Quantitative data come in numbers. Quantitative data analysis assumes, "If it exists, it exists in some quantity and can be measured." Quantitative data provide answers to such questions as "How much?" "To what extent?" and "How many?" In addition the analysis of quantitative data involves looking at relationships between quantities. For example, an evaluator may ask, "Were more positive attitudes about a program associated with having received more information about it?"

Both kinds of data are usually needed in a complete evaluation, and each supports and is complementary to the other. Qualitative data are often transformed into quantitative data by coding procedures. For example, attitudes might be expressed in a variety of ways in a series of interviews but they could probably be classified on a five-point scale ranging from strongly negative to strongly positive. Once quantified in this way, by being expressed as categories, the powerful techniques of quantitative analysis can be employed to search for relationships as well as to summarize the pattern of data. When quantitative relationships are found they often need the illumination of qualitative description and case studies to help us understand how the relationships may have arisen and what they mean.

INSTRUMENTS, MEASURING INSTRUMENTS, or MEASURES. These terms refer to any means by which information is obtained. The following, for example, are all considered measurement instruments: stethoscope, achievement tests (locally made or purchased), observations, interviews, records, reports, checklists, questionnaires.

CASES. The use of the term "case" to refer to a patient or client is common in medical literature but less familiar in educational evaluation. It can be a useful term. It is not always confined to referring to a person. Sometimes data are being collected about classrooms or schools rather than about individuals. The "case" in general is the unit about which data are collected.

VARIABLES. A variable is a type of information, usually the result of a measurement or an observation. The variable "sex," for example, informs us of the gender of a case. The variable "age" informs us of the age of a case. Often we use more complex variables such as "attitude." For example, the question, "Were more positive attitudes about a program associated with having received more information about it?" is about the relationship between two variables: attitude toward the program and information received. For each case, the values for these variables may be different.

SAMPLE and POPULATION. When a poll is taken to predict political voting, not everyone in the population is interviewed, just a small sample. The words SAMPLE and POPULATION are used in the same way in social science and statistics. The population is everybody about whom you are trying to make accurate statements (such as 45.3% will vote for such and such a political party) and the sample is the small subset of the population from whom you actually collect information. As you can imagine, your prediction about the population will be more accurate the larger your sample and the more representative it is. Unlike political pollsters, evaluators usually never do get information on the whole population of interest. If, for example, evaluators have found a relationship between "attitude" and "information" in one particular program one year, they hope to say that, in general, this relationship is likely to occur—in other years and in other instances of the program and so on. They hope to make an inference from the sample they have measured to a larger population. Statistical testing is one way of checking on the acceptability of such generalization. The (unknown) situation in the whole population is often called the 'true' situation.

GROUPS. The term "group" will refer to a group of cases. There may, for example, be an experimental group and a control group. Or cases may be placed in groups on the basis of some characteristic of each case, such as state of health, level of ability, age, or height.

The Chapters

In describing the chapters below, terms are used that may be unfamiliar. They are explained in the relevant chapters and used here for the convenience of being able to indicate content quickly to those who already have some familiarity with data analysis.

The chapter you are reading is Chapter 1, an introduction.

In Chapter 2, ways of describing data from a single variable are presented. Description, summarization, and graphing constitute the first step in data analysis. A study of distributions leads to summary statistics such as the mean and standard deviation and from there to standardized scores (z-scores) and their use in standardized scales such as the IQ scale or reading ages. Box and whisker plots and stem and leaf diagrams are added to more traditional graphical displays.

In Chapter 3, techniques are presented for examining differences between groups of cases: the t-tests, analysis of variance, and the sign test. The emphasis is on not only the statistical significance of differences but also the magnitude of differences. Variations in the dispersions of scores are also considered.

In Chapter 4, relationships between pairs of variables are introduced: the correlation coefficient and the chi-square statistic. Regression and prediction are included in the long section on the correlation coefficient, and procedures for testing differences between correlations are included as well as the usual tests for statistical significance. Measuring inter-rater reliability is another topic in this chapter.

In Chapter 5, the usefulness of statistical procedures in developing measuring instruments is illustrated. Particular attention is devoted to developing reliable attitude scales.

Having learned statistical techniques many people still feel confused when confronted with a large body of data to analyze. With the growth of information technology and the increasing availability of databases on anything and everything, evaluators (and program managers and administrators) will increasingly find themselves provided with the opportunity of analyzing large bodies of data. Chapter 6 provides an approach that can be widely adopted and adapted, using a body of real data. (Examples before Chapter 6 clearly use invented data for purposes of illustration.)

Chapter 7 also uses real data in introducing the technique of meta analysis, a quantitative approach to synthesizing research findings. Some of the recent work of Hedges and Olkin (1985) is presented in simple format in this chapter.

At the end of each chapter, except Chapter 1, there are "Notes for Users of SPSSX." SPSSX is a "statistical package," a collection of computer programs packaged to work together to accomplish statistical analyses. The Statistical Package for the Social Sciences (SPSS) is one of the most widely used packages, especially for survey and social science data, and its latest version, SPSSX, represents 17 years of work by what is now a large corporation. This package is available at almost every large computer site, and a version has recently become available on personal computers (SPSSX PC).

It frequently happens that people start to learn to use statistical packages at about the same time as they start to learn statistics. Indeed, it is advisable to become familiar with some statistical package or easily used programs: Nothing so enhances your willingness to explore data thoroughly as having an efficient way to perform the calculations.

To assist those who are beginning to use SPSSX, there are notes at the end of each chapter on how the statistics dealt with in the chapter can be obtained from SPSSX procedures. These notes do NOT teach SPSSX; they are simply notes to assist those who are becoming familiar with the package. The notes do not deal with the graphics options in the SPSSX system, nor with personal computer implementation of SPSSX. The differences between mainframe and PC procedures should be slight.

Chapter 2
Summarizing a Single Set of Scores

If you have ever tried it, you know how difficult it is to read down a long list of scores and get a firm grasp of what the scores are telling you:

- What is their range?
- What score represents the average?
- Are there more high or more low score?
- Are there any extreme scores?

The first step in data analysis is usually, therefore, to examine the scores obtained on each single measurement and to try to summarize them. In other words, we examine data one variable at a time. (A particular measurement is often called a variable—achievement might be one variable, an attitude measure might be another, blood pressure another.) How do we examine the data? Two steps often are taken to describe and summarize a set of scores: (1) Plot graphs and (2) compute statistics that summarize the set of scores.

The following pages provide an introduction to graphing a DISTRIBUTION of scores (Worksheets 2A and 2B), computing some numbers that summarize how the scores look on the graph, that is, computing SUMMARY STATISTICS (Worksheets 2C and 2D), and then plotting graphs based on the summary statistics (Worksheets 2E and 2F).

This procedure produces a *graph* showing how many times each score has occurred, that is, displaying the *frequency* of each score. The graph illustrates what is called the *distribution* of scores.

First, a horizontal *axis* or line, is drawn on graph paper, allowing each square to represent a score value or values. The score for each case, represented by an X, is then placed on this axis. Xs pile up in a vertical column when several cases get the same score or have scores in the same category. A vertical axis may be drawn, and numbers added to denote the frequency of each score.

Example. A set of scores plotted on a graph:

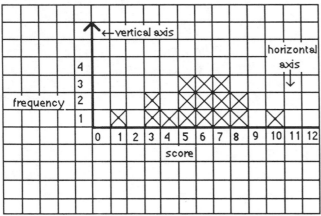

Figure 1

Here, the same scores have been *grouped* into score categories:

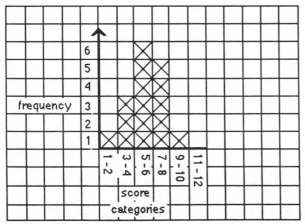

Figure 2

Graph paper is not essential. A rough sketch is often sufficient:

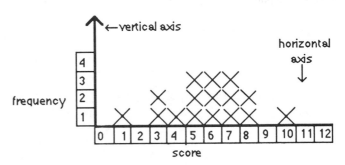

Figure 3

When to Graph Scores

For the following reasons, scores collected from any measurements should be graphed:

(1) *You need to see how the set of scores looks in order to describe it.* Are most of the scores clustered at one end? Or evenly spread? Do the scores seem to form a normal distribution—that is, are there a few high and low scores and many average scores making for a hump-in-the-middle appearance?

(2) *You want to check for outliers.* OUTLIERS are extremely high or low scores. When plotted, such scores appear isolated from the main group of scores. Sometimes an outlier represents an unusual occurrence and should be removed from the data. For example, you might ask a teacher about a student's score that was practically zero and discover that the child had been summoned to the office right after the test started. Or suppose you had a list of gain scores (posttest minus pretest for each participant) with one score showing an enormous gain. Checking pretest papers, you might find that the participant's pretest score had been incorrectly recorded as 05 instead of 50. In general, when you see an outlier, you should ask,

Is this a score from a very unusual case or was there some error in the administration of the measure, the recording of the data, or in computations that may have been performed to yield the score? If the score seems likely to be the result of an error, discard it. Even if the score is valid, you may want to discard it if its inclusion would unreasonably affect the results. For example, if a control group happened to contain a phenomenally bright child whose unusually high scores distort the group's mean, it might be a good idea *not* to include the child's scores in your analysis. Of course, you should mention this decision, complete with rationale, in your report.

(3) *You may need to locate the median score and other quartiles.* A set of scores is well described by stating the *MEDIAN* and *UPPER* and *LOWER* (Sometimes called the first and fourth) *QUARTILES*. These can be easily found by counting off scores from one end of a plotted distribution. The median is the middle score, or 50th percentile point of a distribution: 50% of the scores are above the median, 50% below it. The lower quartile is the point below which lie one quarter (25%) of the scores. The upper quartile represents the point below which three quarters (75%) of the scores have fallen.

Example. Fifty-seven scores are plotted on a graph, as indicated by the postscript n = 57.

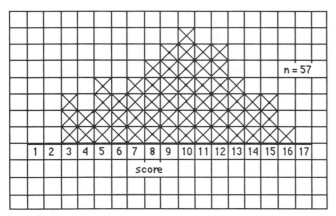

Figure 4

Because half of 57 is 28.5, the median can be taken as the point between the 28th and 29th score. Counting from the left up and down each column locates the 28th and 29th scores. The number along the horizontal axis corresponding to these scores, 10, can be described as the median.

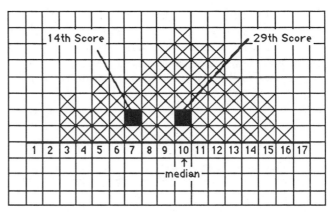

Figure 5

Since 57/4 = 14.25, the lower quartile (below which one-quarter of the scores lie) will appear between the 14th and 15th scores. Since these scores are both 7, the 25th percentile, or lower quartile, can be taken to be 7.

---

(4) *You may intend to use the set of scores for assigning individuals to programs or for dividing them into subgroups.* You may need, for instance, to assign a school's lowest achievers to a compensatory program. Or, if you are selecting a random sample of a district's schools, you might want to first divide them into groups with histories of high, average, and low achievement. Assuring that you sample a proportionate number from each stratum strengthens your claim that the sample is representative of the whole district. In either of these situations, you will need to select CUTOFF SCORES—from performance, achievement, aptitude, or other tests that form the boundaries among the groups you intend to define. Graphing is a good preliminary to choosing cutoff scores. The graph is a picture of how scores tend to group themselves.

Interpreting Graphs

This section describes a few kinds of distributions you might produce using Worksheets 2A or 2B.

1. UNIMODAL: There are a lot of average scores with a few high and low scores on each side

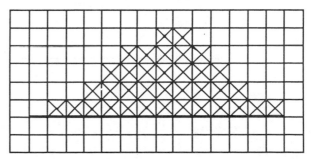

Figure 6

A distribution that looks like the figure will occur often and can be roughly described as a *NORMAL DISTRIBUTION*. (The normal distribution is mathematically defined. A distribution that is close to normal will have certain standard properties that make possible various statistical statements.) Such an array of scores is also *UNIMODAL*. The *MODE* is the most usual score; *UNIMODAL* distributions have just one peak. If there are few extreme scores, the distribution may be steeply peaked.

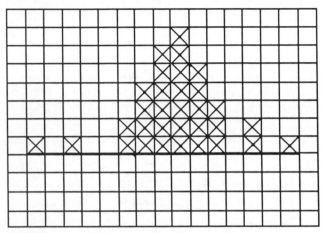

Figure 7

Or, if there are a large number of high and low scores, you might find a flattened distribution.

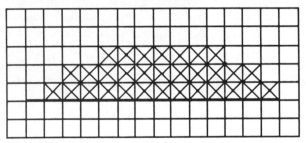

Figure 8

All three of these distributions can be considered *unimodal* and *symmetric*. They will correspond roughly, for most purposes, to a normal distribution.

2. SKEWED: Scores are mainly high or mainly low

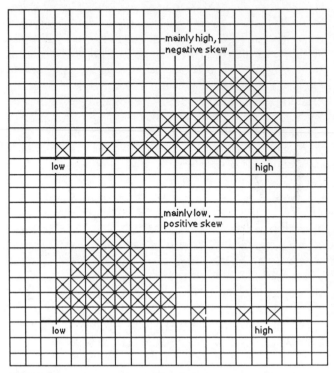

Figure 9

These are called *SKEWED* distributions. The distribution with mainly high scores is called a *NEGATIVELY SKEWED* distribution; the one with mainly low scores is a *POSITIVELY SKEWED* distribution.

A negatively skewed distribution could indicate that the measure producing the scores had a *ceiling*.

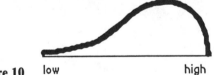

Figure 10

It did not give potentially high scorers a chance to score high enough to produce a more normal distribution. The ceiling is probably a result of the absence of enough difficult items to allow the brightest students to show their strength: However, if the test has been designed to measure *mastery* of certain skills and you expect most of a group students to achieve mastery, then a negatively skewed distribution is what you will want to see.

Notice that a pile of scores at one end of a distribution makes the test *unsuitable* for selection at that end of the scale.

A positively skewed distribution occurs when there are many more low scores on the test than high scores.

Figure 11   low   high

This could indicate a *floor* to the test: The easy items were so easy that almost all individuals answered them correctly, but only a very few students could answer the more difficult questions. It is as though the normal curve were pushed in at the lower end, eliminating very low scores because of several easy items, or perhaps items that could be guessed. If the low scores were all *very* low, this could indicate that almost all the items were difficult.

Notice that skewedness does not only apply to distributions of scores from ability and achievement tests. A skewed distribution can be produced by an attitude scale when almost everyone gives one kind of response.

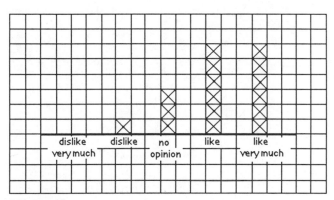

Figure 12

3. BIMODAL: Scores pile up at two different parts of the scale

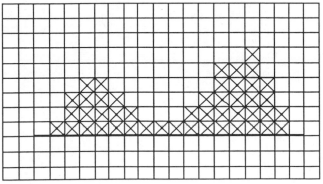

Figure 13

This is called a *BIMODAL* distribution. If an achievement test yields such a distribution, investigate further:

- The test might have a *breakthrough* built into it: Individuals who can answer some items can answer a whole set of other items; individuals who cannot are stumped.
- Program participants may represent two levels of development or experience. For instance, were you to graph results on a spelling test for a group composed of equal numbers of third graders and fifth graders, it would not be surprising if you found two humps in your graph, one mostly from the scores of third graders and the other from the scores of fifth graders.

In most situations, however, it will remain for you to discover the characteristics or differences in experience that best explain the gap between the two performance levels. Differences in background, experience, training, differences in activity prior to taking the test, or other differences between groups explain some bimodal distributions.

Bimodal score distributions from *attitude* measures indicate that respondents are falling into groups with different opinions. If the two modal opinions—the two peaks—are on opposite sides of the neutral point, as in the graph, the bimodal distribution indicates *polarization*.

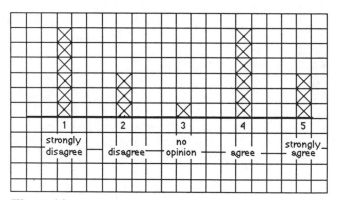

Figure 14

If you should find that your scores yield a bimodal (or perhaps *multimodal*) distribution, you will have to use great care when discussing and summarizing them. For one thing, *when a distribution is clearly bimodal, it cannot be described by reporting a single statistic, such as the median or the mean score*. In the graph above, the mean score is about 3—"no opinion"—but reporting this mean would not at all convey the way the group responded to the attitude question. If a distribution is bimodal, this should be reported and both modes should be noted.

4. RECTANGULAR: Scores occur about equally often all along the scale

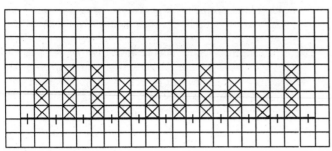

Figure 15

This is called a *RECTANGULAR DISTRIBUTION* and indicates the same numbers of scores at each point on the scale. For an achievement or performance test this would be a strange distribution as there are usually more scores in the middle than scores that are either very high or very low. However, there is a situation in which a rectangular distribution is *expected* and that is if your horizontal axis is not raw scores but is, instead, percentile scores. Plotting percentiles provides a good way to compare your sample with national norms (see *How to Communicate Evaluation Findings*, Volume 9 in the *Program Evaluation Kit*, Chapter 3, for example). There is more information on percentiles, norm groups, and standardized tests later in this chapter.

Steps	Example

1. Prepare a data summary sheet

Make a list of the cases (students, patients, clients, classes, sites, etc.) and the scores you intend to graph for each. Find some graph paper. If there is no graph paper on hand just sketch a graph on ordinary lined paper, keeping all the Xs the same size. Since you should plot a distribution for every set of scores, you can't let absence of graph paper deter you.

1. Prepare a data summary sheet

In this case, a list is made of 26 students and their achievement test scores.

Results on a 20-item test

Student	Score
Arlene Apple	13
Brian Berry	8
Chi Chan	13
David Dear	10
Evan Evans	7
Fred Fink	10
Graham Garden	9
Helen Handler	15
Ivan Inglis	13
John Jones	6
Kevin Kee	6
Linda Lightfoot	4
Marlene Mann	8
Norbert Norris	14
Odette Orme	7
Penny Parker	11
Quinton Quin	10
Rosa Robinson	12
Saul Sanchez	12
Tom Takada	14
Upton Ulm	9
Valerie Venn	11
Wendy Williams	8
Xavier Xerxes	13
Yolanda Young	10
Zelda Zee	12

2. Choose a convenient scale

Decide *how many squares* you are going to need on the horizontal axis. This will determine the scale of the graph. To do this, you will need to do the following:

(a) Decide what *range* of scores must be shown. Do you want the axis to represent

- the range of *possible* scores? This is the range from zero to the top score possible on the test.
- the range of *obtained* scores? This is the range from the highest score on the list to the lowest score on the list.

2. Choose a convenient scale

The achievement test had 20 items, so a 20-square axis is useful. This is the range of *possible* scores. The range of *obtained* scores was 12: from 4, the lowest score, to 15, the highest score.

Steps	Example

(b) Then decide whether each square on the axis will represent a *single* score or a score *category*. Examples of these two types of horizontal scale were shown on page 14.

3. Prepare the horizontal axis

Draw the horizontal axis, and label a convenient number of boxes.

3. Prepare the horizontal axis

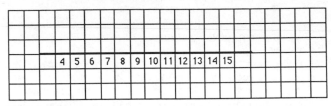

Figure 16

4. Plot scores on the graph

Read a score from the data summary sheet, and mark an X in the box for that score value on the horizontal axis. Repeat for all scores in the list, piling the Xs into a vertical column when several scores are the same.

4. Plot scores on the graph

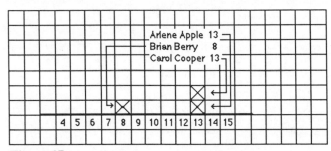

Figure 17

You will not, of course, write in the student's name.

5. Label the graph

Add a *key*, and label the axes and the graph.

5. Label the graph

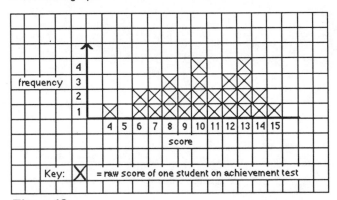

Figure 18

Note: Stem and leaf displays are one of a variety of techniques proposed by Tukey (1977) in his book *Exploratory Data Analysis* (EDA). EDA is now a recognized acronym. The advantage of stem and leaf displays is that the original data can be easily read from the display.

Steps

---

1. *Prepare a data summary sheet*

Example

---

1. *Prepare a data summary sheet*

A list is made of 26 clients and their pulse rates.

Results of pulse rate measurement

Client	Pulse
Arlene Apple	79
Brian Berry	64
Carol Chan	90
David Dear	73
Evan Evans	77
Fred Fink	72
Graham Garden	86
Helen Handler	85
Ivan Inglis	80
John Jones	72
Kevin Kee	71
Linda Lightfoot	78
Marlene Mann	83
Norbert Norris	99
Odette Orme	73
Penny Parker	84
Quinton Quin	98
Rosa Robinson	78
Saul Sanchez	67
Trever Taylor	69
Upton Ulm	96
Valerie Venn	86
Wendy Williams	77
Xavier Xerxes	72
Yolanda Young	74
Zelda Zee	81

Steps	Example

2. Choose a stem

Usually the stem will be composed of tens for two-figure numbers or the first two digits for three figure numbers. You might need to split the stem-categories up to spread out the distribution. This step is often accomplished with some trial and error.

2. Choose a stem

Tens were chosen as a first exploration. The range needed was from 60 to 90.

```
    | 90 |
    | 80 |
    | 70 |
    | 60 |
```

Figure 19

3. Add the leaves

The part of each number that has not been recorded on the stem is indicated by writing it next to its stem, that is, on the appropriate row. Thus 95 might be split into a stem of 90 and a leaf of 5.

3. Add the leaves

```
| 90 | 0 9 8 6
| 80 | 6 5 0 3 4 6 1
| 70 | 9 3 7 2 2 1 8 3 8 7 2 4
| 60 | 4 7 9
```

Figure 20

This display makes the distribution look smooth, with modal values in the 70 to 80 range.

4. Reconsider

(a) Would the display be more informative if the stem were stretched, thus reducing the number of cases on each row by increasing the number of rows?

(b) Should both sides of the stem be used, either to display two subgroups or to label cases?

4. Reconsider

(a) Stem categories were split in two, with "0" to "4" units on one row and "5" to "9" units on the next row up.

```
| 9+ | 9 8 6
| 90 | 0
| 8+ | 6 5 6
| 80 | 0 3 4 1
| 7+ | 9 7 8 8 7
| 70 | 3 2 2 1 3 2 4
| 6÷ | 7 9
| 60 | 4
```

Figure 21

One notices, this time, three scores that are somewhat out on their own in this sample.

(b) It was decided that a male-female split would be useful since female pulses are generally slightly higher than males.

```
 Males              Females
   6 8 9 | 9+ |
         | 90 | 0
       6 | 8+ | 5 6
       0 | 80 | 3 4 1
       7 | 7+ | 9 8 8 7
 2 1 2 3 | 70 | 2 3 4
     9 7 | 6+ |
       4 | 60 |
```

Figure 22

The three highest pulses stand out even more. Interpretation would depend on age and the results of further measurements.

The mean of a set of scores is the average score. It is represented by the symbol $\overline{X}$, read as *x bar*.

$$\text{Mean} = \frac{\text{sum of scores}}{\text{number of scores}} \quad \text{that is,}$$

$$\text{Mean} = \frac{\Sigma X}{n} = \overline{X}$$

Σ is the capital Greek letter "sigma" and stands for "sum of".

Figure 23

The mean score is a balance point. If the scores were weights on a ruler, the mean would be the spot at which the ruler would balance.

Example.

$$\text{Scores}$$

$$
\begin{array}{c}
11 \\
9 \\
9 \\
6 \\
3 \\
2 \\
\hline
\end{array}
$$

$$\Sigma X = 40$$

$$n = 6$$

$$\text{Mean} = \frac{40}{6} = 6.67 = \overline{X}$$

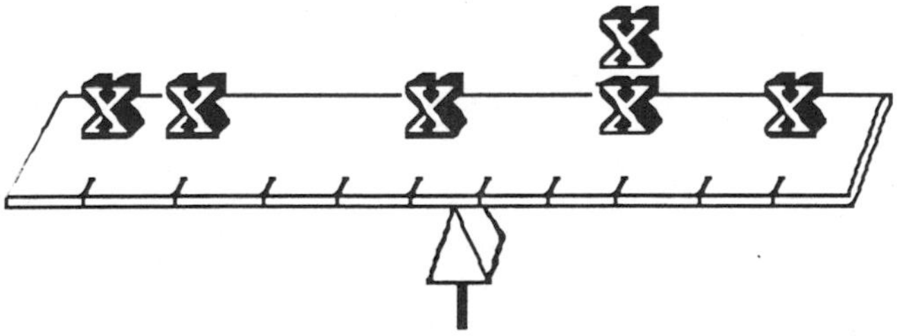

Mean

= 6.67

= balance point

= $\overline{X}$

Figure 24

Symbols for the Mean

If the set of scores for which you have computed the mean is to be regarded as a SAMPLE, then represent the mean as $\overline{X}$ (i.e., as x bar). If the scores are simply to be described, as a whole population, and are not to be used in testing for statistical significance, you might use μ (Greek letter "mu") to represent the mean.

When to Use the Mean

Use the mean when you want to represent a set of scores by using a single numeral. "How can a whole group of scores be well represented by a single number?" you might ask. This depends on the set of scores. If scores are unimodal and tend to cluster fairly close together, then the mean will be a good representative. Otherwise, be wary of reporting only the mean, and make public your doubts of its adequacy. Do *not* use the mean if the distribution of scores is *bimodal*. Watch out for this situation with attitude responses particularly. Be careful, in addition, to check for *outliers* before computing the mean. Since the mean is a balance point, it can be heavily influenced by extremes if you have only a small number of scores.

The mean is an extensively used and useful indicator of group performance. Evaluations often focus major interest on *mean* scores from groups of participants or sites since large-scale programs generally aim at improving the general performance or attitude level of groups receiving various programs rather than concentrating on the performance of individual students.

If you want to describe a set of scores via a single number, however, there is an alternative to using the mean. This is the median, which can be located quickly on a graph showing the distribution of the set of scores. *You may want to use the median rather than the mean if*

- you will *not* need to perform statistical tests that require the mean,
- you need a quickly obtained estimate of group performance, and
- there are outliers that you have not had time to examine.

Unlike the mean, the median is not strongly influenced by outliers.

Steps	Example

Example

The data:

Student	Score on Test
John	4
Mary	8
Susan	6
May	10
David	2

1. Compute the sum

Add up all the scores to get the sum of the scores, sum x.

2. Count the number of scores you just added, and call this number n

3. Divide the sum of the scores (sum X, the result of Step 1), *by the number of scores* (n, the result of Step 2)

The result is the average score $\overline{X}$, the mean.

 Note: If you have so many scores that entering them on a handheld calculator is tedious, you should try to use a micro-computer or, at the very least, a calculator with a paper printout so that you can check that you have entered the scores correctly.

1. Compute the sum

Total = sum X = 30

2. Count the number of scores you just added, and call this number n

 Number of scores = n = 5

3. Divide the sum of the scores by the number of scores

 Mean score = 30/5 = 6

The standard deviation of a group of scores is a number that tells you whether most of those scores *cluster closely around their mean* or are *spread out* along the scale. The standard deviation is useful not only for describing distributions but also for comparing groups. Furthermore, as shown later in this chapter, it provides the basis for *standardizing* test scores by computing, for instance, stanines, IQs, and scale scores.

The meaning of the term *STANDARD DEVIATION* can be understood by considering the meaning of the word *deviation. A deviation is the distance of a score from the mean for its group.* If a group of scores has a mean of 10, then the deviation of a score of 15 is 5 points. The deviation of a score of 6 is –4 points: Six is 4 points *below* 10; 15 is 5 points *above* 10. The *standard deviation,* symbolized simply as *s,* is similar to, but not equivalent to, the average of the deviations of the scores (ignoring the negative signs). (You will see from working through Worksheet 2D why the average deviation cannot be used.) The larger the standard deviation, the further away from the mean the scores are, on average. Thus *the standard deviation of a set of scores is a statistic that shows how much the scores are spread out around the mean. The larger the standard diviation, the more spread out are the scores.*

Example. A distribution with a *small* standard deviation:

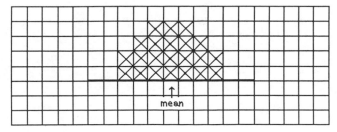

Figure 25

A distribution with a *large* standard deviation:

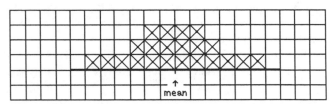

Figure 26

The *variance,* s^2, is simply the square of the standard deviation, that is, the standard deviation multiplied by itself. It is often used in statistical calculations.

Knowing the standard deviation of a group of scores performs two functions for you:

- It gives you a number that indicates the spread of the scores obtained from the administration of a particular instrument.
- It provides a basis for later statistical procedures that you might want to perform, such as tests of the significance of differences between group means.

You will notice, if you look ahead in this book, that the standard deviation occurs in many of the formulas for performing statistical tests.

When to Use the Standard Deviation

Whenever you report the *mean* of a set of scores, report the standard deviation along with it. However, if you have more than, say, 100 scores to deal with, you may find calculation of the mean and standard deviation too time-consuming. If you do not *have* to report them and do not need them for statistical tests, then you might choose to report instead the median and upper and lower quartiles described on page 15 and in Worksheet 2E.

A Slight Complication

There are two formulas for the standard deviation, and therefore for the variance. One formula is for a SAMPLE and the other is for a POPULATION standard deviation. Use the population formula if the data you are using are simply to be described or are to be considered as the whole population. Use the sample value if there is going to be statistical testing.

	SAMPLE	POPULATION
SD symbol:	s	σ (small sigma)
formula:	$s = \sqrt{\dfrac{\Sigma(X-\bar{X})^2}{n-1}}$	$\sigma = \sqrt{\dfrac{\Sigma(X-\mu)^2}{n}}$
variance:	s^2	σ^2

Figure 27

For a population, a lower case Greek letter, sigma (σ) is used for the standard deviation and variance is therefore written as sigma squared: σ^2.

You may wonder why the SAMPLE standard deviation, s, has "n – 1" whereas the POPULATION standard deviation, σ, has "n" in its formula. This slight difference can be explained as follows: The SAMPLE standard deviation is used to *estimate* the POPULATION standard deviation, and you get a more accurate estimate if you use n – 1 rather than just n. This is just one of the facts that users of statistics generally accept on trust from mathematical statisticians. The quantity n-1 is called the DEGREES OF FREEDOM for a set of n scores from which you have computed one mean. You will meet degrees of freedom (often as just "df") in many statistical tables and formulae.

Generally when you report the standard deviation of a small set of scores you should use s rather than σ. As a rough rule of thumb, sample sizes of less than 30 are considered small.

Worksheet 2D

Calculating the Standard Deviation s and Variance s^2

Steps

$$s = \sqrt{\frac{\Sigma(X - X)^2}{n-1}} \qquad \sigma = \sqrt{\frac{\Sigma(X - \mu)^2}{n}}$$

Figure 28

1. Set up a worksheet with 3 columns

Column 1	Column 2	Column 3
Score	Deviation	Squared Deviation
X	$X - \bar{X}$	$(X - \bar{X})^2$

Figure 29

2. Fill in the scores and compute the mean

Write the scores in the first column, add them up and divide by the number of scores to get the mean (as in Worksheet 2C).

Example

1. Set up a worksheet with 3 columns

X	$(X - \bar{X})$	$(X - \bar{X})^2$

2. Fill in the scores and compute the mean

	X	$(X - \bar{X})$	$(X - \bar{X})^2$
	2		
	3		
	4		
	5		
	5		
	5		
Sum	24		
Mean	$24 \div 6 = 4.00$		

Steps	Example

3. Compute the deviations

On each row—that is, for each score—subtract the mean from the score to get the deviation for that score. Write the deviations in the second column.

As a check you can add up the deviations and, apart from rounding errors when the numbers are not simple integers, they should add up to zero. THE SUM OF THE DEVIATIONS IS ZERO. This is a reason why the average deviation cannot be used to express how far the scores are from the mean: The average deviation is zero since the sum is zero. (Of course, one could drop the signs, take the modulus of each number, and then add the numbers and divide by n. However, for various reasons, this is not the strategy adopted as you will see in Step 4.)

3. Compute the deviations

	X	$(X-\overline{X})$	$(X-\overline{X})^2$
	2	-2	
	3	-1	
	4	0	
	5	1	
	5	1	
	5	1	
Sum	24	0	

4. Compute the squared deviations and sum them

We cannot take the average deviation because of the negative signs that make the deviations sum to zero. We get rid of the negative signs by squaring the numbers. (We must later, in Step 6, remember to take the square root to get a reasonable result for the standard deviation.)

4. Compute the squared deviations and sum them

	X	$(X-\overline{X})$	$(X-\overline{X})^2$
	2	-2	4
	3	-1	1
	4	0	0
	5	1	1
	5	1	1
	5	1	1
Sum	24	0	8

5. Divide by n if you are working toward σ (population value) or by (n – 1) to get s (sample value)

The sum of the squared deviations from the mean divided by n or n – 1 yields a statistic called the variance: the mean sum of squared deviations. Let ss represent the sum of the squared deviations from the mean (i.e., ss = Σ $(X - X)^2$). Then population variance = ss/n and sample variance = ss/n – 1.

5. Divide by n if you are working toward σ (population value) or by (n – 1) to get s (sample value)

SAMPLE	POPULATION
The sample variance $= \dfrac{8}{5}$ $= 1.60 = s^2$	The population variance is $= \dfrac{8}{6}$ $= 1.333 = \sigma^2$

6. Take the square root of the variance

The answer you get is the STANDARD DEVIATION. It should make sense as a number that tells you, roughly, how far away from the mean the scores were, on average.

6. Take the square root of the variance

SAMPLE	POPULATION
The sample SD is the square root of 1.60 $s = 1.26$	The population SD is the square root of 1.333 $\sigma = 1.15$

Figure 30

Steps

Example

HANDHELD CALCULATORS: If your calculator has statistical functions, it may well have one key for the sample SD and one for the population SD. Sometimes these are labeled σ_{n-1} (sigma subscript n-1) and σ_n (sigma subscript n), respectively. To check that the keys yield the results you expect, you could enter a small set of numbers for which you have worked out the sample SD and the population SD (using the worksheet) and check the answers given by your calculator. For example, if you enter 2, 4, 6, and 8, the sample SD should be 2.5819 and the population SD should be 2.2360. (You would report these numbers as 2.58 and 2.24, but they are given here as they are likely to show up on the calculator.)

Since calculators differ it is not possible to give exact instructions, but the following *may* be helpful with your calculator:

(1) Clear the statistical register (i.e., get rid of any previous set of numbers that was being accumulated).
(2) Enter the first number and press the summation key, usually labeled Σ. The calculator may respond with a 1, indicating that the first number has been entered and stored.
(3) Continue to enter each of the remaining numbers, following each entry with the summation sign.
(4) Press the appropriate key: either σ_n (sigma subscript n) or σ_{n-1} (sigma subscript n – 1).

Very often you find yourself with data from several groups as, for example, different classes in school, different treatment groups, different age groups. You may wish to look at how these groups differ on some measurement. You could display the actual distribution for each group, but comparisons across the groups might be facilitated by concentrating on summary statistics. There are three kinds of graphs that will be useful here, depending on your purpose.

Steps

---

1. Decide on your main purpose and draw up a table of appropriate data

Purpose A. To indicate the means and standard deviations for several groups, especially where sample sizes are similar and distributions within each group are not strongly skewed. Particularly useful with ANOVA.

Data needed: mean and SD for each group

Purpose B. To indicate the location of the means and how accurately each mean has been estimated.

Data needed: mean, and SE of the mean for each group. [SE of the mean = SD/(Square root of n).]

Purpose C. To display the shapes of the distributions in each group, perhaps with particular attention to outliers.

Data needed: minimum, lower quartile (i.e., 25th percentile), median, upper quartile, and maximum

2. Plot an appropriate graph

For Purpose A. Draw up a table of summary statistics showing the number in each group, the mean and the standard deviation of the scores on the measurement of interest. Construct a graph putting groups on the X axis, and choosing a convenient scale for the Y axis: the measurement of interest.

Draw bars above the group labels on the X axis, at a level indicating the mean for the group.

Indicate the standard deviation (SD) for each group by a rectangle around the mean extending one SD above and below the bar (drawn according to the scale on the Y axis, of course).

For Purpose B. The mean is estimated more accurately the larger the sample. Compute the quantity called the standard error of the mean by dividing the SD for each group by the square root of n, the number in that group. Then draw the same kind of graph as for Purpose A, only making the rectangles represent the standard error of the mean rather than the SD of the scores.

Example

---

1. Decide on your main purpose and draw up a table of appropriate data

The evaluators had posttest data from 4 sites and could not decide which purpose, A, B, or C, was likely to become most important. They therefore decided to plot the data for group 1 in the three different ways and *then* decide which graph they wanted to use in order to compare the four groups.

They plotted the distribution for group 1 (Worksheet 2A) and used that plot to locate the lower quartile (P25, the 25th percentile), the median (P50) and the upper quartile (P75). They used handheld calculators with statistical functions to obtain the mean and standard deviation of the scores and drew up the following set of data:

Site	n	minimum	P25	P50	P75	Maximum	Mean	s	SEmean
1	16	18	28	30	45	70	35	10	2.50

2. Plot an appropriate graph

The three graphs for group 1 were plotted using the same Y-scale.

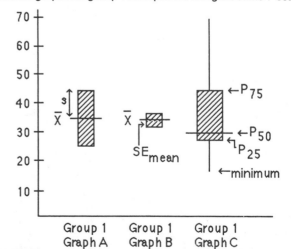

Figure 31

Steps

Example

For Purpose C. Produce box and whisker plots. Box and whisker plots use quartiles rather than means and standard deviations. The box encloses the middle 50% of scores (i.e., it marks off the lower and upper quartiles) and the whiskers might be used to show the range of scores, the minimum and maximum.

You will need to have the scores either rank ordered in a table or plotted as a distribution, as in Worksheet 2A.

To find the lower quartile (LQ) divide the sample size by 4 and then, starting from the lowest score in the distribution, count up this number of scores and note the point on the scale that is about half-way to the next higher score. Call this point the lower quartile. Repeat for the upper quartile (UQ), only counting from the top down. Draw the box and whiskers.

The figure below shows a distribution (such as you might get from following Worksheet 2A) translated into a box and whisker plot.

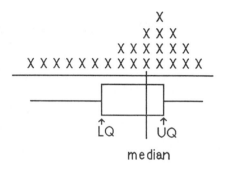

Figure 32

Since box and whisker plots are usually drawn vertically, the one above is "on its side."

Note how the skewed distribution shows up in the difference in the size of the rectangle on either side of the median. A short distance from median to upper quartile indicates that the scores are clustered together in that range. This indicates a skewed distribution.

Rather than extend the whiskers as far as the range, it might be better to extend them only so far as one more interquartile distance, or to the last score within that distance. Other more extreme scores are then marked individually. This avoids a false impression being given by one or two extreme scores. It also calls attention to outliers. The vertical positioning of a box and whisker plot usually makes the labeling of outliers easier.

It was agreed that the box and whisker graph gave the most information, but there was some feeling that graph B might be desirable because site 4 had a much larger sample than the others. It was decided to indicate sample size on the box and whisker graph by making the box width proportional to $\sqrt{n}$ (i.e., to the square root of n).

The data were tabulated for all four sites and then graphed.

Site	n	Min.	P25	P50	P75	Max.
1	16	18	25	30	45	70
2	25	10	20	25	35	60
3	30	20	25	40	45	55
4	100	10	30	50	55	70

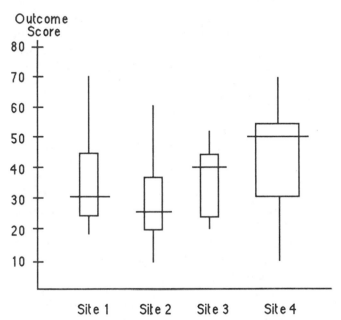

Figure 33

Applications of Data Summary Techniques

The simple technique of computing the mean and the standard deviation for a set of scores provides you with some very useful applications and enables you to understand "standardized scores" such as reading ages and IQ scores. Before coming to these applications it is necessary to introduce several concepts: transformed scores, norm-referenced as opposed to criterion-referenced assessments, and z-scores.

Transformed scores

You will have heard about "scales" in connection with maps: Some maps are large scale and some are small scale depending upon how many miles are represented by each inch. Equally the same map might have been on a scale of kilometers per centimeter, rather than miles per inch. The choice of scale is arbitrary and a choice made for convenience or custom. It does not alter what the map represents, only how large or small it looks on the page.

Similarly the scale used in marking a test is also arbitrary: You could mark a test out of 25 or, by doubling the marks for each question, out of 50. This would be a "simple linear transformation" of the scale.

What, you wonder, is a nonlinear transformation? A nonlinear transformation of a scale *does* alter the general picture. If for example, you decided that only certain questions on a test would have the marks doubled you would change the scale in a nonlinear way. By weighting certain items you could alter the ranking of candidates on the test. That would be a nonlinear transformation of the scores. The pattern of scores would have been altered in the same way.

A simple linear transformation of the scores that you will have used yourself is the percentage transformation. If the test had a total possible of 25, you multiply each score by 100/25—that is, by 4, and then report the scores as a percentage.

> Percentage score = (raw score) × 100/total
> (percentage score equals raw score times 100 divided by total marks possible)

Thus the student who scored 20/25 gets a score of 80%. Transforming scores into percentages is useful in comparing scores on two tests. If a student brought in a report indicating 16/37 for Geometry and 29/40 for Algebra, you could make more sense of these scores by transforming them into percentages: thus for the student,

> the score on Geometry was 16 × 100/37 = 42% (approx.)
> the score on Algebra was 29 × 100/40 = 73% (approx.)

It appears that the pupil got a larger proportion of the test correct in Algebra than in Geometry.

This transformation to percentages is probably a procedure that is quite familiar to you. It can be used here to introduce some important terminology and ideas.

RAW SCORE. The use of the term "raw score" refers to the score on the original scale. It is raw in the sense that it has not been altered or transformed. The transformed scale can be shown graphically by renumbering the original scale. This is illustrated below for the Algebra scale (raw scores were out of 40):

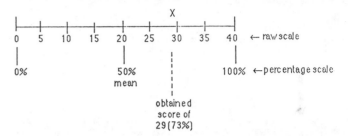

Figure 34

SIGNIFICANT FIGURES. Note also that the percentages were reported using just two figures. The answer our calculator gave for the first percentage was 43.24324-324324, but it would be silly to pretend that all those decimal places mattered! As a rough guide, for calculations illustrated in this book, use three decimal places in calculations but only report results to the nearest whole number for individual scores or to two decimal places for summary statistics.

Criterion-Referenced and Norm-Referenced Scores

When we are willing to interpret a score solely in terms of one individual's performance relative to the content assessed on a test (e.g., 73% correct) then we are using a CRITERION-REFERENCED approach. The score is viewed as a direct measure of the performance of the individual on the content or skill assessed by the test. No reference is made to the performance of other individuals; only to the test as a criterion. If, however, we start to ask how the student did in comparison with other individuals who took the test, then we are beginning to use a NORM-REFERENCED approach. Saying that a pupil who scored 73% correct was at the top of the class is adding a piece of norm-referenced information, comparing the pupil's score with that of others in his or her class. If we report that a score placed the pupil at the 96th percentile on national norms, that too would be a norm-referenced approach. This time the pupil's performance was compared with that of others who had been part of the national sample that the test publishers used in "norming" or "standardizing" the test.

Z-scores

A z-score is obtained by a simple linear transformation of a raw score. That is, it is another kind of transformed score. As we shall see, it has certain advantages over a percentage X score.

A z-score tells you how far from the mean of a distribution the score was, and "how far" is measured in terms of standard deviations. Thus if the z-score is 2.00, the raw score was two standard deviations above the mean. If the z-score was 0.50 then the raw score was half a standard deviation above the mean. If the z-score was 0 the raw score was no distance at all from the mean, that is, it was at the mean. Perhaps you can guess that a z-score of –1.00 would be obtained from a raw score that was one standard deviation *below* the mean.

Note that you cannot compute a z-score unless you have a distribution of scores to which it is referenced.

- A z-score locates a score in a given distribution.
- A z-score tells how many standard deviations away from the mean the raw score is.

$$z\ score = \frac{raw\ score - mean}{standard\ deviation}$$

Since the raw-score-minus-the-mean is called the deviation, we could also write the following:

$$z\ score = \frac{deviation}{standard\ deviation}$$

The z-score is very useful. Although scores are rarely reported as z-scores the z-score underlies many other "standardized" scores and is of use in calculating statistics such as the correlation coefficient (Chapter 4). Just as any set of raw scores can be re-expressed as percentages, any set of raw scores can be re-expressed as z-scores. To transform a scale of raw scores into z-scores we obviously need to know the mean of the scores and their standard deviation. Suppose for the Algebra test the mean was 25 and the standard deviation was 5, then the z-score scale would match up with the raw score scale as shown below:

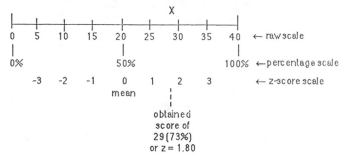

Figure 35

The obtained score of 29 could be expressed as z = 1.80:

$$z = \frac{raw\ score - mean}{standard\ deviation} = \frac{29 - 20}{5} = 1.80$$

In summary, given any distribution of scores, a mean and standard deviation can be computed for the distribution. Using these statistics the raw scores can be transformed into z-scores. As will be shown below, these z-scores underlie some common "standard scores."

Some Commonly Used Norm-Referenced Scales

The IQ scale. The IQ was so called because it originally represented an "intelligence quotient." The quotient was "mental age" divided by the person's actual age. Thus if someone's score on a test was equal to the mean score of 15-year-olds but their actual age was 12, he or she would be said to have an IQ of 100*(15/12) = 125. There were problems with this method due to different variability at different age levels, and the modern IQ is not a quotient but a "deviation IQ." The test is developed using items that are considered to be measures of general ability and it is then given to a representative sample of persons of various ages. This representative sample is known as the NORMING POPULATION because it is the set of scores from which norms are drawn up. The scores for the various age groups in the norming population are then expressed as z-scores so that there is the same variation at each age level. The z-scores are then transformed to a scale in which the mean is called 100 and a standard deviation is represented by 15 divisions on the scale.

- For an IQ scale, the mean = 100
- the standard deviation = 15

(Some adjustment may be made to the shape of the distribution but these need not concern us.) Suppose on the test that was developed the mean score in one age group was 92. Then anyone of that age obtaining a score of 92 would be said to have an IQ of 100, that is, an average IQ. If the standard deviation of scores in that age group was 24, then a person with a score of 92 + 24 = 116 would be said to have and IQ of 100 + 15 = 115, that is, a score one standard deviation above the mean for the IQ scale. The figure below shows the raw score scale, the z-score scale, and the IQ scale for this (imaginary) test.

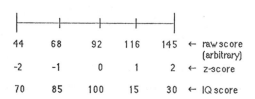

Figure 36

Obviously the numbers do not fit exactly so they have to be rounded. This is done in drawing up the tables to show how raw scores are translated into IQ-scale scores. You can see such tables in manuals for the administration and scoring of IQ tests. These manuals should also describe how the norming population was selected and how large it was.

Grade equivalent scores. Another kind of norm-referencing can be accomplished by relating raw scores obtained on a test to the grade in school of the students tested. (In the United States, school starts with kindergarten at age 5 and then proceeds from grade 1, six-year-olds, through grade 12, 17-year-olds).

If a test is given to students from grades 4 to 6 inclusive, three mean scores could be obtained from the raw data: the mean for grade 4, the mean for grade 5, and the mean for grade 6. The assumption is then made that there are 10 months in an academic year and the scale between each pair of means is divided into 10 parts. Thus if a student obtained a raw score halfway between the mean grade 4.0 (grade 4 tested in month 0, September) and grade 5.0 (grade 5 mean on a test given in September), he or she would be assigned a grade equivalent score of 4.5 (the fifth month—February—of the 4th grade).

For some subject areas that are taught throughout the grades that show steady improvements that we might assume are due to instruction, these grade equivalents are a useful index of achievement. However, they should be interpreted with care. A score that is the same as that of the average student in grade 6 does not mean the student with that score knows grade 6 work. He or she might simply know grade 5 work very well indeed. However, any test can suffer from there being different patterns leading to the same total score, and grade equivalents can give meaning to test scores by providing a comparison with grade groups. In using such scores you should read the manual provided by the test publisher and note how many students were actually tested at each grade level. If there were adequately drawn samples at grade levels 4, 5, and 6, for example, you will feel reasonably happy with the scores in this range (interpolations). You will not want to interpret literally grades much outside this range (e.g., grade equivalent scores of 2, 3, 8, or 9), which will represent extrapolations well outside the range of the actual data.

It is important to note the standard deviation for grade equivalent scores has been found to be about 1.0 (Glass, McGaw, & Smith, 1981, p. 103). Assuming normal distributions this implies that about 68% of any year group will be within one grade of the appropriate grade. A student with a grade equivalent two grades higher than his or her actual grade is likely to be in the group designated "mentally gifted."

Age equivalent scores. In just the same way as described above for grade equivalent scores, age equivalent scores can be developed yielding "reading ages" or "mathematics ages." These are just scores referenced to age norms, that is, to what is normal or average for students of certain ages. The raw scale is transformed to reflect the mean scores for students of certain ages.

The Normal Distribution

The normal curve represents a FREQUENCY DISTRIBUTION and looks like this:

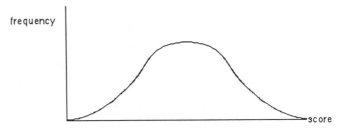

Figure 37

The normal distribution can be *described* in words—it is bell-shaped, symmetrical, its tails are asymptotic—but it is *defined* mathematically by an equation given below. It is an important distribution both for empirical and theoretical reasons. It is found in practice (empirically) that many distributions are roughly the same shape as the normal distribution. This is probably because many measurements are the results of a number of chance factors coming together, and such measurements can be expected, theoretically, to yield normal distributions.

There are four ways in which *you* can obtain access to information about the normal distribution: the equation, if you know quite a bit of mathematics; 100 Xs, normally distributed, if you want an easy introduction; tables of the normal curve for more details; and Pascal's Triangle for fun, which proves useful later.

The equation

The normal distribution is *defined* by this equation:

$$Y = \frac{N}{\sigma\sqrt{2\pi}} \times e^{(-x^2/2\sigma^2)}$$

where Y = frequency of x
  x = X – mean of X = deviation of X
  N = total frequency

Figure 38

If you know some calculus you will be able to show that it is at the point at which $X = \sigma$ (sigma, the standard deviation) that the curve changes from curving outward to curving inward:

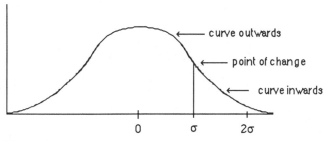

Figure 39

Without calculus, that is just an easy fact to remember and helps you to sketch the curve correctly.

One hundred Xs, normally distributed

Below are 100 scores distributed normally. A smooth curve over them would be approximately a normal curve.

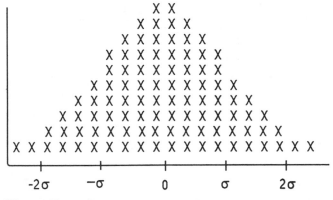

Figure 40

You can derive many correct statements about the normal curve from these 100 scores. For example, what percentage of scores lies within one standard deviation of the mean, if scores are normally distributed? If you count, you will find that there are 68 Xs in the range shown. Since this is 68 out of the total 100 Xs, the answer to the question is 68%.

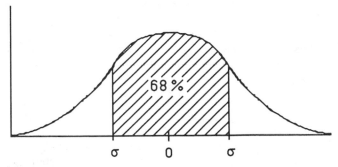

Figure 41

By counting Xs you can confirm the following statements:

- Only two% of scores are higher than 2 standard deviations above the mean (i.e., higher than z = 2.00).

  If we interpret this in terms of an IQ scale in which (sigma) = 15, it means that only 2% of IQ scores are expected to be above 130 (a criterion for "mentally gifted").
- The percentage of individuals you would expect with IQs between 70 and 85 is 16%. Such information might be important in planning a program for this range of ability (70 = $-.2\sigma$ and 85 = $-\sigma$).
- A percentile score indicates what percentage of a group had lower scores than the given score. If someone had a score that was one SD above the mean, (i.e., a z-score of 1.00), his or her percentile score would be 84. (By counting Xs you can see that 84% were below a score of one sigma. You know that half the distribution contains 50 Xs so you only needed to count the 34 between 0 and 1 sigma.)
- A percentile score of 31 represents a z-score of –0.50. (Count 31 Xs from the left tail of the distribution.)

These few examples indicate that, whenever one can reasonably assume a normal distribution, one can relate z-scores to probabilities and proportions. Because the normal curve is so important and useful in this way, a self-instructional program is provided in Appendix A in order to strengthen your understanding of these relationships.

Tables of the normal curve

Obviously the 100 Xs only yield approximate answers. They represent what is called a "discrete" distribution. Only certain discrete values are represented. The normal curve itself is a continuous distribution with all values represented. Should you wish to find accurate answers to questions about the relationship between percentiles, z-scores, and probabilities you will use a table. There is probably one in every textbook on statistics, and one is provided here in Appendix 2.

One unfortunate aspect of the normal distribution tables in textbooks is that they come in a variety of formats and with a variety of titles ("the standard normal distribution," "the standard normal cumulative distribution function," "the unit normal distribution," and so on). The important thing to check is how the table has been constructed. Do this by looking at the proportion that is associated with a z-score of 1.00. You may find any (or all) of three quantities associated with z = 1.00, these being the quantities indicated in the figures below:

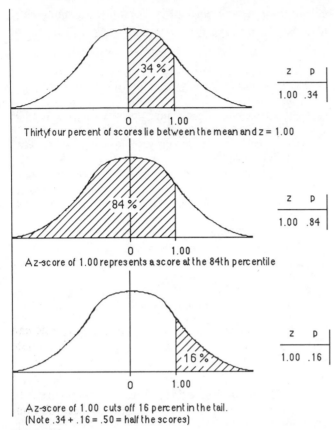

z	p
1.00	.34

Thirtyfour percent of scores lie between the mean and z = 1.00

z	p
1.00	.84

A z-score of 1.00 represents a score at the 84th percentile

z	p
1.00	.16

A z-score of 1.00 cuts off 16 percent in the tail.
(Note .34 + .16 = .50 = half the scores)

Figure 42

Clarify this point before using a table. Which area (i.e., proportion) is the table reporting?

Pascal's Triangle

The relationship of this triangle to the normal distribution might seem a little obscure but treat it as a game and don't worry about the meaning to begin with. Here are the first three rows of Pascal's Triangle:

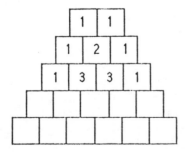

Figure 43

You can see how it is built up. The first line consists of 1 and 1. To construct each row you add up the numbers above to the left and the right. Thus you always start with a 1 (from adding nothing +1). A triangle with more of the rows completed is shown below.

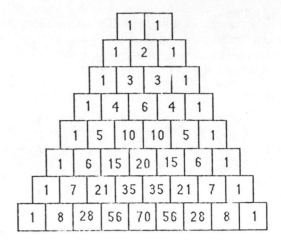

Figure 44

If you take any row of Pascal's Triangle you can draw a normal curve from it, more or less. The graph below takes data from row 8:

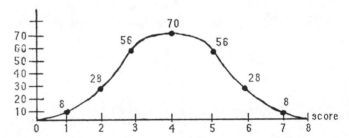

Figure 45

This property of Pascal's Triangle will be useful for the sign test in Chapter 4.

Stanines

Standard scores such as those on an IQ type of scale give an impression of accuracy that is not warranted and lead to the danger that someone will interpret an IQ, say, of 105 as higher than an IQ of 102 whereas they are essentially equivalent; the difference between them is more likely to be due to errors of measurement than to a real difference. To avoid this kind of pseudo-accuracy, scores are sometimes grouped into larger categories. The larger categories also have the advantage of yielding fewer numbers in a long list, so that they are more easily scanned by eye.

The STANINE is one way of grouping standard scores in 9 large categories (STA NINE = standard of nine). The 100 Xs display shows you the percentage in each stanine group.

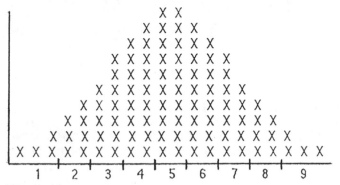

Figure 46

Either by counting Xs or by consulting the Table C.2, you can see that the percentage expected in each stanine is as follows:

```
* * * * * * * * * * * * * * * * * * * * * * * * *
  STANINE                     1  2  3  4  5  6  7 8 9
  PERCENTAGE EXPECTED    4  7  12 17 20 17 12 7 4
* * * * * * * * * * * * * * * * * * * * * * * * *
```

Notes for SPSSX Users

The procedure that will provide you with the data to plot a distribution is called FREQUENCIES. Indeed it will plot the distribution for you if you include the command HISTOGRAM. The distribution will not look like the ones in the chapter because SPSSX puts the score axis vertical rather than horizontal. (Turning the hardcopy output through 90 degrees will yield the more familiar format.)

Not only does FREQUENCIES give you a distribution, it also provides all the descriptive statistics you will need. In order to obtain statistics for box and whisker plots you can ask for PERCENTILES. For example, you want graphs of the distribution of scores on two variables: PRETEST and POSTTEST, and summary statistics for tables and for plotting box and whisker graphs. An appropriate procedure would read

```
* * * * * * * * * * * * * * * * * * * * * * * * *
  FREQUENCIES VARIABLES = PRETEST, POSTTEST
    /STATISTICS = DEFAULT, SEMEAN
    /PERCENTILES = 25 50 75
* * * * * * * * * * * * * * * * * * * * * * * * *
```

The DEFAULT on the statistics command provides the mean, standard deviation, minimum and maximum. SEMEAN provides the standard error of the mean.

To obtain z-scores you must use the CONDESCRIP-

TIVE procedure. Not only will it compute z-scores, it will also use them in the same run and/or save them in the system file. OPTIONS 3 causes z-scores to be computed and labeled by a z at the front of the variable's original name.

```
* * * * * * * * * * * * * * * * * * * * * * * * *
  CONDESCRIPTIVE PRETEST POSTTEST
    OPTIONS 3
    SAVE OUTFILE = filename
* * * * * * * * * * * * * * * * * * * * * * * * *
```

[use the SAVE OUTFILE, with its associated FILE HANDLE, to save a system file that will have the z-scores on it, labeled ZPRETEST and ZPOSTTES]

If you had a measurement on several groups (as in Worksheet 2E) then you could either get the numbers or graphs out separately by using a SPLIT FILE command or you could use a procedure that splits the data into groups. For example, suppose you had POSTTEST as a measurement from each of three classes that are indicated by the variable CLASS. To use the approach of splitting the file you could use

```
* * * * * * * * * * * * * * * * * * * * * * * * *
  SORT CASES BY CLASS
  SPLIT FILE BY CLASS
  FREQUENCIES etc. as shown above
* * * * * * * * * * * * * * * * * * * * * * * * *
```

To obtain the data on which to base a graph to show how accurately the means have been estimated use ONEWAY (one-way analysis of variance), which prints out 95% confidence intervals on the mean for each group. Rounded appropriately these can be used to plot the graph. (The 95% confidence interval is used like the SE of the mean in Worksheet 2E. It is simply 1.96*(standard error of the mean).

```
* * * * * * * * * * * * * * * * * * * * * * * * *
  ONEWAY POSTTEST BY CLASS(1,3)
    STATISTICS ALL
* * * * * * * * * * * * * * * * * * * * * * * * *
```

To obtain box and whisker plots or stem and leaf displays, you have to turn to a rather complex procedure because, being written more recently than many of the simpler programs, it contains these newer types of data display. The procedure is MANOVA (multivariate analysis of variance).

```
* * * * * * * * * * * * * * * * * * * * * * * * *
  MANOVA POSTTEST BY CLASS(1,3)
    /PRINT = OMEANS
    /PLOT = BOXPLOTS, STEMLEAF
* * * * * * * * * * * * * * * * * * * * * * * * *
```

Chapter 3
Examining Differences Between Groups

Here are some examples of the kinds of questions dealt with in this chapter:

- Did clients using drug A show lower cholesterol levels than drug B clients?
- Did phonics-emphasis program students do better in the end-of-year reading test than experiential-emphasis students?
- Were females reporting the same levels of stress as males?
- Was there a significant change in efficacy during the course of the delinquency prevention program?
- Which method, A, B or C, produced the best results on the outcome measure?

All these questions involve examining the differences between a variable measured in two or more groups. Sometimes the groups will have been randomly assigned experimental and control groups (referred to as E-group and C-group) and in other situations the groups will simply be naturally existing groups such as patients at various clinics, students in different classrooms, different sexes, different socioeconomic status groups, and so on. Sometimes "control" groups may have received no treatment at the time of the experiment; in other studies the control group may have received a competing treatment. Sometimes there are more than two groups to be examined. These important differences in the DESIGN that has been adopted for the evaluation do not affect the statistical tests much: It is in the *interpretation* of the results that you will need to consider carefully the implications of the design that was adopted.

Since this chapter is about differences between groups it is appropriate to ask what kind of differences between groups will be examined. You will recall that the distribution of scores in a group is well described by reporting the mean and standard deviation. Consequently there are two obvious questions to ask about the differences between two or more groups: (1) Were the means different? and (2) Were the standard deviations different?

Most of the chapter will be concerned with differences between the means, but it is also important to keep an eye open for differences in standard deviations. For example, one result of an intervention might be to spread out the scores on an outcome measure, that is, to increase the standard deviation. If, for example, a method of teaching was very effective for slower students but held back more able students, one would expect the standard deviation to be smaller on posttest scores than on pretest scores. The

group would have been made more homogeneous on that particular achievement variable. On the other hand, some other method of teaching might result in some students racing ahead and others doing very little: the standard deviation of scores on the same test given as a pretest and a posttest would show an increase; the group would be more spread out in its achievement. Unfortunately the procedures for testing the differences between standard deviations are slightly more tricky than those for testing differences between means. (The tests for differences in variances are affected by the shape of the distributions, whether they are normal or not. The tests for differences between means are also based on models that assume normally distributed variables but the tests for means are usually very little affected by non-normality: They are said to be ROBUST to violations of the assumption of normal distribution.)

Nevertheless, some methods for comparing variances will be presented, just to give a rough guidance to the size of differences that might be notable and also to encourage attention to standard deviations (indicating VARIABILITY) as well as to means (indicating the general LEVEL or LOCATION of the data.)

Remember to Graph Results

Before selecting the worksheet you need for examining differences, be sure not to neglect the first critical step in data analysis: displaying the raw scores graphically. Whenever you intend to compare scores from two or more groups, plot the distributions in a way that makes it easy to catch a profile of each group's performance. Below, as a reminder, are three examples of ways of displaying the distributions or summary data from an experimental and a control group.

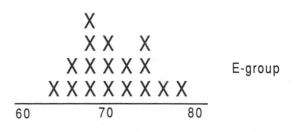

Example 1. Posttest distributions

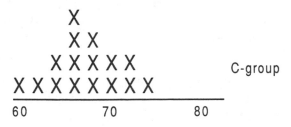

Example 1. Continued

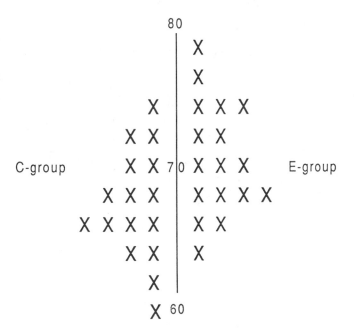

Example 2. Posttest distributions

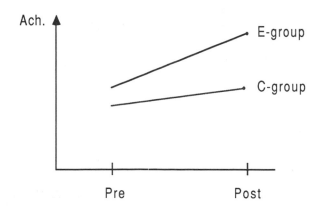

Example 3. Pretest and posttest means

Selecting the Procedure You Need

The next figure presents a decision tree to guide you to the worksheet you need for testing the differences between means. (The relevant tests for variances will be presented in the same worksheets where appropriate.)

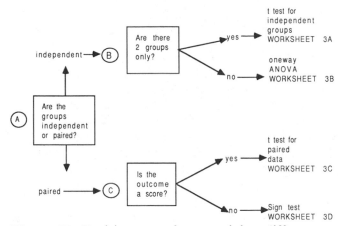

Figure 47. Decision tree for examining differences between groups

Decision A. Are the groups independent or paired? ("Correlated" or "uncorrelated" are terms also used sometimes.)

> Groups are "independent" unless the cases in the groups have been deliberately matched or paired in the design or the "two" groups are in fact the same group measured on two occasions.

Let us consider each of these possibilities in turn. Cases might have been paired in a matched-pairs-random-assignment design (see *How to Design a Program Evaluation*, Volume 3 in the *Program Evaluation Kit*, p. 15), which is a very strong and useful design. In this design, cases are matched on the basis of some characteristic that is known to correlate with the outcome measure. *Then* one of each pair is randomly assigned to the experimental or control group. Another kind of matching is POST HOC matching, in which the groups you have to use for E- and C-groups were naturally occurring groups (e.g., classroom groups, teaching sets, clinic groups) rather than randomly assigned groups and you pick out of these groups pairs of cases that match on some variable related to the outcome variable. This is a weak design, a fall-back measure, adopted as a makeshift tactic when groups cannot be randomly assigned. For example, if you were examining the outcome of treatment A and treatment B respectively, you might compare the outcomes for patients from one clinic with a group from the other clinic that were matched for age, sex, and severity of presenting condition. You would match for those variables, such as age and sex, that you thought would have affected the response to treatment. Although POST HOC matching and non-equivalent control groups do not provide evidence as strong as true (i.e., randomly assigned) control groups, it is better to have this kind of quasi-control group than none at all.

The other way in which paired data arise is when the same group is measured twice (a REPEATED MEASURES design). You could call the "groups" the posttest group and pretest group; each posttest score can be paired with the score obtained by that case on the pretest. In other words, you need the paired data (i.e., the "matched" or "correlated") t-test if you are examining CHANGE scores, or GAINS from pretest to posttest.

Looking at the worksheets will make these concepts clearer.

In short, you are dealing with matched groups, or paired data, if each CASE in one group can be matched with a case in the other group based on some characteristic that makes the two cases likely to produce similar results on the outcome measure. Clearly, if cases in the groups being compared were matched, then each group will have an equal number of cases in it. If groups have *unequal* sample sizes this tells you immediately that you need the *independent* t-test.

Decision B. If you do not have paired groups you have independent groups. If you have just *two* independent groups a t-test is used to test whether or not the means should be considered different (to test for "statistical significance"). If you have more than two means to examine then you need to use a procedure called ANOVA, which stands for analysis of variance. Despite its name it is used to test for differences among *means*.

Decision C. If you have paired data and if your posttest (or "outcome measure") is a SCORE variable, then you will need the t-test for paired data (sometimes called the correlated or dependent t-test).

If the outcome measure was not a score but some kind of judgment, the sign test might be appropriate. The only information required for this test is which one of each pair was the higher on the outcome measure. In other words, the sign test is the method of choice if the outcome can be expressed as a simple comparison between the cases in each pair.

Section 1: Comparing Scores From
Two Independent Groups

Use these worksheets when comparing the mean scores of unmatched groups. The groups being compared may or may not have the same number of members.

Introduction to Worksheet 3A

Testing the Statistical Significance of the Difference Between Two Means: The t-Test for Unmatched Groups

The t-test is a test to see if there was a statistically significant difference between the mean scores of two groups—say, an experimental (E) group and a control (C) group. Some of the logic underlying the *t-test* is explained in the following paragraphs.

Suppose a group of students composing a class have all been taught in the same way all year. You arrive in April and randomly divide the class into two subgroups, giving both the same test. You would not expect to find that the scores of the two random subgroups are very different. On the other hand, the mean scores of these subgroups are not likely to be *exactly* the same either. Because all scores are susceptible to errors and variability, any two sets of test scores—even from essentially the same group—will have slightly different means. Just *how* different the two means turn out to be will depend upon the following:

(1) The sizes of the subgroups. The larger the number in each subgroup, the more you can expect the mean of each subgroup to be the same as the mean of the whole original group.

(2) The variability of the scores. The wider the variation you find among the scores, the more likely it is that the means will be, by chance selection, quite a bit different.

The t-test is designed to help you take into account these two factors—group size and score variability—when interpreting the difference you have observed between groups. If a t-test were applied in the situation just described, you would expect it to show that, given the variability of scores in the two groups, the difference between means was *not* big enough to reach statistical significance. You would conclude that the two subgroups were not really different on the variable measured (achievement, in this example).

Now, suppose that a group of students has been divided randomly into two groups. One has been taught by what you have been told is a good method, and the other group has been taught by a method that you suspect to be much poorer. Again, you give a test, and find the means for the two groups. Sure enough, as expected, one group has a higher mean score than the other. But you have to consider the possibility that this difference is no more than would be expected anytime you measured two small samples; that the two groups are in reality performing equivalently.

One way to see if the difference is too large to be just due to sampling would be to pool all the scores from both groups and keep selecting random subgroups and recording the difference between the means. If the differences between pairs of groups obtained in this way were smaller than the difference found when you divided the students according to how they were taught, then you would conclude that teaching method had really made a difference. This procedure would work well, but it would be very time-consuming.

The t-test is a quick way of accomplishing the same end by applying what amounts to the same procedure. It answers the question, Is the *obtained* difference between the means bigger than the differences you would expect to obtain if the two groups were actually equivalent? In other words, is the difference you obtained bigger than the differences that could be expected to occur by random sampling?

To apply a t-test to the difference between means, you calculate an *obtained t-value* by inserting into a formula the obtained difference between means and its associated standard deviation, representing the variability of scores. You then check the obtained t-value against a *tabled t-value*. The tabled t-value is read from a table organized according to the number of cases in each group. If the obtained t-value is larger than the tabled t-value, the obtained difference between means is larger than would be expected if the groups were not really different. It is said to be "statistically significant."

When to Use the t-Test

The t-test is most often used in conjunction with research and evaluation designs to scrutinize differences in scores—achievement, attitude, or whatever—between experimental and control groups. You might want to use a t-test to check if *pretest* scores of two randomly composed groups were equivalent. The two groups can be considered equivalent if the obtained t-value is *less* than the tabled t-value. This indicates *absence* of a statistically significant difference on the measure used. A true, randomly selected, control group will almost always turn out to be equivalent to the randomly selected experimental group. In the case where you are using a *non-equivalent control group*—one *not* formed by random assignment—a test for significant pretest differences is essential. Conclusions about the final effects of a program will be strengthened if a t-test of the difference between E- and C-group *pretest means* shows *no* statistical significance. This indicates the E- and C-groups probably started out equivalent at least on what was measured by the pretest.

You should compute a t-test to check if the differences in *posttest* scores between two groups, usually an E- and a C-group, were statistically significant.

The t-test has non-design uses as well, all of them situations where you want to know if score differences between two groups on some measure are significant. You might want to test, for example, whether males and females are achieving equally well in a certain program. A t-test will tell if the males' mean score is significantly different from the females' mean score. You can use a t-test to examine the difference between *attitudes* of certain parent groups or between *program implementation* practices at different sites.

In general you can use a t-test to search out statistically significant differences between any two groups you can identify on any measure you can administer—though how you *interpret* the results will differ from one situation to another. Note, however, that the t-test does not tell you whether or not a statistically significant difference is an *important* difference. To get a sense of the importance of the difference in means you will consider the *size* of the difference and you will also compute an "effect size."

**Testing the Statistical Significance of the
Difference Between Two Means:
The t-Test
for Unmatched Groups**

Steps

Preview

Below is a formula for t. The following steps explain how to calculate t using this formula. When you have a value for t, called your *obtained t-value*, you will compare it with a value in a table. If your obtained t is larger than the *tabled t*, then the difference between the means is statistically significant.

$$t = \frac{\overline{Y}_E - \overline{Y}_C}{s_d} \qquad \text{where}$$

$\overline{Y}_E$ = E-group mean

$\overline{Y}_C$ = C-group mean

s_d = a standard deviation (Read as "s sub d." This is the standard deviation of the differences you would get by repeated random sampling from the data.)

1. Prepare input data

For each group, compute the mean score $\overline{Y}$, and the standard deviation, s, and record these values in the Descriptive Statistics Table below along with the number, n, of scores of each group. As you work through the following pages, you will be able to refer back to this table if you forget what quantity a symbol stands for.

	Number of scores	Mean of scores	Standard deviation
E-group	$n_E =$	$\overline{Y}_E =$	$s_E =$
C-group	$n_C =$	$\overline{Y}_C =$	$s_C =$

Example

Background

The students in one classroom were randomly assigned to cover the semester's social studies by one of two methods: projects or regular classwork. Those working in the projects method were the E-group, and those doing regular classwork were called the C-group. At the end of the semester, they all took a 50-item test on the social studies curriculum.

1. Prepare input data

The Descriptive Statistics Table shows that the 12 E-group students had a mean score of 30 on the posttest, and the 15 C-group students had a mean score of 36. Thus the C-group students had a higher mean score.

	Number of scores	Mean of scores	Standard deviation
E-group	$n_E = 12$	$\overline{Y}_E = 30$	$s_E = 6$
C-group	$n_C = 15$	$\overline{Y}_C = 36$	$s_C = 4$

Steps	Example

2. Compute $\bar{Y}_E - \bar{Y}_C$, the difference between group means

Subtract the mean of the C-group from the mean of the E-group and record the result here:

$$\boxed{} = Y_E - Y_C$$

3. Compute s_d

$$s_d = \sqrt{\left[\frac{s_E^2 (n_E - 1) + s_C^2 (n_C - 1)}{n_E + n_C - 2}\right] \left[\frac{1}{n_E} + \frac{1}{n_C}\right]}$$

Here are ten substeps for computing s_d using an electronic calculator. The procedure first produces the values that belong inside each square bracket; then it multiplies these quantities and takes the square root.

a.   Multiply s_E by itself then multiply the result by (n_E −1) --the number that is *one less* than the number of scores in the E-group. Put the result here:

$$\boxed{} = s_E^2 (n_E - 1)$$

b.   Multiply s_C by itself, then multiply this result by (n_C −1). Put the result here:

$$\boxed{} = s_C^2 (n_C - 1)$$

c.   Add the results of Substep a and Substep b and put the sum here:

$$\boxed{}$$

d.   Add n_E and n_C and subtract 2 from the sum. Put the result here:

$$\boxed{} = n_E + n_C - 2$$

This is called the degrees of freedom, (df).

e.   To produce the quantity inside the first square bracket in the equation, divide the result of Substep c by the result of Substep d. Put the result here:

$$\boxed{} = s_p^2$$

(This quantity is the square of the "pooled" standard deviation).

f.   Now, enter 1 on the calculator. Divide it by n_E. Put the result here:

$$\boxed{} = \frac{1}{n_E}$$

g.   Enter 1 on the calculator. Divide it by n_C. Put the result here:

$$\boxed{} = \frac{1}{n_C}$$

h.   To produce the quantity inside the second square bracket in the equation, add the results of Substeps f and g and put the sum here:

$$\boxed{} = \frac{1}{n_E} + \frac{1}{n_C}$$

Example

2. Compute $Y_E - Y_C$, the difference between group means

30 − 36 = −6

3. Compute s_d

(a)

$6 \times 6 \times 11 = 396$

(b)

$4 \times 4 \times 14 = 224$

(c)

$396 + 224 = 620$

(d)

$12 + 15 - 2 = 25$

(e)

$620/25 = 24.6$

(f)

$1/12 = 0.08$

(g)

$1/15 = 0.07$

(h)

$0.08 + 0.07 = 0.15$

Steps	Example

i.   Now multiply the result of Substep e by the result of Substep h. Enter the result here:

     ☐

(i)

     $(24.6)\,(0.15) = 3.72$

j.   Find the square root of Substep i. This is s_d. Enter it here:

     ☐ $= s_d$

(j)

     $\sqrt{3.72} = 1.93$

     $s_d = $ $\boxed{1.93}$

Steps	Example

4. Compute t

Divide the result of Step 2 by the result of Step 3, Substep j. This value is your obtained t-value. Enter it here:

☐ = obtained t-value

Notice that if $\overline{Y}_E - \overline{Y}_C$ was negative, your obtained t-value will be negative.

4. Compute t

Obtained t-value =

$-6/1.93 = -3.11$

Steps	Example

5. Find the tabled t-value

Using Table C.3 you need to find the critical or tabled t-value. This is found by first locating the correct "df" value, the degrees of freedom, which is the quantity $n_E + n_C - 2$ [the result of Step 3d]. The critical value will be one of the numbers on the row for the appropriate df. You need to decide whether you are making a one-tailed or two-tailed test. If you believed that one group would score higher than the other (e.g., that the E-group would outperform the C-group) and it did, then use a one-tailed test. If you made no prediction either way, use a two-tailed test. The traditional level of significance to report is the .05 level. Having selected a column by level of significance and one tail or two tail, the critical value can be read at the intersection of this column with the row for the df.

☐ = tabled t-value

5. Find the tabled t value

The row was for df = 25. The teacher conducted this experimental comparison of projects with regular classwork in order to see which worked better. He had *not* made a prediction as to which method would work best, so he used a two-tailed test. He chose the traditional .05 level and read the critical value as 2.06 from Table C.3.

two tail	**.05**
df	
¦	
¦	
¦	
¦	
¦	↓
25 ————————→	**2.06**
¦	
¦	

one tail	

tabled t-value = ☐ **2.06**

6. Interpret the result

(a) Statistical significance

The obtained t-value may have been negative. Ignore the negative sign if there is one, and compare the absolute size of the obtained t-value with the tabled t-value. If the obtained value is larger than the tabled value, then the difference between the two groups was statistically significant in the conventional sense. If the obtained t-value was *not* larger than the tabled t-value, you must report that "the difference between group means was not statistically significant at the .05 level."

6. Interpret the result

(a) Statistical significance

Since 3.11 is larger than 2.06, the result was statistically significant. The C-group, doing regular classwork, had done significantly better than the E-group.

Steps	Example

(b) Size of the difference

Examine the practical significance of the result. If the E-group did better than the C-group, *how much* better? Did the average gain represent valuable extra learning or significant change, or just a gain of a few items? Making such a judgment is often difficult. Before you report your results, meet with administrators, staff, and possibly community members to find out what magnitude of gain they would consider exciting.

(c) Effect size

The difference in the *raw scores* (computed in Step 2) is important in the interpretation of the results from *one* experiment or evaluation study. But the interpretation of this raw difference depends upon knowing the outcome measure well. Furthermore, different evaluations of the same intervention might have used different outcome measures so that the RAW differences would not be comparable. What we need is some STANDARDIZED mean difference so that we can get a sense of how much difference an intervention has made compared with the differences generally found for this intervention, or, indeed, for other interventions. For this purpose we use the effect size, a standardized mean difference:

THE EFFECT SIZE (ES)

$$ES = \frac{\overline{Y}_E - \overline{Y}_C}{s_p}$$

DEFINITION OF EFFECT SIZE:

$$ES = \frac{(\text{Mean of E group}) - (\text{Mean of C group})}{\text{pooled standard deviation}}$$

COMPUTATION OF EFFECT SIZE FROM t:

$$ES = \sqrt{\frac{1}{n_E} + \frac{1}{n_C}} * t$$

$$= \text{(the square root of the result of step 3h) times (the t value)}$$

Step 7: Examine variances

(You doubtless recall that the square of a standard deviation is the "variance" of the scores, so examining variances amounts to investigating standard deviations.) In order to investigate vari-

---

(b) Size of the difference

The teacher tentatively concluded that an advantage of 6 points in favor of the regular-classwork group, on a test of only 50 items, was indeed educationally significant. He thought, however, that the test, based on general concepts, might have given undue weight to aspects of the curriculum stressed most heavily by the regular program. Perhaps it neglected important learning produced by working on projects. He resolved to devise an outcome measure that might better reflect project-related learning and also to investigate attitudes next time he ran the experiment.

(c) Effect size

$$ES = \sqrt{0.15} \, (-3.11)$$

$$= -1.204$$

This was a very large effect size that caused further alarm over the progress of E-group pupils on the work measured by the test, that is, the outcome measure.

7. Examine variances

$$F = \frac{6^2}{4^2} = \frac{36}{16} = 2.25$$

Steps

ability of scores on the outcome measure, examine the standard deviation for each group and test for the statistical significance of the difference between the variances. The *F* test is used to answer the question, Do two variances appear to be random samples from the same population? To conduct the F test, call the group with the larger standard deviation group 1, and the group with the smaller standard deviation group 2. The ratio of the squares of the standard deviations, with the larger value "on top," is the F statistic:

Significance of the difference between two standard deviations
$$F \; = \; \frac{S_1^2}{S_2^2}$$
$$F \; = \; \frac{\text{variance of scores from group 1}}{\text{variance of scores from group 2}}$$
Group 1 is the group with the larger variance which is put "on top" as the numerator Group 2 is the group with the smaller variance, which is put below as the denominator
The critical value is found from table C.4 using df for numerator $\quad = \; n_1 \, - \, 1$ and df for denominator $\quad = \; n_2 \, - \, 1$

Example

The critical (tabled) values for 11 and 14 degrees of freedom were approximately 2.56 at the .05 level and 2.07 at the .10 level. Thus the variances were not significantly different at the .05 level but were significantly different at the .10 level. It might be worth considering the possibility that the larger variance in the F group arose because projects suited some pupils but were not a good learning method for other pupils. Further investigation would be needed, including interviews with pupils.

Further Topics Relating to Statistical Testing

Before presenting the other worksheets, three further topics will be considered. EFFECT SIZES, important measures of *how much* difference an intervention makes, will be further described, and some concepts generally applicable to statistical testing (TYPE I and TYPE II errors and CONFIDENCE LIMITS) will be introduced.

More About Effect Sizes

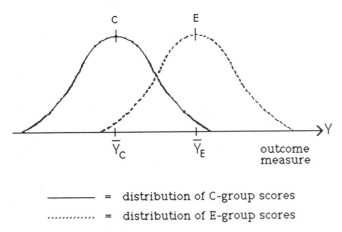

——— = distribution of C-group scores

.... = distribution of E-group scores

The figure above shows the EFFECT SIZE (ES) in a situation in which the E-group did better than the C-group. The distribution of results on Y, the posttest (outcome measure) is indicated by curve C for the control group. The greater the impact of the experimental program, the more the E-group's distribution will be shifted to the right, toward the higher scores. The EFFECT SIZE is a standardized index of this shift in the E-group's distribution. Using a standard deviation calculated by combining the data from within each group (the "POOLED" standard deviation), the C-group distribution is converted to z-scores. The EFFECT SIZE is then the z-score for the mean of the E-group.

If an ES were 1.00 it would imply that the E-group distribution had been shifted to the right by a whole standard deviation. You may recall from Chapter 2 that would also imply that the average E-group member had an outcome score higher than 84% of C-group members. As you can imagine, an ES of 1.00 is unusually large. It's an effective intervention that has such a large impact! Generally ESs are less than 1.00. For further discussion of the interpretations that can be applied to ESs see Chapter 7.

Type I and Type II Errors

(This section will make more sense if you have worked through the self-instructional materials in Appendix A). For those who can stomach it, significance testing can be made a little more complex than simply testing at the .05 level, as presented in Steps 5 and 6 of Worksheet 3A. However, in becoming slightly more complex it becomes considerably more reasonable.

Rather than stating that a difference was or was not "statistically significant" at the .05 level, we can indicate *what level* of significance was obtained: .05 or .07 or .23 or .001 for example. This level of significance, call it the "p value," indicates the probability that your obtained value, or one larger than it, would show up if (a) random samples (of the same size as yours) were repeatedly drawn and if (b) there were actually no difference. That is, it tells the probability of a value as large or larger than the obtained one showing up in random sampling "*under the NULL HYPOTHESIS*", that is, given the condition of no "true" difference.

How is this done? The self-instructional program in Appendix A showed how the probabilities could be associated with scores if the distribution of scores was known. The probability of a given t-value can be computed if the distribution of possible t-values is known. Mathematical statisticians have worked out the distribution of t-values under the null hypothesis for samples of various sizes.

The figure below sketches one of these t distributions. It shows a t-value of 2.2 located in the distribution. Such an obtained value would be statistically significant at approximately the .025 level on a one-tailed test because it lies in the part of the "tail" of the distribution that contains only .025 (2.5%) of the sampling distribution. If we have to consider the other tail as well then the "significance level" would be reported as .05, the significance level on a two-tailed test.

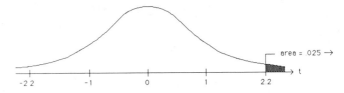

When must you consider the probability as "ONE-TAILED" as opposed to "TWO-TAILED"? You can only use a one-tailed test if before seeing the data, you predicted which mean would be the higher mean. If, for example, you were evaluating a treatment expected by prior evidence or by theory to be effective, you could ask, "Was the E-group mean significantly *higher* than the C-group mean?" and use a ONE-TAILED test. If the effect of the treatment was unknown, the question would be, "Was the group mean significantly *different* from the C-group mean?" and the test would be TWO-TAILED—that is, the differences could show up as positive or negative, in either tail.

If the obtained t-value is way out in one or other tail of the t-distribution expected under the null hypothesis, then the inference we draw is that the value was not actually derived from this null hypothesis distribution. The idea of the null hypothesis is rejected and instead it is suggested that there was a "true" difference.

This decision might be a mistake: The inference might be wrong. Extreme values *can* occur by random sampling. The p value indicates how likely it would be in the long run that such a mistake would be wrong: It represents the probability of making an error of the kind called a TYPE I error. A TYPE I error is made when the null hypothesis is wrongly rejected. In the context of a t-test for the significance of the difference between two means, a type I error occurs when we decide that the sample indicated that there was "true" difference when "in fact" there was not. The terms "in fact" and "true" refer to the reality we assume exists but that we never know about, so we never know whether or not we have made a type I error—not, at least, on the basis of one set of results. We only know *the probability* of making such an error due to *one* of the ways of being misled: being misled by the variability we inevitably find in samples.

Once a t-value has been obtained, the associated p value can be read from tables that have been drawn up to represent the distribution that would result from repeated random sampling. For t-tests the distribution of t-values is recorded in Table C.3 (just as the distribution of z-values is recorded in Table C.2). For large samples, the sampling distribution for t approaches a normal curve. For smaller samples the t-distribution is flatter, and thicker in the tails than the normal curve.

Table C.3 can be used to find, approximately, the level of significance of the obtained t-value. Of course, if you have a statistical package to analyze your data, it will very likely print out the exact p value, such as p = .07, or p = .23). This makes life easier. For those without this facility the following box illustrates the process of obtaining something near to an exact p value from Table C.3, using the value of t obtained from Worksheet 3A:

Locating the exact p value for a t-test as nearly as possible with Table C.3.

The obtained t-value was 3.11 and the quantity ($n_E + n_C - 2$) was 25 (this latter quantity, depending upon the sample size, is called the degrees of freedom.)

Using Table C.3, we look along the row for df = 25 to find the largest tabled t-value that is still smaller than the obtained value (ignoring the sign of the obtained value). We find the value 2.78 and, looking to the top of the column, find this is associated with a two-tailed probability of .01.

We can therefore report: t = –3.11, p < .01 (two-tailed test).

Having obtained the exact probability, more or less, how is it to be used? To begin with, this p value, representing the risk of a type I error, should be reported along with the sample sizes, means, standard deviations and t-value. You then have to decide whether to treat the difference as a "true" difference or not. Traditionally differences have been treated as "true" if p was less than or equal to .05. So a p value of .03 or .002 would be "statistically significant" but a p value of .07 or .12 would not be. However, the .05 level is an arbitrary cutoff point. It is a level that keeps the type I error rate down to .05. But there is another kind of error: failing to "believe in" or accept a difference that is in fact true. Failing to detect a true difference is called a TYPE II error.

As you can imagine, as you weigh up whether or not to infer that there was a true difference, you have to weigh up the costs associated with TYPE I or TYPE II errors. The more you avoid a TYPE I error, the more likely it is that you will make a TYPE II error. The less willing you are to believe in a difference on the basis of the sample, the more likely you are to overlook a difference that *is* there.

What you would want to do, if possible, is to consider the costs and benefits associated with a decision to believe in the difference or not believe in it. If claiming a difference leads people into risk (e.g., into taking a drug that may have strong side effects) then you would want to be very careful to avoid claiming a difference that was not there. You might then want to set a stringent p value, say p < .001, *and* to consider carefully whether the *size* of the difference merited the risk of the side effects.

On the other hand, if the drug were harmless and cheap, your major concern might be to detect even a small improvement due to its use and you would therefore be willing to take a greater risk of a type I error and accept the difference as true if p were, say, .10 or .20.

Another situation in which you might want to consider p values as large as .20 would be in testing for differences among PRETEST means. Your concern there is to locate differences if they exist. You need a test with POWER. The power of a test is the probability that it will detect a true difference (analagous to the power of a microscope). Power can be increased by accepting larger p values as indicative of true differences.

However, let us not play the numbers game too much. The numbers are a guide, but it is the design and measurements employed in a study that are decisive in providing usable information. Turning to this broader purview, the following steps can be used to increase the power of a test, to improve the amount of information it provides:

- improve the reliability of the measurement instruments (by, for example, using longer tests or more raters or developing better items or procedures; see Chapter 5 for assistance)

- increase the effect size if possible (perhaps by improving the treatment, or by running the evaluation for a longer time, or finding something that has a synergistic effect)
- locate and measure moderator variables and include them as factors in the design
- increase the sample size, preferably aiming for equal numbers in the experimental and control groups

These basic principles of good design should be used to increase power in addition to the following statistical strategies:

- use a more liberal p value (e.g., .10 rather than .05)
- use one-tailed tests if possible, rather than two-tailed tests

In summary, the p value represents one piece of information—the probability that the result could have arisen due to sampling variation. If you decide to treat an obtained value as a true difference, to act on this information, then you run the risk of making a TYPE I error. On the other hand if you accept the null hypothesis you might have made a TYPE II error: failing to detect a true difference. The balance you try to strike between type I and type II errors will depend upon the costs associated with each error, costs that have to be evaluated in each situation. Sometimes you may simply present and discuss the data and let users make up their own minds about the risks of each kind of error.

Confidence Intervals

Using Worksheet 3A you can test for the statistical significance of a difference between two means. However, it may often be the case that statistical significance is not really of interest to your audience: They wish to know *how much* difference there was. Consequently the worksheet advised examining the difference in the light of what was known about the measurement used. (For example, if the difference were on an achievement test one might consider the number of items on the test that such a difference represented.)

In the absence of any other information, the observed difference is your best guess as to the true difference, the difference you would find if the entire population could be measured rather than just a sample. Clearly the observed difference from one investigation is not totally accurate. It may be helpful to report the observed difference to your audience in a way that indicates how accurate or inaccurate it is. This can be done by reporting confidence intervals on the estimate. If, for example, you said a difference was 8 plus or minus 2, this would indicate that you expected the true difference to lie between 6 and 10. If, on the other hand, you said the difference was 8

plus or minus 9, this would imply that the true difference was somewhere between –1 and 17, Because this latter confidence interval includes zero as a possible difference, it is equivalent to saying that the null hypothesis might be true: There might be zero true difference, the difference was not "statistically significant." Thus confidence limits actually are an alternative to statistical significance: They provide the same information, only in a way that, it is often argued, is more meaningful. Some journals may even require confidence intervals rather than significance tests.

The problem with a shift to confidence intervals arises when we try to choose a *level* of confidence: 95% confidence intervals are traditional but this does not mean they are any more appropriate than their equivalent—the routine choice of the .05 level for statistical significance. If, as recommended earlier, the actual "significance level" is reported, then the statistically knowledgeable reader can simply deal with this as one of many possible threats to the internal validity of the investigation and he or she may be able to choose between the risks of TYPE I and TYPE II errors.

However, it might sometimes be helpful to report confidence intervals. The way to do this is described below.

95% confidence interval for the difference between means

Find the tabled t-value for the appropriate degrees of freedom (i.e., for the quantity $n_e + n_c - 2$) from column 3 in Step 5. Call this the "tabled-t."

The .95 confidence interval for the difference in means is the obtained difference plus or minus the quantity "tabled-t times s sub d":

That is, the interval FROM

$$\text{diff.} + (\text{tabled-t} \times s_d)$$

TO

$$\text{diff.} - (\text{tabled-t} \times s_d)$$

where s_d is the value computed in Step 3j of Worksheet 3A.

The meaning of the confidence interval

If repeated random samples were taken, of the kind used in the investigation, and for each sample a confidence interval were computed, it could be expected that, in the long run, about 95% of these confidence intervals would "capture" the true difference; that is, the value of $\mu_E - \mu_C$ would lie within about 95% of these confidence intervals. You cannot know for sure whether your particular sample has captured the mean, but it is fairly likely.

ANOVA is a technique for examining differences among independent means. The t-test (Worksheet 3A), for examining differences among *two* means, is simply a special case of the more general approach represented by ANOVA. When you want to ask if *three or more* means were significantly different, you will want to use ANOVA. You might, for example, be comparing outcome scores from three kinds of treatment, or asking if four different sets of instructions were equally effective. In these cases the GROUPS that are being compared have received different "treatments" or interventions and can be thought of as TREATMENT GROUPS. In other situations you might be comparing scores among PRE-EXISTING GROUPS, such as clients from different clinics, or students from different ethnic backgrounds. Whether the groups are treatment groups, defined by the kind of intervention or treatment they have received, or pre-existing groups, defined by some characteristic they share, will make no difference to the statistical procedures; it will only affect the interpretation.

So, for ANOVA, you will have SCORES from several GROUPS. These scores could be displayed as distributions, as below, showing the scores of four groups, A, B, C, and D. (Capital Ys have been used whereas previously we have used capital Xs for raw scores. We use Ys here to emphasize that the scores are the scores on the dependent variable, such as a posttest.)

```
group A:                Y
                  Y Y Y Y Y
                Y Y Y Y Y Y Y
              _____ >>

group B:                      Y
                        Y Y Y Y Y
                      Y Y Y Y Y Y Y
              _____ >>

group C:              Y
                  Y Y Y Y Y
                Y Y Y Y Y Y Y
              _____ >>

group D:                Y
                    Y Y Y Y Y
                  Y Y Y Y Y Y Y
              _____ >>
```

Were the means significantly different?

What is meant by this question? Even if the four groups were *not* different on the variable measured by the Y score, it would be surprising if the four means were exactly equal. They would differ because they are small samples. What we want to ask is, How unequal should the means be for the differences between them to be considered more than sampling variation?

We answer this in two ways: by testing for statistical evidence and by examining the magnitude of the differences.

Statistical significance. The test for statistical significance will tell us how unlikely the observed differences would be in a set of random samples from a single population. If such differences would be very unlikely then we would note that the differences among means were statistically significant. This statistical significance is assessed by an F test in which the variance of scores caused by the way the means differ BETWEEN GROUPS is compared with the variance of scores found WITHIN each group. The variance is called the MEAN SQUARE and represented by MS. You may remember from Chapter 2, page 26, that

$$\text{sample variance} = \frac{\text{sum of squares}}{\text{df}} = \frac{\text{SS}}{n-1}$$

This quantity is called the mean square, MS.

The test for the significance of the difference between the means uses the ratio of two variances:

$$F = \frac{\text{MS BETWEEN}}{\text{MS WITHIN}}$$

A method for computing this F ratio is described in Worksheet 3B.

Magnitude of the differences. Graphing the results will be important in examining the sizes of the differences, as will considering what the differences mean in terms of the actual measure used. It may also be useful to express the differences in terms of effect sizes.

One-Way ANOVA:
Comparing Three or More Groups

Steps	Example

Three teachers were discussing new trends in the teaching of history. One "traditionalist" rejected new approaches and declared that lecture-and-notes was entirely sufficient. One teacher favored creating atmosphere and a feeling for the times with liberal use of audio-visual materials, and the third felt there may be some mileage in the use of "original sources," particularly to stimulate insight into problems in the interpretation of historical events.

They were keen to explore the effects of the three teaching approaches, so they selected a curriculum unit, agreed on objectives, and randomly assigned 36 pupils to make three equivalent groups of 12. On an immediate posttest results were similar to those shown in the table below. (Small, simple numbers have been chosen to make the computations clear and only 18 scores are presented.)

student	group	posttest
001	trad (A)	7
002	trad (A)	7
003	trad (A)	9
004	trad (A)	9
005	trad (A)	11
006	trad (A)	11
007	a-v (B)	2
008	a-v (B)	2
009	a-v (B)	5
010	a-v (B)	5
011	a-v (B)	8
012	a-v (B)	8
013	orig (C)	2
014	orig (C)	2
015	orig (C)	4
016	orig (C)	4
017	orig (C)	6
018	orig (C)	6

Steps

Example

1. Compute the means and standard deviations for each group

You almost always need to know descriptive statistics for groups so this is a good starting point for any further analysis of the data.

1. Compute the means and standard deviations for each group

SUMMARY STATISTICS FOR THE THREE
TREATMENT GROUPS on the posttest

group	n	mean	SD
trad (A)	**6**	9.00	1.789
a-v (B)	**6**	5.00	2.683
orig (C)	**6**	4.00	1.789

2. Graph the distributions and the summary statistics

Graph the distributions in a way that facilitates comparisons between the groups and graph the summary statistics using one of the methods suggested in Chapter 2.

2. Graph the distributions and the summary statistics

DISTRIBUTIONS OF SCORES IN THE
TREATMENT GROUPS

GROUP A

```
                          x       x           x
                          x       x           x
    1   2   3   4   5   6   7   8   9  10  11
```

GROUP B

```
        x           x           x
        x           x           x
    1   2   3   4   5   6   7   8   9
```

GROUP C

```
        x       x       x
        x       x       x
    1   2   3   4   5   6   7   8   9
```

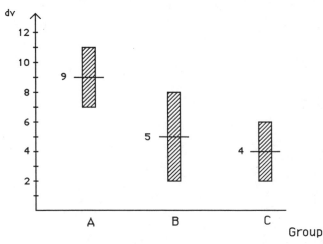

Steps	Example

3. Compute the within-group SS and df

Steps

Within each group (i.e., for each group separately), compute the sum of the squared deviations from the mean. Rather than computing these directly they can be obtained from the standard deviations using the formula below:

For group A:

$$SS_A = s_A^2 \times (n_A - 1)$$

The within-groups df is the group-size minus one:

$$df_A = n_A - 1$$

When these values have been computed, sum them to give totals for the WITHIN groups statistics:

$$SS \text{ within} = SS_A + SS_B + SS_C \text{ etc.}$$
$$=$$

$$df \text{ within} = df_A + df_B + df_C \text{ etc.}$$
$$=$$

Example

OR

$$(SS_A = \Sigma (Y - \bar{Y}_A)^2$$
$$= 2(7-9)^2 + 2(9-9)^2 + 2(11-9)^2$$
$$= 8 \quad + \quad 0 \quad + \quad 8$$
$$= 16.00$$

$$s_A^2 = (n_A - 1) = (1.789)^2 \times 5$$
$$= 16.00$$

Working similarly for the other groups yielded data recorded in the table of summary statistics:

SUMMARY STATISTICS FOR THE THREE
TREATMENT GROUPS on the posttest

group	n	mean	SD	SS	df
A	6	9.00	1.789	16	5
B	6	5.00	2.683	36	5
C	6	4.00	1.789	16	5

Summing to give totals for the WITHIN group statistics:

$$SS \text{ within} = SS_A + SS_B + SS_C$$
$$= 68$$

$$df \text{ within} = df_A + df_B + df_C$$
$$= 15$$

(Note that df within = N − K)

4. Compute the between-group SS and df

Steps

The between group SS is the SS you get if

(1) you replace every score with the mean for the group which that score belongs to and
(2) you then treat the entire set of scores as one set of data.

The between groups degrees of freedom is the number of the groups minus 1.

$$df \text{ between} = K - 1$$
where K = the number of groups

Example

Replacing every score with the mean for the group to which that score belonged:

THIS:

A	B	C
7	2	2
7	2	2
9	5	4
9	5	4
11	8	6
11	8	6

BECOMES:

A	B	C
9	5	4
9	5	4
9	5	4
9	5	4
9	5	4
9	5	4

Steps	Example

Example side:

The mean of all scores was 6.00

BETWEEN GROUP = SUM OF SQUARED
SUM OF SQUARES   DEVIATIONS FROM THE MEAN

For the data above, right:

$$SS_B = 6(9-6)^2 + 6(5-6)^2 + 6(4-6)^2$$

$$= 54 \quad + \quad 6 \quad + \quad 24$$

$$= 84$$

df between = number of groups -1
$$= K-1$$
$$= 3-1$$
$$= 2$$

5. Complete the ANOVA table and look up F in Table C.4

It has become traditional to report the ANOVA in a table with these headings:

SOURCE	df	SS	MS	F
between groups				
within groups				

5. Complete the ANOVA table and look up F in Table C.4

SOURCE	df	SS	MS	F
between groups	2	84.00	42.00	9.265
within groups	15	68.00	4.53	

"Source" refers to the source of variation. In the case of a one-way ANOVA, the sources are WITHIN or BETWEEN groups.

The F value, as already stated, is the ratio (MS between/MS within). If the obtained F value was larger than the tabled value in Table C.4, then the differences among means was statistically significant at the indicated level. The tabled or critical F value is found from Table C.4 by locating the column using df between (from the above table) and the row by using df within, for the level of significance chosen.

The obtained F value was greater than the tabled F for the .05 level. (The tabled F was 3.68.) Therefore, for this sample, the differences among means were statistically significant at the .05 level.

6. Examine differences between variances

Below are two tests for the statistical significance of the difference between variances from independent groups. The first one, the simpler of the two, answers the following question: How likely is it, given samples of the size used, that the ratio of the largest variance to the smallest variance would be as large as that obtained, if the groups were simply random samples from a single population? Unfortunately it should only be used when there are the same number of cases in each group, in other words, when sample sizes are equal. (If sample sizes are unequal see the Bartlett test, below.)

6. Examine differences between variances

| Steps | Example |

THE Fmax TEST

For variances from independent groups of equal size

$$F_{max} = \frac{\text{largest variance}}{\text{smallest variance}} = \frac{s^2 \text{ largest}}{s^2 \text{ smallest}}$$

NOTES:

Each s is calculated using $(n - 1)$ (i.e., it is the sample value estimating a population value). For critical values at the .05 level consult table C.5 in Appendix C. To enter the table use the same $(n - 1)$ as was used in the computations of the s values.

For unequal sample sizes there is the Bartlett test:

THE Fmax TEST

For variances from independent groups of equal size

$$F_{max} = \frac{(2.683)^2}{(1.789)^2} = 2.25$$

NOTES:

The critical value at the .05 level was 10.8 (table C.5 in Appendix C). The differences in variances were not statistically significant.

THE BARTLETT TEST
for homogeneity of variances

$$B = \frac{2.30259}{C}[df_w \log_{10} MS_w - \Sigma(df \log_{10} s^2)]$$

$$\text{where } C = 1 + \frac{\Sigma(\frac{1}{df}) - \frac{1}{df_w}}{3(k - 1)}$$

The summations are over groups.

---

7. Examine pairs of means

Note that a significant F value only implies that somewhere among the means there was at least one that was significantly different from another. It may be of interest to compare the means in pairs to locate the ones that were significantly different from others. There are a number of "range tests" for doing this. The following is one of the simplest and most useful: the Tukey test for "honestly significant differences."

Tukey's HSD Range Test

To apply Tukey's HSD test:

(1) Look up Q in Table C.6.
(2) Compute the quantity Q $\times$ SQRT (MSwithin/N) = HSD = honestly significant difference.

(3) Complete the table showing differences among all possible pairs of means.

---

7. Examine pairs of means

Tukey's HSD Range Test

(1) Looking up q in Table C.6 for df within = 15 and 3 means gave q = 3.67 for .05.
(2) These gave values for HSD of

$$3.67 \times \text{SQRT } [(MS \text{ within}/N)]$$
$$= 3.67 \times 0.502$$
$$= 1.84$$

(3) Completing the table showing differences among all possible pairs of means:

Steps

Example

Group	A	B	C
A			
B	-4.0*		
C	-5.0*	-1.0	

(4) Star those differences that are larger than the HSD. The differences that are starred were statistically significant at the .05 level. That is, the risk of a type I error in claiming these differences to be true was less than .05 per experiment.

(5) If one group was a no-treatment or competing treatment control group, express the means of the other groups as effect sizes against the control group mean, using the square root of the MS-within as the pooled standard deviation.

(4) The differences starred were statistically significant at the .05 level. That is, the risk of at least one type I error in claiming these differences to be true was less than .05 per experiment, using two-tailed tests.

(5) Effect sizes for the pairs of means were added to the table, treating the traditional treatment as the control against which the others were compared. Effect sizes are shown above the diagonal:

Group	A	B	C
A		-1.88	-2.35
B	-4.0		-0.47
C	-5.0	-1.0	

6. Interpret differences between means, raw and standardized

The interpretation will depend heavily on how the groups were constituted, that is, on the *design* of the investigation. If groups were randomly assigned and other threats to internal validity are controlled by the design, it might be possible to say that one "treatment" *caused* better results than the another. If groups were non-equivalent the interpretation should be more cautious and should speak more of an *association* of good outcomes with such and such a treatment.

6. Interpret differences between means, raw and standardized

Since the groups were randomly assigned, they can be considered to have been "equivalent" before the teaching experiment. Thus some of the differences in posttest scores could be attributed to the effects of the teaching. Unfortunately, the "teaching" consisted not only of three different methods but also of three different teachers. The different *teachers* might have accounted for some of the differences in learning outcomes, and there was no way in this experiment to disentangle the effects of the teacher from the effects of the method. To put it technically: Method and teacher were confounded.

The following conversation illustrates some of the problems of interpretation.

TRADITIONALIST: As I expected, my group did best: a mean of 9 as opposed to means of 4 or 5. You can't beat the old chalk and talk approach. Why do you think it's been around so long?

Steps	Example
	METHODOLOGIST: [without a lot of conviction] The results of a small experiment must be treated with great caution.
	EXPERIENTIALIST: Sounds like a load of jargon. Can we ignore the results?
	METHODOLOGIST: Well, not really. The means we've obtained are still the best estimate of the effects of the three methods, given that we haven't any other controlled experiments to go by. There's another interpretation, though: that the means indicated that he was a better teacher than you or I. In other words, it wasn't the method, it was the teacher. The two things—teacher and method—were confounded, you see.
	TRADITIONALIST: OK, we must obviously repeat the experiment and YOU do the chalk-and-talk and I'll use your original sources. I'll bet chalk-and-talk will still win.
	EXPERIENTIALIST: But you might not try to teach well if you were using a method you didn't agree with.
	METHODOLOGIST: In other words there's another factor to be considered in future experiments: the teacher's attitude toward the method to be used.
	TRADITIONALIST: Why do we need more experiments? Is it because you didn't like the outcome of this one?
	METHODOLOGIST: Not at all. Experiments always need replicating before we can have any confidence in the results. That's standard scientific practice.
	EXPERIENTIALIST: Well, I think we should change the test. I don't think it was fair to the experiential approach. A lot of the questions were about facts.
	TRADITIONALIST: Well YOU helped to create the test and you agreed that it was fair. You maintained that your students would learn the facts through their "experiences." You can't object now, just because you've seen the results.
	EXPERIENTIALIST: I can and I do!
	METHODOLOGIST: We could improve the experiment by having two independent teachers examine each item on the posttest and declare whether it favored one or other of the methods. Then we could examine the outcomes by groups of items as well as by the whole test. It would increase the credibility of the outcome measure.
	EXPERIENTIALIST: For that matter I think we should look at attitudes, not just at what they've learned. Enjoyment of a subject counts for something doesn't it?
	METHODOLOGIST: It counts for a lot, I quite agree. We could include an attitude measure next time, though it would be difficult to construct one just out of the blue. We should get someone independent to interview some of the students from each group, probing for indications of effects we haven't considered and also trying to get some ideas about the enjoyment of each method.
	TRADITIONALIST: Who's going to spend all that time?
	EXPERIENTIALIST: We could get some of the older students involved. It would be a good experience for them, and the students might be more honest with them than with a grownup. I think *enjoyment* is *very* important so we should try to measure it.
	TRADITIONALIST: The students enjoy my methods as much as yours. I don't need measurements to tell me that. And the idea of repeating the experiment just seems like a waste of time to me.

Steps	Example
	EXPERIENTIALIST: I don't agree with you at all about the students' enjoyment. Several students said to me. . .

EXPERIENTIALIST: I don't agree with you at all about the students' enjoyment. Several students said to me. . .

METHODOLOGIST: [interjecting] This disagreement is one reason why more experiments are not a waste of time. We're nowhere near any agreement on the interpretation of the data, let alone a good understanding of the effects of these different approaches. Furthermore, if the traditional chalk-and-talk approach really is consistently better than other approaches—even if used by teachers who would prefer some other approach—then we need to know that. It would be a very serious matter to go on teaching in a way that made students achieve less than they might, don't you agree? We do need more evidence. I suggest we run the experiment again on the unit we teach next term and this time we'll toss coins to decide who teaches by what method . . .

TRADITIONALIST: [interjecting] How's that going to help? Method and teacher will still be confounded. We'd need lots of groups of teachers all randomly assigning themselves before we'd have anywhere near enough evidence.

METHODOLOGIST: Yes, that's what I was about to say. We'll invite other teachers in other schools to run similar experiments and then we'll have a conference to compare results. We could even do a meta analysis. [Chapter 7]

EXPERIENTIALIST: Well, at least it would mean that teachers would find out about the experientialist approach. That can't be a bad thing.

TRADITIONALIST: I can just see what will happen. You two, for example, will slip a lot more chalk-and-talk into your methods now you've seen how much better my students did.

METHODOLOGIST: Well, what you're saying there is that we need some implementation measures and you're absolutely right. Why don't we make videos? Then there's a record of exactly what has happened; it can be analyzed in many ways. We may decide, for example, that we're asking a completely wrong question. We may decide that what needs to be examined for any lesson is the demand for active responding, or the amount of student talk, or the extent of individualization, or the embedding of the instruction in students' experiences.

EXPERIENTIALIST: I think we need a fourth approach, which consists of all three approaches in equal quantities: Variety is the spice of life. I bet that approach would win on both attitudes and achievement.

TRADITIONALIST: This is getting ridiculously complicated.

METHODOLOGIST: Why shouldn't it be complicated? Is there a rule that says social science has to be easy and simple? We're still learning to *do* social science, as is clear from the debates about how it should be done.

Here's another complication: One method might suit certain kinds of students more than other kinds, depending upon their preferred learning style or personality or something we haven't thought of. Still, with enough experiments, enriched by the qualitative data from videos and interviews, we might begin to assess whether "aptitude treatment interactions" are substantial or not. Here's to a few multi-factor ANOVAs! [beyond the scope of this book, but see notes for SPSSX users]

Steps	Example
	Note to the reader. One reason for including the above conversation is to illustrate that the analysis of the data from one evaluation often raises as many questions, if not more, than you started out with. Furthermore the analysis rarely leads to an unchallengeable conclusion. Data analysis in particular, and evaluation in general, simply contributes *a little* to the accumulation of evidence and theory.
	It should be noted that if your evidence does not become part of the retrievable information available to evaluators and researchers, it is essentially lost. It may have been useful locally but it will not have helped in the accumulation of knowledge. If you do not publish your evaluation results, send them to a document storage and retrieval service such as the Educational Resources and Information Center (ERIC) for education or a DATABASE, as these become available, for social or medical studies. See Newton (1987) for a report relevant to the above invented data and for an attempt to encourage the publication of small-scale experiments.

Comparing Scores From Matched Groups

Use this section when comparing results from two groups, the members of which have been, or can be, matched. Since each member of one group is matched with a member of the other group, the numbers in each group will always be the same.

Testing the Statistical Significance of the Difference Between Two Means: The t-Test for Paired Data

The t-test is a way of testing whether or not two groups can be considered to be equivalent on some measure. The mean score on the measure is computed for each group, and a t-test is used to see if the difference between the two means is large enough to be considered statistically significant or whether the difference is of a size that could easily have occurred in random samples.

Suppose you have found that the experimental (E) group's mean was higher than that of the control (C) group. Someone might argue that *any* two groups will generally yield different means when tested. The two groups are not *really* different on the measure; they just appear to be. The observed difference in means is just a reflection of the way sample means always differ slightly from the population mean, μ. The purpose of the t-test is to see to what extent this argument is tenable. The t-test indicates whether the difference in means is greater than would have occurred just because of the only-to-be-expected variation in obtained sample means. If the difference is so large that you would find it fewer than 5 times out of 100 when indeed there was no *real* difference

between the E-group and C-group's performance, then it is called statistically significant at the .05 level.

Note, however, that the t-test does not tell you whether or not a statistically significant difference is an *important* difference. You or your evaluation users will have to judge that for yourselves by examining differences and asking if they are large enough to be considered substantively important.

When to Use the t-Test for Paired Data

Use this test when you need to know if the difference between the results from two *matched* groups is statistically significant, that is, not just a chance result. The pairing, or *matching*, should have been done on the basis of some characteristic likely to be related, positively or negatively, to the outcome measure you are using.

You should also use this test if you wish to see if there have been significant changes in a *single* group between pretest scores and posttest scores. Each person's posttest is matched with his or her own pretest to form the pairs.

Testing the Statistical Significance
of the Difference Between Two Means:
The t-Test for Paired Data

Steps

Preview

You are going to calculate a value called t.

$$t = \frac{(\bar{d})(\sqrt{n})}{s_d}$$

This *obtained t-value* will then be compared with a t-value from a table. If your obtained t-value is *larger* than the *tabled t-value*, then the difference between the means is statistically significant.

1. Prepare a pair-difference table

Pair	E-group member's score	C-group member's score	Difference in scores
1 2 3 . . n			

Each different score is obtained by subtracting the score obtained by one member of the pair from the score obtained by its partner in the pair. It will be best to subtract the C-group score—the score obtained by the member of the pair who is part of the C-group—from the E-group score.

A positive difference is then a difference in favor of the E-group. A negative difference is a difference in favor of the C-group. Usually some differences will be negative and some positive.

Example

Background

Thirty trainees had been formed into 15 matched pairs on the basis of pretest scores. One of each matched pair was assigned to the E-group, the other to the C-group. At the end of the training, scores were as shown in the posttest scores columns of the table in Step 1.

1. Prepare a pair-difference table

Pair	Posttest scores E-group	Posttest scores C-group	Difference in outcome scores
1	58	56	2
2	43	44	— 1
3	71	65	6
4	52	56	— 4
5	49	46	3
6	50	48	2
7	50	51	— 1
8	49	41	8
9	42	44	— 2
10	78	71	7
11	52	53	— 1
12	69	70	— 1
13	40	36	4
14	38	42	— 4
15	68	68	0

Steps	Example

2. Compute the mean of the set of difference scores

Use Substeps a through d below to calculate the mean of the numbers from the right-hand column in Step 1. This mean of the differences is represented by a d with a line over the top, $\bar{d}$, called a "d bar." This figure is also equal to the *difference between the first group's mean and the second group's mean*. It represents how much better one group did on the average.

Notice that there are positive and negative d's.

(a) Add up the positive d's.

$\boxed{}$ = sum of positive d's

(b) Then add up the negative d's.

$\boxed{}$ = sum of negative d's

(c) Combine (this means adding a negative number) the results of Substep b and Substep a to obtain the total, or overall, difference.

$\boxed{}$ = total d

(d) Divide the result of Substep c by the number of pairs. The result is d.

$\boxed{}$ = $\bar{d}$

3. Calculate $(\bar{d})(\sqrt{n})$

The number of pairs is n. It is the same as the number of d's used in Step 2. Find the square root of n; then multiply that number by d, computed in Step 2.

$\boxed{}$ = $(\bar{d})(\sqrt{n})$

---

2. Compute the mean of the set of difference scores

(a) Positive d's

$$\begin{array}{r} 2 \\ 6 \\ 3 \\ 2 \\ 8 \\ 7 \\ 4 \\ 0 \\ \hline 32 \end{array}$$

(b) Negative d's

$$\begin{array}{r} -1 \\ -4 \\ -1 \\ -2 \\ -1 \\ -1 \\ -4 \\ \hline -14 \end{array}$$

(c)

$$32 - 14 = 18$$

(d)

$$18/15 = 1.2$$

$$\bar{d} = 1.2$$

3. Calculate $(\bar{d})(\sqrt{n})$

$$n = 15 >$$
$$\sqrt{n} = 15 = 3.87$$
$$(\bar{d})(\sqrt{n}) = (1.2)(3.87) = 4.64$$

Steps	Example

4. Compute S_d, the standard deviation of the difference scores

S_d (read as "s sub d") can be calculated by applying Worksheet 2D to the data (treat each d as an X) or by entering the data on a handheld calculator or into a microcomputer program.

4. Compute S_d, the standard deviation of the difference scores

$$S_d = \sqrt{\frac{200.8}{14}} = 3.787$$

Step 5. Compute the obtained t-value

Divide the result of Step 3 by the result of Step 4.

5. Compute the obtained t-value

$$t = 4.647/3.787 = 1.23$$
$$\text{obtained } t = 1.23$$

6. Look up critical t-value

Refer to Table C.3 at the back of the book. Locate the row for df = n − 1, where n is the number of *pairs* (not necessarily the number of persons for whom there are data).

Choose the appropriate column, according to whether you are making a one-tailed or two-tailed test and according to the level of significance at which you are testing (.05 is traditional).

(Alternatively follow instructions on p. 51 to locate the level at which the results were significant.)

= tabled t-value

6. Look up critical t-value

With 15 pairs the df figure was 14. Using a two-tailed test and the .05 level of significance, the tabled t was 2.14.

tabled t-value = 2.14

7. Compare the obtained t-value with the tabled t-value

Is the obtained t-value as large as the tabled t-value?

7. Compare the obtained t-value with the tabled t-value

The obtained t-value was *not* as large as the tabled t-value.

Steps	Example

8. Interpret the statistic

If the obtained t-value is *larger* than the tabled t-value, then the difference between the mean scores of the two groups is statistically significant.

If the obtained t-value is *not as large* as the tabled t-value, then there is not strong evidence for saying that one group did better than the other group. The difference between mean scores of the E- and C-groups is not statistically significant. It could be just a chance difference.

Examine the practical significance of the result. If the E-group did better than the C-group, *how much* better? Did the average gain represent valuable extra learning significant changes or just a gain of a few items? Making such a judgment is often difficult. Before you report your results, perhaps you could meet with administrators, staff, and possibly community members to find out what magnitude of gain they would consider exciting.

8. Interpret the statistics

The t-test showed that the difference between the two groups was not large enough to reach statistical significance. The evaluator had to conclude that as far as *these* test results showed, the E-group program neither improved scores nor depressed them relative to the control group. Both E- and C-group programs appeared to be equally effective.

The effect size was calculated by computing the standard deviation for all 30 scores (i.e., the pooled SD) and dividing this into $\bar{d}$, the mean difference (which is also the difference in means).

$$ES = \frac{1.2}{11.61} = 0.10$$

The ES was small but in favor of the E-group.

Comparing Two Groups If the Outcome Measures Are Comparisons Rather Than Scores: The Sign Test

Suppose the experimental E-group and the control or competing C-group were formed by first matching individuals or units on some characteristic, and then assigning them randomly to either the experimental or control group. At the end of the program, the matched cases are examined to see whether the scores from the E-group tend to exceed their matched partners who had been in the C-group. In this case, the *sign test* provides a very simple, easily computed test of the significance of the differences between two groups of matched pairs when these differences are based on simple comparisons between each pair. A *simple comparison* is one that says which member of the pair is higher on some dimension. For example, one individual in each pair might be *judged* to be more assertive, or to have a more positive attitude toward school or to be more employable. A simple comparison makes no effort to say *how much* more assertive, or *how much* more positive; only the *direction* of the comparison is recorded. The sign test examines all the comparisons between the members of two groups and decides whether the number of comparisons in favor of one group is unlikely to be due to sampling variation. An excess of comparisons in favor of the E-group would indicate that the group had probably been affected by the program.

When to Use the Sign Test

Use the sign test when your situation matches one of the following:

(1) Participants in the E- and C-groups are or can be matched on some relevant pre-program characteristic(s), something likely to be related to the expected outcome.

(2) The outcome measure is a comparison rather than a score. For example, the outcome measure is a judgment of higher or lower, but not of *how much* higher or lower. The sign test is particularly useful with measures that only allow a *qualitative* judgment, such as an observer's opinion about some feature of the program implementation or supervisor or expert's ratings of the relative quality of papers.

When interpreting results from the sign test, be careful to note that the test does not tell you whether or not the significant difference you have found is an *important* one.

**Comparing Two Groups If the Outcome
Measures Are Comparisons
Rather Than Scores:
The Sign Test**

Steps

Preview

You will calculate a number that indicates how probable your particular results would be if the comparisons made between the pairs had been random.

If it turns out that the result was highly *improbable*, then this indicates a statistically significant result rather than simply the variation you would expect in small samples.

1. Prepare a list of pairs and their outcome results

Start with a list of the pairs of cases that were originally matched and are now to be compared. Each pair consists of an E-group member and a C-group member.

Record the result of the outcome comparison in this way: Write down a "+" if the E-group member exceeded the C-group member. Record a "–" if the C-group member was higher. The "+" indicates that a comparison is in favor of the E-group; the "–" indicates a comparison the other way. If the pair comparison showed no difference, record a zero.

Example

Background

A regional in-service course on effective public speaking was being offered during April and had to be evaluated. Supervisors were asked to nominate pairs of teachers whose public speaking skills were of about the same "quality." One of each pair was randomly offered the in-service course. Five weeks after the course finished, the regional in-service director visited each office and heard special presentations given by one of each pair of the originally nominated staff. After listening to the presentations, he noted which had the better quality. He was not informed which member of each pair had received the in-service training.

1. Prepare a list of pairs and their outcome results

Pair number	Judgment of quality
1	+
2	+
3	0
4	+
5	0
6	–
7	–
8	0
9	–
10	+
11	–
12	+
13	0
14	–
15	0
16	0
17	0
18	+
19	+
20	+

Key:

+ Speaking skills of staff members of who has had in-service course was judged superior to that of who had not had the course

– staff who has had no in-service course was judged superior

0 unable to judge one superior to other

Steps	Example

2. Prune the list

Eliminate any pairs in which there was no discernible difference on the posttest.

Step 2. Prune the list

Pair number	Judgment of speaking skill
1	+
2	+
~~3~~	~~0~~
4	+
~~5~~	~~0~~
6	-
7	-
~~8~~	~~0~~
9	-
10	+
11	-
12	+
~~13~~	~~0~~
14	-
~~15~~	~~0~~
~~16~~	~~0~~
~~17~~	~~0~~
18	+
19	+
20	+

3. Find x

(a) Count the number of "+"s and the number of "–"s, and record these here:

☐ = number of "+"s

☐ = number of "–"s

(b) Compute the sum, which is the number of pairs to be used in the analysis.

☐ = n

(c) Determine which is smaller—the number of "+"s or the number of "–"s. Let the *smaller number* be x, and write it down.

☐ = x

4. Test the significance of the result

If you have 25 or fewer pairs, use the table below. Go down column (n) until you locate the number of pairs to be used in your

3. Find x

(a)

number of "+"s = 8

number of "–"s = 5

(b)

n = 13

(c)

x = 5

4. Test the significance of the result

The value read from the table for 13 pairs was 3. Since the value of x was 5, which is *larger* than 3, a statistically significant result had

Steps	Example

analysis. If x is *equal to or smaller* than the corresponding number in the second column, then there is a statistically significant result. If x is *larger* than the appropriate number in the second column, a statistically significant result has not been established.

not been established. It could not be said that the results of the in-service were clear to a visitor.

Table for the Sign Test
When There Are Fewer Than 26 Pairs

Number of pairs used in analysis (n)	Value that x must not exceed for significance at 10%
5	0
6	0
7	0
8	1
9	1
10	2
11	2
12	2
13	3
14	3
15	3
16	4
17	4
18	5
19	5
20	5
21	6
22	6
23	7
24	7
25	8

Number of pairs used in analysis (n)	Value that x must not exceed for significance at 10%
5	0
6	0
7	0
8	1
9	1
10	2
11	2
12	2
13	(3)
14	3
15	3
16	4
17	4
18	5
19	5
20	5
21	6
22	6
23	7
24	7
25	8

If you have more than 25 pairs, compute z using this formula:

$$z = \frac{n - (2x + 1)}{\sqrt{n}}$$

Substeps for computing z:

(a) Double x

$\boxed{}$ = 2x

(b) Add one

$\boxed{}$ = 2x + 1

(c) Subtract the result of Substep b from n, the number of pairs

$\boxed{}$ = n − (2x + 1)

(d) Compute $\sqrt{n}$

$\boxed{}$ = $\sqrt{n}$

(e) Divide Substep c by Substep d to obtain z

$\boxed{}$ = $\dfrac{n - (2x + 1)}{\sqrt{n}}$ = z

The next September, however, the course was offered again to a larger number of randomly selected staff from pairs nominated by office directors. The computations were as follows:

Number of "+"s	=	28
Number of "−"s	=	11
n	=	39
x	=	11

(a)

$2x = 22$

(b)

$2x + 1 = 23$

(c)

$n - (2x + 1) = 39 - 23 = 16$

(d)

$\sqrt{n} = 39 = 6.24$

(e)

$z = \dfrac{16}{6.24} = \boxed{2.56}$

If z is *equal to or larger* than 1.64, you have a statistically significant result at the 5% or .05 level.

Postscript to the Sign Test

Rather than relying on tables to give critical values for a pre-set p level (p = .10 in the tables above in Worksheet 3D) you can work out the exact probabilities using Pascal's Triangle, introduced in Chapter 2. The example for the following mini-worksheet works out exact possibilities for a sample size of 6.

The z value of 2.56 is *larger* than 1.64. This time, therefore, the result was statistically significant. The in-service course seemed to have improved the quality of staff's public speaking.

The evaluator suggested that the positive results the second time might have been due to the fact that the in-service course was given at a time when staff were more likely to be making a variety of presentations and therefore were more motivated and got more practice.

Steps	Example

Background

In five out of six pairs in a matched-pairs experiment, the E-group member of the pair was rated higher than the C-group member on a measure of psychological adjustment.

1. Find the row corresponding to the sample size

For a sample size n, find row n, counting from the top down. Note that the second number on each row is also the number of the row. Therefore the row you want has your sample size as its second element.

1. Find the row corresponding to the sample size

row = row 6

2. Sum the row, to give Σ_f

This is the sum of the frequencies with which various combinations of results can be expected. The first row, for example, sums to 2, and if you have one pair, the results you could get would be either one + one or one –. So there are two possible outcomes for one comparison.

On row two, the sum is four because there are four possible outcomes if you have comparisons from two pairs:

- first and second pair both positive
- first positive and second pair negative
- first negative and second pair positive
- first and second pair both negative

The possible distribution of results for n = 2 is shown graphically below:

2. Sum the row, to give Σ_f

$$\Sigma_f = 1 + 6 + 15 + 20 + 15 + 6 + 1 = 64 \quad (\text{which is } 2^6)$$

Graphically, for n = 6, the possible distribution of results is as shown below:

possible results:	--	+– or –+	++
		X	
	X	X	X
number of plusses:	0	1	2
p values per element:	.25	.50	.25

possible results:	–––	––+ ––+ in any order	––– –++ –++ in any order	––– +++ +++ in any order	––+ +++ +++ in any order	–++ +++ +++ in any order	+++ +++
number of plusses:	0	1	2	3	4	5	6
p values per element:	.016	.094	.234	.312	.234	.094	.016
cumulative one tail p:	.016	.110	.344	.656	.890	.984	1.000

Steps	Example

3. Divide each element of the row by Σ_f.

This gives the probability associated with the set of results represented by the element. For example, for two pairs, the chance of both being positive *if either outcome is equally likely* would be 0.25 (one chance out of four). The plot of possible outcomes represents the distribution *under the null hypothesis*.

Notice that the outcomes can be expressed in terms of the number of comparisons that are + or – (in one direction or the other as shown in the second section of the figure below.)

4. For x positive results, sum the probabilities up to and including x

		X	
	X	X	X
possible results:	– –	+ –	+ +
		or – +	
number of plusses:	0	1	2
p values per element:	.25	.50	.25

This sum is then the one-tailed significance value (p value) for the sign test.

3. Divide each element of the row by Σ_f.

The results for this step were written onto the above diagram as p values.

4. For x positive results, sum the probabilities up to and including x

The p values were summed on the last row of the diagram above. For 1 or 0 pluses, the one-tailed probability was .11, which was thus the level of significance attained.

Notes for SPSSX Users

Worksheet 3A: t-Test for Unmatched Groups

To compare, say, math scores from school 1 and school 3 using the uncorrelated t-test the procedure would be:

```
T-TEST GROUPS=school(1,3)/VARIABLE=math
```

and this procedure also gives you the F ratio to compare variances.

Worksheet 3B: ANOVA

The data showing the scores and the groups have to be in the familiar cases-by-variables matrix for SPSSX analysis. Thus ANOVA data, for example, might appear as in the table below.

```
TABLE:  Data for worksheet 3B
```

cases	variables: group	score	
id	school	math	<---- variable names

Using the data above, the following procedure would provide the analysis of variance, test for the homogeneity of the variances, and compute the 95% confidence limits on the means, which provides useful data for drawing graphs. All three schools would be compared.

```
ONEWAY mathBYschool(1,3)
       /RANGES=TUKEY
STATISTICS ALL
```

The RANGES option yields a comparison of each mean with every other mean (using Tukey's HSD) so that you can see exactly where the most statistically significant differences in the data were located.

For an ANOVA that takes account of more than just one factor that affects the scores, the format is as shown below, adding SEX as a second factor:

```
ANOVA mathBYschool(1,3)sex(1, 2)
STATISTICS ALL
```

Note that range tests are not available for multifactor ANOVA. (They can be worked out by hand following a statistics book).

Worksheet 3C: The Paired-Data t-Test

When the paired-data t-test is needed *because the same group has been measured twice*, this presents no problems. For example, if there had been not just one score but two scores for the cases in the table above, then the following procedure would test for the significance of any differences between, say, score 1 and score 2 (which might have been pretest and posttest for example):

```
T-TEST PAIRS=score1,score2
```

Notice that the scores compared were two columns, i.e., two variables.

If, therefore, you have a matched pairs design you must *make the pair the unit of analysis* by putting each pair on its own row, as a case. The *pair* becomes the case. Thus the data from Worksheet 3C might be entered as follows:

pair	data from e-group member			data from c-group member		
01	e id	e score 1	etc	c id	c score 1	etc

The paired t-test would be obtained by:

```
T-TEST PAIRS=escore 1,cscore1
```

Worksheet 3D: The Sign Test

The same arrangement of data would be used for the sign test. The sign test is one of a large group of "non-parametric" statistics. The distributions expected under the null hypothesis are computed for these statistics without assuming normal distributions or equal variances, assumptions that underlie the "parametric" statistics such as the t and F tests. Hence the term NPAR, standing for non-parametric, in the procedure for the sign test:

```
NPAR TESTS SIGN=escore1, WITHcscore1
```

Chapter 4
Examining Relationships Between Variables

Was reading achievement related to the amount of time spent in the remedial reading laboratory? Were children's self-esteem scores related to their positions in class? Were students who scored high on a scale measuring attitude to test Y actually doing well in test Y (i.e., were attitudes and achievement related)? Was failure to complete a course of treatment related to housing location? Was the choice of optional courses related to an index of home background?

Each of these questions is about the relationship between two measures. There are various statistics that can be calculated to indicate the extent to which measures are related and the two most widely used ones will be introduced here. Which one you should use depends upon the kinds of measurements you are trying to relate:

- If the measures are scores or ranks, use r, Pearson's product-moment correlation coefficient (Worksheet 4A).
- If the measures are categories, use chi-square (Worksheet 4D).

The correlation coefficient is particularly important in quantitative work. It has many applications and is the basis of several advanced statistical techniques. It is often used in *prediction*. For example, if two measures are related, then knowing a person's score on one of the measures would mean that you could have a good guess at his or her score on the other measure, even if that measurement was still to be made. Thus you can use one measure to predict scores on the other measure. Because it is such a widely used and important statistic several pages are devoted to it here. You are urged to work through the graphical introduction (Worksheet 4A) and the explanations before applying r. There are situations in which it should not be used, as will be quite clear when you realize how it works.

Because qualitative data can often be expressed as categories, chi-square lends itself to the analysis of qualitative data as well as the analysis of quantitative data. Again, it is a useful and important statistic but there are situations in which it is not applicable.

The Correlation Coefficient

The correlation coefficient is used when you have two scores for each person in a group. For example, you may have measured achievement in English and in mathematics on the same set of students. Table 1 presents a small example of such data: scores on test X and test Y for 10 persons.

TABLE 1
Test X and Test Y Scores

Person	Test X	Test Y
Arlene Apple	1	8
Bnar Bevy	3	4
Carol Cooper	3	10
David Dear	4	8
Evan Grass	5	10
Freda Fink	5	16
Grahm Garden	6	12
Helen Harker	7	10
Ivar Inglis	7	10
John Jones	9	12

The correlation coefficient is best understood by reference to the graph you could use to display these scores. Each set of scores could be separately displayed as a distribution, as in Figure 48. However, those graphs fail to show how the scores were *related*: Were those scoring high on test X also scoring high on test Y? To show how the scores were related, we put one distribution at right angles to the other (Figure 49) and plot a "scattergram." The scattergram is plotted in this way: Reading from the table we see that person AA had 1 on test X and 8 on test Y. So follow the horizontal axis (which we have decided will represent text X) along till the score 1 is reached. Draw a vertical line through this score. Then go up the vertical axis, which represents test Y, to 8 and draw a horizontal line through the score. Where these two lines cross make a dot. You can see that this dot represents *both* the scores of the first person: 1 on test X and 8 on test Y. Continuing in this way with all the other scores will yield the scattergram. To understand this scattergram is to understand correlation.

The horizontal axis is often called the X axis and the vertical axis is called the Y axis. If one of the measurements was collected before the other, then it is usual to put that measurement on the X axis.

It is often convenient to draw a line on the scattergram in order to show the general trend in the data. In Figure 50, this line has been added. It is called a regression line, and the r of regression has become the symbol for a sample "correlation coefficient," an index of the extent to which scores are related.

Before we look at how r is calculated, notice one more feature of the scattergram—the way it can be used for prediction. Suppose you knew someone had scored 2 on test X. What score would you predict for test Y for that person? You would use the regression line as follows:

Look along the test X axis to the score 2 then sketch a line up to the regression line and make a dot. That dot represents your best guess as to the person's scores, so you can now read the test Y score off the graph by looking across to the test Y axis. In this case, you find that the test Y score most likely associated with a score of 2 in test X is 8. Note that, by using this procedure, you have predicted a test Y score of 8 on the basis of two sources of information:

(1) the person's test X score and
(2) the general relationship between test Y and test X scores as represented by the scattergram and Table 1.

The score of 8 in test Y is a PREDICTED score, predicted on the basis of the two sources of information just noted. It can also be called an EXPECTED score, it represents the score you would expect *on the basis of the two sources of information noted above.*

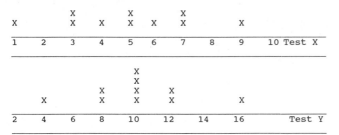

Figure 48. Distributions on test X and test Y

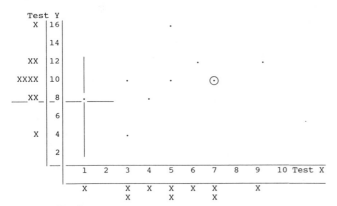

Figure 49. Scattergram

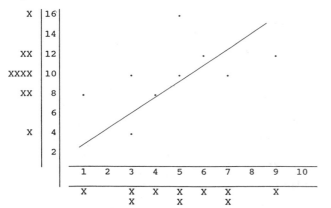

Figure 50

So what is this correlation coefficient: How is it calculated, how does it help us to draw the regression line, and how is it interpreted? Because you know about z-scores from Chapter 2, the correlation coefficient is very simple to define: It is the average product of the z-scores:

$$r = \Sigma \ \frac{z_x \times z_y}{n}$$

z_x is a z-score for variable X

z_y is the z-score the same person got on variable Y

n is the number of persons (or whatever is represented by each dot on the scattergram)

Σ means the SUM of what follows

$z_x \times z_y$ means z_x multiplied by z_y (which is called the "product" of z_x and z_y)

Look at Worksheet 4A and you will see the correlation coefficient computed for the data in Table 1. It would be a good idea at this point to make up some graphs of your own and compute correlations. Can you chose a set of points on a graph so that the coefficient comes out negative? (If you haven't time to discover this for yourself by plotting and thinking, just read on to find the answer.)

How does this statistic, the correlation coefficient, behave? Study column 1 of Figure 51. It shows the value of the correlation coefficient for several scattergrams. If the X and Y values are actually on a straight line (row [a], which would almost never happen in practice) the correlation coefficient has its largest value, 1.00, and one variable can be exactly predicted from the other. If the two variables show no linear realationship then the value of the correlation coefficient is zero (row [d]), and knowing X would not help you to predict Y at all. In between these two extremes there can be any decimal values. The larger the numbers in the decimal the more strongly the variables are related. Thus the relationships shown on row [b] are stronger than the relationships shown on row [c]. You can see from the graphs that a strong relationship exists when the points are close to the regression line. When points are close to the regression line you can expect that if you predict a score on the regression line you will not be far out—the points already obtained are not far from the line. But when you predict a point on the regression line for a weak correlation, you haven't as much confidence in it: The actual point may be quite far from the one you predicted, the one on the line.

The second column of Figure 51 illustrates correlations with the same numbers as in the first column but negative rather than positive. What does the negative sign imply? It implies that persons who scored *high* on one variable scored *low* on the other variable. For example, you might expect to get a negative correlation between the time taken to do a set of mathematics problems and the students' ability measures: *less* time is associated with *more* ability.

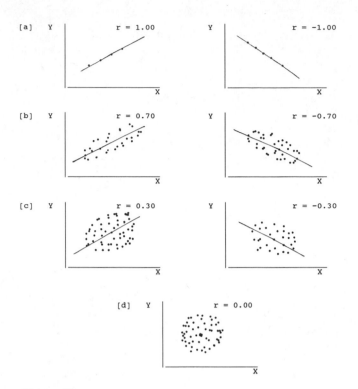

Figure 51

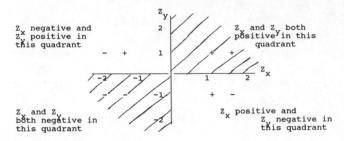

Figure 52. Showing how the sign of the product $z_x \times z_y$ varies from quadrant to quadrant

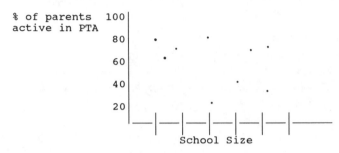

Figure 53. Scores showing a negative relation (–.30)

Why does the value of r turn out negative when low scores on X are associated with high scores on Y and vice versa? This is easily understood if you think of how points would look on a scattergram if we transformed all the scores to z-scores and plotted z_x against z_y, as in Figure 52. If most scores were in the top right quadrant (high scores associated with high scores) and in the bottom left quadrant (low scores associated with low scores) the *products* of these scores would be positive because either both scores were positive, or both were negative and the product of two negative numbers is positive (e.g., $-1 \times -2 = 2$). For a negative correlation most scores would lie in the other two quadrants and their the products would always be negative. For a zero correlation the points would be scattered in all four quadrants and positive and negative products would cancel each other out when they were summed, thus yielding r = 0.00 approximately.

Let us consider another example of a negative correlation, one that raises the question of the UNIT OF ANALYSIS. It might be the case that the percentage of parents participating in school activities decreases with increasing school size; that is, *smaller* schools show a *larger* percentage of parents participating in school activities than do larger schools. If you collected school size and parent participation data from a large number of schools and computed the correlation coefficient, it might be r = –0.30, a weak and *negative* relationship. The graph of a negative correlation slopes downward rather than upward, as shown in Figure 53, a hypothetical example.

In this example each dot represents not the scores of a *person* but the mean scores for a *school*. The school was the "unit of analysis." On other occasions you might use classrooms as the unit of analysis, or teachers or school districts.

It is important to remember that the correlation coefficient is only completely satisfactory as an indicator of a relationship if the relationship is more or less LINEAR, that is, if the trend in the scattergram is well represented by a straight line. As an example of a situation in which a straight line would not be appropriate, consider the following. It may be that *moderately anxious* persons do better on tests than persons who are so lacking in anxiety that they do not really wake up and try. This suggests a *positive* correlation between achievement and anxiety— *higher* anxiety associated with *higher* achievement. But if people are *very highly* anxious rather than just moderately anxious, they may make mistakes and thus lower their achievement. In this case, *higher* anxiety may then become associated with *lower* achievement—a *negative* correlation. Figure 54 shows the postulated situation.

Here, *use of the correlation coefficient would be inappropriate* since the graph is not a straight line. Calculation of r would yield a very low, nonsignificant value even though there was a strong but *curvilinear* relationship.

The size of the correlation coefficient shows how well a *straight line* fits the data when the two measures are plotted on a graph.

Achievement

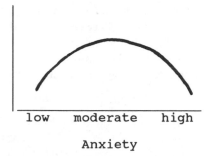

low   moderate   high

Anxiety

Figure 54. Hypothetical relationship between anxiety and achievement

Interpreting Correlation Coefficients

You have decided that it makes sense to look for a linear relationship (straight line relationship) between two measures and have computed a correlation coefficient, using Worksheet 4A or a computer program. How do you interpret it? Here are three pieces of information that you will generally want to consider as soon as you have obtained a correlation coefficient: the direction of the relationship, the statistical significance of the correlation, and the strength of the relationship.

The Direction of the Relationship

This is determined simply from the sign: If the correlation coefficient is positive then the interpretation is that people who had high scores on one measure tended also to have high scores on the other measure. Notice that high scores were simply *associated with* high scores; high scores on one measure cannot be interpreted as having *caused* high scores on the other measure simply because they were correlated. "Correlation is not causation."

The Statistical Significance of a Correlation Coefficient

You can imagine that if you correlate two sets of scores you are unlikely to come up with a correlation of exactly zero even if there were really no relationship between the variables measured by the scores. This idea of no "real" relationship between the variables is called the null hypothesis—the hypothesis that the "true" correlation is zero. To be more precise, the null hypothesis is the hypothesis that the POPULATION correlation coefficient is zero. The data we have and from which we calculate the r are only a SAMPLE of all the possible data. As you will recall, a sample value is usually represented by a Roman letter, (r in this case) and the population value (which you can think of as the true value that you would find if you could collect all the data) is represented by a Greek letter. The Greek letter closest to r

is "rho," written ρ = rho = symbol for the POPULATION correlation coefficient.

How large must r be to persuade us that rho is not really zero? Table C.7 helps in answering this question. For example, the critical values shown in this table for the 0.05 two-tailed test are such that, if we took lots of samples of the size indicated, and if rho *were* zero, only .05 of the samples would yield the correlation we find in our one sample (the "obtained value"). If the obtained value disregarding the sign is larger than the .05 critical value in the table we then say that the correlation was "statistically significant at the .05 level." This statement only means that the kind of variability we get when we take samples is not likely to explain a correlation as high as the one we have found; it's as unlikely as .05. (Note that the statement could also be taken as indicating the probability that we are wrong in claiming that there is a correlation, because there is a 5% chance that such a value *would* show up in a sample even when the true correlation, rho, was zero. Indeed, .05 is called the TYPE I ERROR RATE; it represents the probability that, due to the variations one inevitably gets in sample statistics, we might be led to claim a correlation when there wasn't one. This error rate is often reported as a probability (e.g., "$p < .05$").

You might find yourself wondering, "Why the .05 level?" Why not .10 or .20 or .01 for the p-value? Or why pick out any critical level; why not just report how likely it is that your obtained value would occur due to sampling variation? To some extent the .05 level has become a convenient tradition or rule of thumb. One factor that probably contributed to this practice was the fact that the original tables had to be drawn up without the aid of computers. This computation required considerable labor and a large amount of printing to tabulate the results. Consequently only a few key critical values were presented, usually .05 and .01 and .001.

Nowadays, however, when so much data analysis is done on computers, which can tell you the exact likelihood of your sample value or one larger having occurred if rho were actually zero, it is preferred practice to report this level of significance rather than simply saying whether or not the correlation was "statistically significant at the .05 level." However, if your computer does not produce the exact p-value, use Table C.7. In summary, to give your readers some guide as to how the correlation coefficient should be interpreted, report it in either of the following formats: If the exact p-value is known,

$$r = .36 \ (n = 30, \ p = .04)$$

If the exact p-value is not known the same information might be reported

$$r = .36 \ (n = 30, \ p < .05)$$

Notice, from Table C.7, that for 100 cases a correlation of .19 is statistically significant at the .05 level. But a scattergram for a correlation of .19 illustrates that it does not allow very accurate predictions to be made. It is still a weak correlation even if it is statistically significant. Is a correlation of this size important? How large does a correlation have to be before we pay attention to it?

The Magnitude of the Correlation: The Strength of the Relationship

Some rough guidance on how to describe correlations can be obtained from Figure 55.

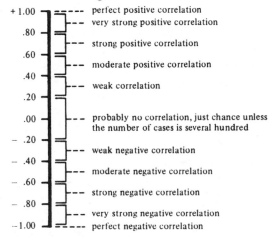

Figure 55. The range of possible correlations and their usual interpretations

However, whether a correlation of some particular size is important or not depends upon the circumstances—in particular it depends upon how it is to be used. Below are some points to consider in trying to get a sense of the importance of a correlation of a given size.

Proportion of predictable variance

The proportion of the variance in Y that is predictable from X is r squared, where r is the correlation between X and Y. Thus if the correlation was .80 between X and Y, we could say that the proportion of PREDICTABLE VARIANCE was .64, or 64%. This is often referred to as the "explained" variance or the proportion of variance "accounted for." Notice that even a strong correlation leaves a large amount of variance "unexplained."

The term "predictable" variance is preferable to the commonly used term "EXPLAINED VARIANCE" or "VARIANCE ACCOUNTED FOR" because these expressions seem to imply that one understands *how* X causes or explains Y. The term "prediction" should not have that implication. For example, the rising of the sun each morning must have been predicted by early homo

sapiens but it is unlikely they understood or could explain the correlation between time and sunrise. Knowing that variables are related allows one to make predictions, but being able to lay claim to prediction does not mean that one can lay claim to understanding.

Proportion of predictable variance = r^2

You will recall that "variance" is the square of the standard deviation, that is, s^2. The predictable variance is the variance of the predicted Y scores, which are of course on the regression line. The unexplained variance is the variances of the RESIDUALS scattered above and below the regression line.

In short, one way to evaluate the magnitude of the correlation is in terms of the proportion of predictable variance; this is usually called the "proportion of variance accounted for" or the "proportion of explained variance."

Standard error of estimate

Sometimes you are not interested in the total amount of variance to be predicted but in the prediction of individual scores. Here you need to consider the standard error of estimate, which is the standard deviation expected in Y scores for a given X score. In other words, you will consider the correlation between X and Y in terms of the accuracy with which it allows you to predict Y scores.

$$\text{Standard Error of estimate} = s_y\sqrt{1 - r^2_{xy}}$$

Prediction/selection for individuals versus groups

If you are using correlations to make statements or decisions about *individuals*, then you need stronger correlations than if you are investigating *groups*. The proportion of error in a statement about an individual score is likely to be larger than in statements about the mean score for a group. Thus, for example, you might not wish to make predictions based on a correlation of .60 for individuals, but such a correlation might be adequate in predicting *group* differences.

The correlation coefficient as an Effect Size

A dichotomous variable can be used in correlations. If there was an experimental and control group, these could be represented as two points on the X axis. The outcome variable Y would then be two sets of points, one for the E-group and one for the C-group. The regression line could be computed as usual, with the X variable having one of two values according to which group the case was in.

To convert r to an effect size use the following equation:

$$\text{Effect size} = \frac{2r}{\sqrt{1 - r^2}}$$

The conversion could help you compare r with expected effect sizes and thus interpret its magnitude.

Preview

To illustrate the computation of a correlation coefficient a very small set of data, Table 1, is used. As you will see, one cannot have much confidence in a correlation on such a small sample. The point, however, is to show how easy the computation is and how the correlation works.

Steps	Example

1. Set up a table or spreadsheet

Set up a table or spreadsheet with the columns shown below, where X and Y are the variables for which you wish to compute the correlation: r_{xy}. Enter the data you have for X and Y into the columns as raw scores.

1	2	3	4	5	6
Case	X	z_x	Y	z_y	$z_x * z_y$
Sum					
Mean					
σ					

2. Compute mean and standard deviation for X and Y

Use a calculator or Worksheets 2C and 2D to compute the mean and SD for X and the same for Y. Be careful to compute σ, not s.

3. Re-express each X as z_x and Y as z_y

Using the mean and sigma for X, column 3 was completed by entering the value for z_x.

1. Set up a table or spreadsheet

1	2	3	4	5	6
Case	X	z_x	Y	z_y	$z_x * z_y$
AA	1		8		
BB	3		4		
CC	3		10		
DD	4		8		
EE	5		10		
FF	5		16		
GG	6		12		
HH	7		10		
II	7		10		
JJ	9		12		
Sum					
Mean					
0					

2. Compute mean and for X and Y

Using a handheld calculator and the key for the population standard deviation (σ_n), the following values were computed.

$$\bar{X} = 5.000 \qquad \bar{Y} = 10.000$$
$$\sigma = 2.236 \qquad \sigma = 2.966$$

3. Re-express each X as z_x and Y as z_y
For example, for the first row:

$$z_x = \frac{X - \text{mean } X}{\sigma_x}$$

so

$$z_x = \frac{1 - 5}{2.236} = -1.789$$

Steps	Example

Similarly for column 5: $z_y = \dfrac{8 - 10}{2.966} = -0.674$

4. Compute the product $z_x \times z_y$ for each case

On each row multiply z_x by z_y and record the result in column 6.

4. Compute the product $z_x \times z_y$ for each case

1	2	3	4	5	6
Case	X	z_x	Y	z_y	$z_x * z_y$
1		−1.789	8	−.674	1.206
3		−2.023	4	−.894	1.808
3		0.000	10	−.894	0.000
4		−0.674	8	−.447	0.301
5		0.000	10	.000	0.000
5		2.023	16	.000	0.000
6		0.674	12	.447	0.301
7		0.000	10	.894	0.000
7		0.000	10	.894	0.000
9		0.674	12	1.789	1.206
					4.821

5. Sum the products and divide by n

Sum column 6 values and divide by n, the number of cases. The result is the correlation coefficient between X and Y for this sample.

5. Sum the products and divide by n

$$r = \frac{4.821}{10}$$

Therefore, r = .48

6. Test for statistical significance: Is it different from zero?

As discussed in the text, a correlation coefficient for a sample is unlikely to be exactly 0.00 even if the "true" (i.e., population) value was 0.00. We need to ask how likely it was for a sample of this size to yield the observed value, or one larger, if the population value were zero. If it was as unlikely as .05 (5 times out of 100) then we say the correlation was statistically significant at the .05 level. Table C.7 in Appendix C gives critical values for several levels of statistical significance.

6. Test for statistical significance: Is it different from zero?

Using Table C.7

6.1

Look down the sample size (n) column to find the number that is your sample size (or the nearest number to it). You will use the row for that number.

Using Table C.7

6.1

Looking down the sample size (n) column, the number that was the sample size is 10.

6.2

Look along the row until you find the decimal that is smaller than your obtained value and as near to it as possible, *ignoring the sign of your obtained correlation* (i.e., disregarding a negative sign on the obtained correlation.)

If all the values are larger than your obtained value, then report that the correlation was "not statistically significant, (p > .10). If you find a value that is smaller, then continue.

6.2

No value was less than .48 so the correlation was not statistically significant at the indicated levels (p > .10).

Steps	Example

6.3

If you had predicted that the correlation would be positive and it was, or you had predicted it would be negative and it was, then look to the bottom of the table to read the level of statistical significance for a "ONE-TAILED TEST." Otherwise, if you had not been able to predict the direction of the correlation, look up to the top of the table for the level of statistical significance on a "TWO-TAILED TEST."

7. Be warned: Correlations are "slippery statistics"

The scattergram should be examined for outliers, which can have a strong effect on the correlation, especially with small numbers. Consider also all the issues raised in the text of this chapter about subgroups and other factors that may affect the correlation. One way to appreciate how the correlation might vary from sample to sample is to set CONFIDENCE LIMITS, as explained below.

8. [optional] Set confidence limits on r

You are going to set a lower and an upper confidence limit on r, the sample correlation coefficient. The wider the interval between these two values, the more uncertain one is about the actual population value for the correlation coefficient. The confidence limits indicate the kind of size that rho (the "true" or population value) might be. These values illustrate how little confidence we can have in a value of a correlation coefficient obtained from small samples.

(The above paragraph indicates how one interprets confidence limits. If you wish to know more precisely what they are, you could consider the following statement: If you repeatedly sampled the population from which r is drawn, and each time put .95 confidence limits on the r obtained, then in the long run 95% of those confidence intervals would contain the true population value that r is estimating.)

Calculating the upper and lower confidence limits for r is made difficult by the asymmetric shape of the sampling distribution for r. Fisher (1921) had the insight to find a transformation of r that would give a normal sampling distribution. This is the r to Z transformation. The strategy is to convert r to Z, set confidence limits on Z, and then translate these Z values back to r.

8.1. Convert r to Z

Set up a table as below. To obtain Z for a given value of r either look up Table C.8 in Appendix C, or enter r into a calculator and then press the keys to give "arc tanh" or "inverse hyperbolic tangent."

```
-----------------------
|   r     |     z     |
|_____|_____|
|_____|_____|
|         |           |
| enter r -----> > Z  |
|_____|_____|
|         |           |
|_____|_____|
```

6.3

Test X and Text Y were cognitive tests, and it would have been safe to predict that cognitive tests would be positively correlated. Therefore, a one-tailed significance test could have been applied.

7. Be warned: Correlations are "slippery statistics"

With this small sample, subgroups did not enter the picture. By way of illustration, however, suppose there had been one more case with the values 9 on X and 2 on Y. If you re-compute the correlation including the 11th case, the correlation becomes 0.03. With small numbers just one or two points can cause a large change in r!

8. [optional] Set confidence limits on r

8.1. Convert r to Z

Using a calculator, the value 0.48 was entered and INV HYP TAN keys were entered, which yielded a value of 0.52.

```
_____
|    r    |      Z      |
|_____|_____|
|_____|_____|
| .48 ------>> .52      |
|_____|_____|
|_____|_____|
```

Steps	Example

8.2. Compute σ for Z

The standard deviation for Z values based on a sample of size n is

$$\sigma_Z = \frac{1}{\sqrt{n-3}}$$

8.2 Compute σ_z for Z

The standard deviation for Z values based on a sample of size 10 is

$$\sigma_Z = \frac{1}{\sqrt{10-3}} = .38$$

8.3. Compute upper and lower CLs for Z

For the .95 confidence limits the quantity 1.96σ should be added or subtracted from Z:

upper .95 CL = Z + 1.96σ
lower .95 CL = Z − 1.96σ

Place the lower CL in the lower box and the upper one in the upper box. (This is quite arbitrary but it organizes the figures neatly.)

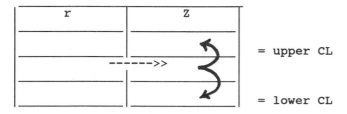

This gives two Z values, which must now be converted back to r values.

8.3. Compute upper and lower CLs for Z

The upper and lower confidence limits on Z were computed from the equations:

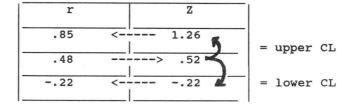

8.4. Convert Zs back to correlations

To obtain r for a given value of Z either look up Table C.8 in Appendix C, or enter Z into a calculator and then press the keys to give "tanh" or "hyperbolic tangent."

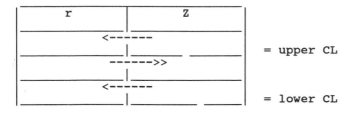

The values of r are the lower and upper 95% confidence limits on r, the obtained value. If the confidence interval includes zero (i.e., if one limit is positive and the other is negative) then this tells you that the obtained correlation was not statistically significant at the .05 level. Thus CLs are an alternative way of testing for statistical significance.

Notice two things: (1) The confidence interval is not symmetrical about r. The obtained correlation will be closer to one limit than to the other limit.

8.4. Convert Zs back to correlations

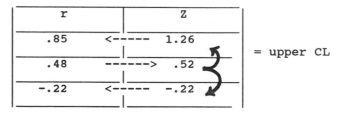

The result showed the obtained correlation was not statistically significant at the .05 level and suggested the true value, p, may lie within the range −.22 to .85.

Steps	Example

Confidence Limits Around r = .60 for 25 Cases

```
    +1.00 |
      .80 | <-----upper confidence limit, .80
      .60 | <-----obtained r
      .40 |
          | <-----lower confidence limit, .27
      .20 |
      .00 |
    - .20 |
```

(2) The confidence interval is broad. Unless the sample size is several hundred, the confidence interval will usually be considerably greater than .1, that is, it will not be merely a range across the second decimal place. In view of the slippery nature of the correlation coefficient, it would be good practice to report correlations to one decimal place only. Unfortunately, the common practice has developed of reporting to two decimal places.

Steps

Preview

$$z_y = rz_x$$

Therefore, $\left(\dfrac{Y - \bar{Y}}{\sigma_Y}\right) = r\left(\dfrac{X - \bar{X}}{\sigma_X}\right)$

Therefore, $Y = \dfrac{r\sigma_y X}{\sigma_x} + \bar{Y} - \dfrac{r\sigma_y \bar{X}}{\sigma_x}$

which can be written as $Y = BX + C$
which is the equation of a straight line with slope B and intercept C.

    The slope is called the "raw score regression coefficient" and is often represented as B. You can see that

$$B = \dfrac{r\sigma_y}{\sigma_x}$$

The intercept is called the "constant," because for a given set of data it is a number and doesn't change as X or Y changes. The constant is

$$C = \bar{Y} - \dfrac{r\sigma_y}{\sigma_x}\,\bar{X}$$

Once you have computed the regression equation you can draw the regression line on the graph. The regression line always goes through the point $(\bar{X}, \bar{Y}$—the two means) so you only need to find one other point to fix the line.

Example

Preview

The same small set of data that was used in Worksheet 4A is used here, in order to make the computations easy to follow.

Steps	Example

1. Compute r and tabulate descriptive statistics for X and Y

Follow Worksheet 4A to obtain the sample correlation coefficient r. Then tabulate the values that you will need for the regression calculations:

Variable	n	mean	σ	r
X	10	5.00	2.236	.48
Y		10.00	2.966	

1. Compute r and tabulate descriptive statistics for x and y

Variable	n	mean	σ	r
X	n	X̄ X	σ_x	r_{XY}
Y		Ȳ	σ_y	

2. Locate the point (X, Y) and label it G

You plot G just like any pair of scores: trace along the X axis till you arrive at the mean, X then draw a perpendicular line through the point. Follow the Y axis to the mean, Y, and draw a horizontal line. Where this intersects the vertical X line is the point representing the mean on each scale: the point $(\bar{X}, \bar{Y})$. (You will only need to draw the lines mentally after a while, in plotting points.)

2. Locate the point (X, Y) and label it G

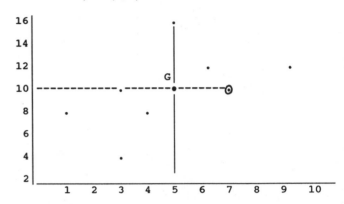

3. Compute the slope (the raw score regression coefficient)

$$\text{Slope} = \frac{r\sigma_y}{\sigma_x} = \boxed{} = B$$

that is, multiply r by σ_y and then divide by σ_x.

3. Compute the slope (the raw score regression coefficient)

$$\text{Slope} = (.48) \times \frac{2.966}{2.236} = \boxed{0.64} = B$$

4. Compute the constant

$$\text{constant} = \bar{Y} - B \times \bar{X} = \boxed{} = C$$

that is, multiply B (from step 4) by $\bar{X}$ and then subtract this quantity from Y.

4. Compute the constant

$$\begin{aligned} \text{constant} = \bar{Y} - B \times \bar{X} &= 10 - (.64)(5) \\ &= 10 - 3.2 \\ &= 6.8 \end{aligned}$$

5. Write down the regression equation and use it to find K

Write down the regression equation:

$$\hat{Y} = B \times X + C$$

that is, the value predicted for Y if the score on X was X is B times the X score plus the constant C

To find a point K suitable for using to draw in the regression line put in a suitable X value. It is suggested that you put in the value of X that is two standard deviations above the mean for X, that is, the

5. Write down the regression equation and use it to find K

$$\hat{Y} = .64 \, X + 6.8$$
$$\begin{aligned} \text{If } X = X + 2\sigma_x \\ = 5 + 2(2.236) \\ = 9.472 \end{aligned}$$

Steps

Example

value X + $2\sigma_X$. Multiply this value by B and add C to it and call the result Y_k, the Y value predicted for an X value of $(X + 2\sigma_X)$. Plot this point and label it K.

then Y = .64(9.472) + 6.8
Y = 12.86

Thus we have a point K at (9.5, 13) approximately.

6. Draw the regression line through G and K

These steps have provided a method for drawing the regression line but what does it represent? You can think of it as being the best guess, given any X, of what Y would be. But some readers might want to know what it is mathematically. Here is an explanation. A "residual" is the difference between a predicted value and an obtained value—it represents the amount by which your prediction was "out." The regression line is drawn so as to make the sum of the squared residuals as small as possible, that is, to minimize what is called the residual sum of squares: the "SS residuals." A satisfactory explanation of how we know that any particular line minimizes the sum-of-squares for the residuals requires calculus, but you can simply accept that using the correlation coefficient to draw the line produces a line that minimizes the SS residuals.

It might have struck you that just as you can predict Y from X so you can also predict X from Y—there are TWO regression lines! Each line goes through one of the perpendicular or horizontal tangents to an ellipse that can be drawn around the scatter of points, as shown below.

6. Draw the regression line through G and K

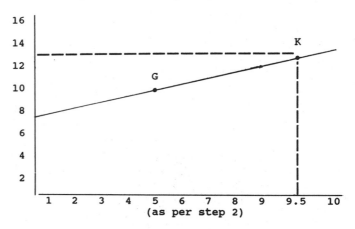

Check: The regression line should "cut" the Y axis at C = 6.8. It did!

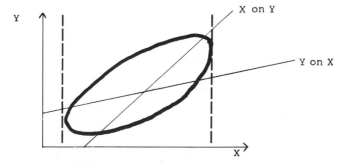

7. Cross-validate if possible

The regression equation is an *optimistic* equation; it represents the best prediction for the sample on which it was calculated. You must expect that it will not predict so well when applied to some other sample. Yet, application to other samples is sometimes exactly what we wish to do with a regression equation.

If possible, apply the equation to predict scores on a sample that is *not* the one on which the equation was computed and see how well it predicts.

Further Topics and Applications for the Correlation Coefficient

The Effect of Subgroups with Different Correlations

Two groups may have the same means on two variables and yet the variables may be related differently. For example, the SLOPE of the regression line might be different for males and females. In such a situation one might need to use two regression lines for prediction or control: one for males and a different one for females. But once again we must remember that most sets of data are SAMPLES and we cannot expect two samples to give *exactly* the same statistics even if they are drawn from the same population. We have to ask how likely this difference in slopes would be if the correlation for one group was "really" equal to the correlation of the other group; if, in other words, the population correlations were equal.

This question can be answered by computing a z score. If the z value is larger than 1.96 then the difference in the correlation coefficients is "statistically significant at the .05 level"—that is, it seems to be larger than would arise from sampling variation. This kind of result, a z larger than 1.96, would suggest that separate analyses for each group might be needed. However, you would also need to look at how much actual practical difference the difference in correlations would make, and also at how small the samples would become if you split up the group into two subgroups.

The calculation of the z value is quite simple, but before it is done each correlation must be re-expressed as "Fisher's Z" (see page 86). To change a correlation r into Z you can either look up Table C.8 in Appendix C or, if you have a calculator that has trigonometric functions, you can enter the value of r and then press the keys to give the inverse of the hyperbolic tangent (arc tanh) and the value of Z will appear. Try this out checking your answers with Table C.8 if you plan to use a calculator. Suppose the two correlation coefficients (from which the regression lines can be worked out) are r_1 and r_2 and they arose from groups of size n_1 and n_2. Re-express these as Z_1 and Z_2 and then compute the z-score using the equation below:

To test the significance of the difference between independent correlations:

$$z = \frac{Z_1 - Z_2}{\sqrt{\frac{1}{N_1 - 3}} + \sqrt{\frac{1}{N_2 - 3}}}$$

Look up the obtained z-score in a table of the normal curve (Table C.1) to find the associated probability, or use Table C.2.

The Question of the Best Predictor

Sometimes you may want to test the significance of the difference between *correlated* correlation coefficients. For example, you may wish to answer the question as to which of two variables (X and Y) best predicts a third variable (Z). You will need to have data on the correlations between the three variables, measured on one sample (sample size = N, say).

Let r_{xz} be the correlation of variable X with variable Z let r_{yz} be the correlation of variable Y with variable Z and let r_{xy} be the correlation of variable X with variable Y—in other words, the correlation between the two predictors. Compute a t-value from the following equation and look up the critical value using df = N-3.

To test the significance of the difference between dependent correlations:

$$t = r_{xz} - r_{yz}\sqrt{\frac{(N-3)(1+r_{xy})}{2(1 - r_{xy}^2 - r_{xz}^2 - r_{yz}^2 + 2r_{xy}r_{xz}r_{yz})}}$$

(Hotelling, 1940)

If the obtained t is larger than the critical t then it would seem reasonable to suggest that whichever variable had the stronger correlation with Z was the better predictor.

For example, for a particular Philosophy syllabus you might wonder which would be the better predictor: a verbal or a nonverbal ability test. Suppose the correlations were as shown below:

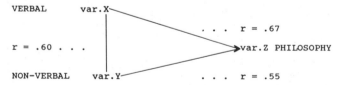

If the size of the sample used to obtain these correlations was 80, then the t-value would work out as 0.828, quite non-significant. Thus on the basis of this sample you could note that the correlation with the verbal test was higher but state that the difference was not statistically significant (p > .05).

The Effect of Not Being Able to Measure Accurately

There is error in every measurement. The amount of error in a particular measurement is indicated by various estimates of the "reliability" of that measurement. A test with a low reliability of .64 has more error than a test with a higher reliability, such as a reliability of .85.

The reliability of a measurement can be expressed as a correlation coefficient. For example, to estimate how reliable a test is from one occasion to another, the test is given twice and the two sets of results correlated. If the results on occasion 2 were exactly the same as on occasion 1, the correlation between the two sets of scores would be 1.00. Due to errors of measurement this never happens, and the test-retest correlation will be considerably less than 1.00. You can imagine that if a test does not even correlate with itself very highly, due to errors of measurement, it will not correlate with other tests as highly as it might were it not for errors of measurement. We say the correlation is "attenuated due to errors of measurement." There is a correction that can be applied for the unreliability of the measurements, giving the correlation that would be expected if each variable could be measured without error:

$$r_{XY} = \frac{r_{XY}}{\sqrt{r_{XX}r_{YY}}}$$

Example. A short attitude-to-school measure was used in an exploratory study of gender differences in schools. It correlated .35 with sex, and the evaluator wondered if a longer measure would be worth developing. The internal consistency of the attitude-to-school scale was only .40. What would the correlation with sex be if attitude-to-school had been measured with perfect reliability?

r = .35
r = 1.00 = reliability of the sex measurement
r = .40 = reliability of the attitude-to-school scale
r_{XY} = .55 = correlation if variables were measured without error

The evaluator might decide that, since this represented an upper limit of the correlation that could be expected, the topic should not be pursued. As with other ways of making inferences beyond the data, this correction should be used with caution.

Inter-Rater Reliability

The difference between agreements on levels and agreements on ranks. The correlation coefficient is sometimes used to examine the extent to which raters or judges agreed on something. For example, if a patient's mental state was assessed by clinical interviews and expressed on one or more rating scales, one might ask whether different psychologists would have made the same ratings. In such a case, if the measurement is important enough to warrant the effort, it might be desirable for two psychologists to interview each patient (or to sit in on the same interview) and come to independent assessments or ratings. It would then be possible to report to what extent their independent

ratings agreed. The measurement would be more convincing if it was seen that there was a high measure of agreement between the two ratings.

Suppose the ratings of ten patients were as shown in Table 2. There was a large amount of agreement, and this can be shown in two ways: by listing the discrepancies and summarizing them, and by reporting the correlation coefficient between the two sets of ratings. It is important to note that a high correlation does not necessarily indicate lack of discrepancies in the ratings. For example, the same *correlation* would be obtained if rater 2 had given all the ratings 1 point lower but there would be more for *discrepancies*.

The correlation coefficient indicates agreements on ranking but the discrepancies indicate the extent to which the raters agreed on the LEVEL.

In addition to showing another application of the correlation coefficient, this example serves as a reminder that the size of the correlation coefficient represents how nearly the points lie on a line. This represents a measure of the extent to which the two sets of scores are *ordered* in the same way (high scores with high scores in a positive correlation for example). This is a different question from whether the scores are at the same *level*, that is, have the same means.

TABLE 2
Clinical Ratings of 10 Patients

Patient	Rater 1	Rater 2	Discrepancy
A	7	6	1
B	6	6	0
C	6	7	-1
D	5	4	1
E	5	5	0
F	4	4	0
G	4	4	0
H	3	3	0
I	2	1	1
J	1	1	0
Mean	4.3	4.1	
S.D.	1.9	2.0	

Correlation between rater 1 and rater 2 was 0.95

Discrepancies
Exact agreements = 60%
Ratings within 1 scale point = 100%

The correlation measures the strength of the relationship, not the agreement between the levels of the scores.

The Effect of Having Data on Restricted Groups

Referring to Figure 56, suppose the correlation between two variables is quite strong, the points scatter in quite a thin cigar shape. But suppose you only have data for those cases above a certain point on the X variable—say, above X_B. Then the correlation will be quite low, as indicated by the way the dots appear more like a circle than a cigar. *Restriction in range on a variable almost always results in its correlation with another variable being less than it would be if a full range of data were available.*

This situation arises quite often in practice. For example, if students are all in remedial classes, the range of their scores on cognitive variables will probably be restricted.

Or consider the following dispute. Students are selected for a course on the basis of certain scores on an entry test. Assume for the sake of argument that it is a valid test. Only students above X_B on the entry test are accepted. Then someone collects scores on an important test that shows how well the students are doing on the course. The correlation between the entry test and the course test is very low so the person declares that the entry test is no use, since it predicts poorly the performance on the course. "Cognitive tests generally correlate about .60 or better," this person declares (correctly), "yet the entrance test only correlates .20 with our course test."

The low correlation is true enough and *does* mean that the entry test cannot be used to predict performance on the course test with much accuracy. However, that does not mean that the entry test was a poor selection test. As can be seen from Figure 56, the low correlation is almost inevitable within a restricted sample; but in its function as a selection instrument, the entry test might have served its purpose quite well: The correlation was strong across the entire range, and if students had been admitted who had done poorly on the entry test they would have done poorly on the course.

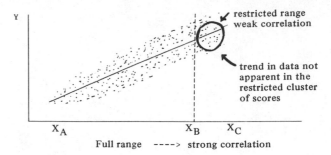

Figure 56. Effect of restriction of range on the correlation coefficient

A formula has been provided by mathematicians to extrapolate from the correlation obtained on the restricted sample to what might have been expected on a full range sample. Like any extrapolation, it should be used cautiously but it can nevertheless serve as a useful reminder of one reason a correlation may be surprisingly low: restriction in range on one or other of the variables.

$$r_u = \frac{r_R(S_u^2/S_R)}{1 - r_R^2 + r_R^2\left(\dfrac{S_u^2}{S_R^2}\right)}$$

where r_u = unrestricted (full range) correlation

r_R = correlation obtained on restricted range

s_u = unrestricted standard deviation

s_R = restricted range standard deviation

Steps	Example

Preview

If one knows what to expect, one knows when to be surprised. The aim of this worksheet is to compute, for each case, a PREDICTED SCORE. When the predicted score is compared with the actual score the difference between them is called the residual. Large residuals may be surprising or informative. Specifically, we have:

RESIDUAL score = OBTAINED score – PREDICTED score

$$d = Y - \hat{Y}$$

Notice the use of the "hat" symbol, ^ , over the Y to mean PREDICTED Y.

The prediction of Y will be made on the basis of some variable X that is related to Y and can therefore be used to predict scores on Y. Notice also that this is equivalent to investigating Y "controlling for" X.

1. Compute the regression equation

1. Compute the regression equation

$$\hat{Y} = .64 \, X + 6.8$$

2. Tabulate X, and predicted Y values

2. Tabulate X, and predicted Y values

Use the regression equation to yield a predicted Y, that is $\hat{Y}$, for each case by entering the value of X for the case into the equation. Tabulate.

1	2	3	4
Case Number	X	Y	$\hat{Y}$

1	2	3	4
Case	X	Y	$\hat{Y}$
AA	1		7.4
BB	3		8.7
CC	3		8.7
DD	4		9.4
EE	5		10.0
FF	5		10.0
GG	6		10.6
HH	7		11.3
II	7		11.3
JJ	9		12.6

Steps	Example

3. Compute residuals

Tabulate actual Y values and for each case, subtract the predicted score from the actual score—that is, compute

$$d = Y - \hat{Y} = \text{residual}$$

3. Compute residuals

1	2	3	4	5
Case				
	X	Y	$\hat{Y}$	d
AA	1	8	7.4	0.6
BB	3	4	8.7	-4.7
CC	3	10	8.7	1.3
DD	4	8	9.4	-1.4
EE	5	10	10.0	0.0
FF	5	16	10.0	6.0
GG	6	12	10.6	1.4
HH	7	10	11.3	-1.3
II	7	10	11.3	-1.3
JJ	9	12	12.6	-0.6

4. Investigate residuals

The residuals represent the discrepancy between the expected score and the obtained score. Note that the expected score was not "expected" on the basis of a personal judgment or the weight of prior evidence or on clinical insight—unless one of these was the X variable; it was the score "expected" on the basis of (1) the score for the case on the X variable and (2) the general pattern of scores in the sample on which the regression equation was calculated.

Which cases were better or worse than expected?

You might find it helpful to rewrite the table, rank ordering the cases by their residuals. Then you can easily pick out those who did "better than expected" and those who had lower than expected Y scores. If the Y test was some kind of achievement and the X a measure of ability, you might define large positive residuals as over-achieving and large negative residuals as under-achieving. You might follow up this statistical analysis with interviews conducted with the over-achieving and under-achieving groups. Or you might ask the teachers of the students in these groups what they recalled about these particular students. In this way, you might build up hypotheses about the factors that led to a good response to the course of instruction and factors associated with a poor response—valuable information for a formative evaluation. Note that whoever was conducting the interviews should not be aware of whether a student was an over- or under-achiever. It would also be best to stratify by ability in making the comparisons: That is, compare like with like. Put another way, do not ask, "What leads to large positive residuals?" but "What leads to large positive residuals among students of high ability, and also among students of low ability?"

Which groups had the best mean residuals?

Sometimes the data fall into treatment groups or groups defined by sex or some other variable. You can see which groups tended to have the higher residuals by computing the mean residual for each group.

4. Investigate residuals

Which cases were better or worse than expected?

When residuals were rank ordered, the following list resulted:

Case	Residual	
FF	6.0	higher than predicted
GG	1.4	
CC	1.3	
AA	0.6	
EE	0.0	achievement on Y as predicted
JJ	-0.6	by X
HH	-1.3	
II	-1.3	
DD	-1.4	
BB	-4.7	lower than predicted

Cases could be simply classified as indicated on the list. The standard error of estimate was 2.6, hence residuals smaller than this value were considered to be pretty much as predicted.

Steps	Example

With which other variables did the residuals correlate?

You can also correlate the residuals with other score-type variables.

5. Issue warnings

The residuals must be taken as indicative, not as established findings. They are only as good as the linear regression model on which they are based.

Sample Size

Remember that the correlation coefficient, on which the computation of residuals depends, is a slippery statistic, and very much more so the smaller the sample. One really needs a hundred or more cases to obtain fairly stable regression equations.

Errors in X

Point out that the method assumes no error in the measurement of X and discuss the reasonableness of this assumption.

Stability

If you have been able to use CROSS-VALIDATION you will have some idea how well the regression equation works from one sample to another. You will also need to be concerned about how STABLE the results are from one occasion to another (i.e., across time). This would be particularly so if the residuals were to be used as an index of "effectiveness" (as in school effects research) or in any other judgmental way. One should strive for rather sound models and data before risking judgments, particularly if others are at risk from the judgments.

The chi-square test is used with measures that place cases into categories. The test indicates whether the results are roughly what one would expect if two measures were *not* related. An example will make this clear. Suppose one measure classifies cases into *program* categories—students are in either the E-group math program or the C-group math program in their secondary school. There are 80 students in the E-group and 100 in the C-group:

```
        Math Program Category
        E-Group         C-Group
```

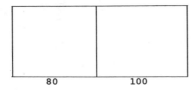

```
           80            100
```

A teacher suggested that their response to the program might depend on which primary school they had recently attended. The evaluator therefore needed to check whether E- and C-groups differed in the proportions of pupils from the three primary schools.

Now suppose that among these students (80 + 100 = 180 total), you knew that 45 were from school A, 45 from school B, and 90 from School C. These categories are listed down the left-hand side of the table, and the total number in each group is indicated outside the table at the right-hand side:

```
                      Math Program Category
                      E-Group          C-Group

Primary School
            A                                      45

            B                                      45

            C                                      90
                                                 -----
                                                  180
```

The numbers outside the box are called MARGINALS. The small blank boxes will form a CONTINGENCY TABLE when the number of students in each category is entered in each "cell." Now, what do you expect the numbers filling the cells will turn out to be? If there were *no* relationship between a student's math program and primary school, then, for the 80 students in the E-group, you would expect about 20 to be from School A, 20 from B, and 40 from C. Why? Because these figures—20, 20, and 40—would keep the figures inside the contingency table consistent with the proportions in the marginals: –45, 45, 90. Thus the *expected distribution*, if math program and primary school attended were not related, would look like Table 3.

TABLE 3

"Expected" Distributions if Math Program and Primary School Were Unrelated

	E-Group	C-Group	
A	20	25	45
B	20	25	45
C	40	50	90
	80	100	180

Since half the students were from School C, you would expect half of the E-group students to be from School C. Likewise for the C group.

Note how the same frequency *pattern* runs down both columns in the contingency table and down the marginal column at the right. Even though the E- and C-groups have a different number of members, the *proportions* of these members form the same distribution pattern as the marginals.

But what if the frequencies, the numbers in the cells, looked like Table 4?

TABLE 4

Observed Distributions, Math Program

	E-Group	C-Group	
A	30	15	45
B	25	20	45
C	25	65	90
	80	100	180

Steps	Example

Overall, half the students were from school C, but in the E-group the proportion was much less than half, only 25 out of 80.

A chi-square test compares the observed distributions with the distributions that would be expected if there were no relationship between the two sets of categories. Here, the test would compare Table 4 with Table 3. The test shows whether the observed distribution is sufficiently different from the expected distribution to be unlikely to have occurred by random sampling.

When to Use Chi-Square

Make up a contingency table and apply the chi-square test whenever you want to decide whether membership in one set of categories is or is not related to membership in another.

The numbers contained in each cell of the contingency table always represent a tally (i.e., a frequency count) of how many cases have the features named in the column and row headings for that cell. Here are some examples of questions that might be asked and the contingency tables that you would set up to answer them.

Examples.

QUESTION	CONTINGENCY TABLE		
Were E-group and C-group Physics teachers about equivalent in academic qualifications in Physics?	Qualifications	E-group	C-group
	Higher degree in Physic		
	First degree with Physics major		
	Science degree, not physics major		
	Other		

QUESTION	CONTINGENCY TABLE		
Were drugs A and B prescribed to similar proportions of each of each socio-economic status group?	SES Group	Drug-A	Drug-B
	High		
	Medium		
	Low		

Example

QUESTION	CONTINGENCY TABLE		
		Program	
	Ethnicity	E-Group	C-Group
Were the E-Group and C-Group similar in ethnic composition?	Black		
	Caucasian		
	Chicano		
	Oriental		
	Other		

QUESTION: Were children in different classrooms expressing different career preferences?

CONTINGENCY TABLE:

Career Preferences	1	2	Classrooms 3	4
Professional				
White Collar				
Blue Collar				
None Stated				

Errors to Avoid When Using Chi-Square

The chi-square test is only applicable if your contingency table has mutually exclusive and exhaustive categories, and each observation is independent of the other observations.

The chi-square test has often been inappropriately used. Asking the following questions will help you avoid errors:

(1) Are you sure that the categories naming the cells of your contingency table are mutually exclusive? Have you eliminated ambiguities about which cell each case belongs in? Are the lines of demarcation between categories clear and definable? Does each case fall into one and only one cell?

(2) Does your contingency table include every possible category into which cases may fall? (i.e., Are the categories exhaustive?) Be particularly careful to include, where necessary, the category called "other" or one that records absence of a characteristic.

(3) Were the observations independent? The fact that a case falls into one cell should not influence where other cases are found. In particular, observations would *not* be independent if they were repeated measurements of the same case. Counting the same case more than once is a common error when using chi-square and is usually referred to as the error of repeated measures. A good way to ensure that you have not made a repeated-measures error is to look at the sum of the marginals of your contingency table. This sum should equal the number of cases in your study.

(4) Is the expected count in any one cell of the contingency table less than 5? Recent work has removed some previous concerns about small expected cell frequencies. Nevertheless, you would not generally want to be making statements about groups of less than 5 or 6 cases. Sometimes it is necessary to rethink the categories in the contingency table, perhaps combining some together to avoid any cell becoming too small. Taking the example of the Physics teachers, you might have found very few with higher degrees in Physics, so that it would be better to combine the first two categories into one category representing "a major or higher degree in Physics." The table would then be a 3-by-2 table rather than a 4-by-2 table.

Steps	Example

Preview

You will make up two contingency tables for the same set of data: one table in which you record the *observed* distributions, and a second table in which you use the marginals to put down *expected* distributions. Then the numbers in these two tables are used to calculate a statistic called chi-square. The bigger this number is, the more likely it is that there is a significant relationship between the two sets of categories.

1. Draw up the observed contingency table from the raw data

Background

The evaluator of an early primary school program wanted to test the hypothesis that children's adjustment was related to their preschool experience.

She collected ratings from teachers of each child's school adjustment. She then divided children into categories according to the kind of preschool they had attended.

1. Draw up the observed contingency table from the raw data

Type of Preschool	Poorly Adjusted	Well Adjusted	
State	40	60	100
Private	10	10	20
Parent-run	5	15	20
No Pre-school	10	30	40
Not Known	15	45	60
	80	160	240

2. Make up the expected distributions using the marginals from the raw data

(a) Set out the contingency table with only the observed *marginals* entered on the table. The marginals, you will remember, are the *total numbers* in each category. On the contingency table, these totals are written in the margins opposite the category to which they refer. The example shows a 2-by-4 contingency table, but you can use the same procedure for any size of table.

2. Make up the expected distributions using the marginals from the raw data

(a)

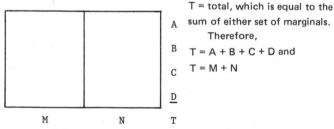

T = total, which is equal to the sum of either set of marginals. Therefore,

$T = A + B + C + D$ and

$T = M + N$

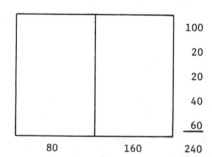

(b) Calculate the expected frequencies in the first column by computing the following:

$$[\text{column total}] \times \frac{[\text{row total}]}{[T]}$$

(b)

This yields the proportion of the column total expected from each row marginal. In the symbols for the above contingency table, the first entry in the first column is as shown:

Steps		Example

$M \times \dfrac{A}{T}$		A
		B
		C
		$\underline{D}$
M	N	T

Filling in the whole first column, you have:

$M \times \dfrac{A}{T}$		A
$M \times \dfrac{B}{T}$		B
$M \times \dfrac{C}{T}$		C
$M \times \dfrac{D}{T}$		D
M	N	T

$80 \times \dfrac{100}{240}$		100
$80 \times \dfrac{20}{240}$		20
$80 \times \dfrac{20}{240}$		20
$80 \times \dfrac{40}{240}$		40
$80 \times \dfrac{60}{240}$		$\underline{60}$
80	160	240

(c) Fill in all the other columns using the same procedure for each cell:

$$[\text{column total}] \times \frac{[\text{row total}]}{[T]}$$

Thus:

(c)

$M \times \dfrac{A}{T}$	$N \times \dfrac{A}{T}$	A
$M \times \dfrac{B}{T}$	$N \times \dfrac{B}{T}$	B
$M \times \dfrac{C}{T}$	$N \times \dfrac{C}{T}$	C
$M \times \dfrac{D}{T}$	$N \times \dfrac{D}{T}$	$\underline{D}$
M	N	T

$80 \times \dfrac{100}{240}$	$160 \times \dfrac{100}{240}$	100
$80 \times \dfrac{20}{240}$	$160 \times \dfrac{20}{240}$	20
$80 \times \dfrac{20}{240}$	$160 \times \dfrac{20}{240}$	20
$80 \times \dfrac{40}{240}$	$160 \times \dfrac{40}{240}$	40
$80 \times \dfrac{60}{240}$	$160 \times \dfrac{60}{240}$	$\underline{60}$
80	160	240

Steps	Example

(d) Complete the calculations in each cell, and assign each cell a number as in the example to the right. You now have a table of *expected frequencies*.

(d)

[1] 33.33		[6] 66.67		100
[2] 6.67		[7] 13.33		20
[3] 6.67		[8] 13.33		20
[4] 13.33		[9] 26.67		40
[5] 20.00		[10] 40.00		60
80		160		240

3. *For each cell of the contingency table, compute this quantity:*

$$\frac{\left(\begin{array}{l}\text{observed} \\ \text{frequency}\end{array} - \begin{array}{l}\text{expected} \\ \text{frequency}\end{array}\right)^2}{\begin{array}{l}\text{expected} \\ \text{frequency}\end{array}}$$

This can be written as follows:

$$\frac{(O - E)^2}{E}$$

Note that the top quantity is squared.

It is convenient to work with a 6-columned table like the one shown in the example. Fill in the first three columns from the tables; then use the calculator. Work across each row. You really don't need to write down columns 4 and 5, but they are shown so you can check that you are working correctly.

Add up the *quantities* in column 6. The total is chi-square, the required statistic. It has the symbol χ^2 (= greek letter chi).

3. *For each cell of the contingency table, compute this quantity:*

$$\frac{\left(\begin{array}{l}\text{observed} \\ \text{frequency}\end{array} - \begin{array}{l}\text{expected} \\ \text{frequency}\end{array}\right)^2}{\begin{array}{l}\text{expected} \\ \text{frequency}\end{array}}$$

1	2	3	4	5	6
Cell	O	E	O-E	$(O-E)^2$	$\frac{(O-E)^2}{E}$
1	40	33.33	6.67	44.5	1.33
2	10	6.67	3.33	11.1	1.66
3	5	6.67	-1.67	2.8	0.42
4	10	13.33	-3.33	11.1	0.83
5	15	20.00	-5.00	25.0	1.25
6	60	66.67	-6.67	44.5	0.67
7	10	13.33	-3.33	11.1	0.83
8	15	13.33	1.67	2.8	0.21
9	30	26.67	3.33	11.1	0.42
10	45	40.00	5.00	25.0	0.63

$$\chi^2 = 8.25$$

Steps

Example

4. Check whether your chi-square value is larger than the tabled chi-square

To do this, you first need to figure out a number that you need in order to use the chi-square table: the df number—degrees of freedom. To find the df number, imagine a row and a column from the contingency table are blotted out and count the number of remaining cells. The number is the df number.

Example. A 3-by-3 contingency table

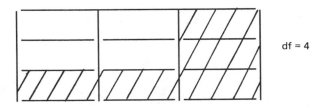

df = 4

Example. A 2-by-3 contingency table

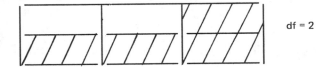

df = 2

Now locate the tabled chi-square in Table C.9 (Appendix C) by going down the left column to the appropriate df number, then selecting the chi-square value from one of the columns.

4. Check whether your chi-square value is larger than the tabled chi-square

For 4 degrees of freedom, the critical value for chi-square at the .05 level of significance is 9.49. The obtained value was less than this critical value.

5. Interpret and report the statistic

If your obtained value of chi-square was greater than that in the .05 column in Table C.9, you can conclude that the relationship between the category that defined the columns and the category that defined the rows was statistically significant at the .05 level. This can be reported by displaying the contingency table, recording chi-square underneath it, and commenting in the text, "Analysis of the contingency table showed there was a statistically significant relationship between the two sets of categories (p < .05).

5. Interpret and report the statistic

The evaluator reported the observed frequencies, adding the percentage of students who had been rated poorly adjusted or well adjusted.

Steps

Sometimes you will find a significant χ^2 value and wonder if there was a strong relationship among all categories in the rows and columns or if *some particular subset of categories* caused the significant relationship. To examine this question, check column 6 of the table in Step 3. If all cells had roughly equal values, then the significant chi-square probably did not result from the influence of any particular cells. On the other hand, if most cells had small values but there were just one or two comparatively large values, then it is among these large values that you might find the source of the significant relationship.

A Final Word of Caution

Whether a relationship is established with a correlation or a chi-square, be careful to avoid a trap into which many researchers and evaluators have fallen: *Remember that establishing the existence of a relationship between two measures does not tell you what has caused it.* If, for instance, it has been shown that students who spend more time in the reading lab have higher reading achievement scores, what interpretation can be made? Was the reading lab improving reading, or were better-reading students choosing to spend more time in the reading lab or being sent to the reading lab more often by teachers? In general, if there is a relationship between X and Y, this does not tell us whether X causes Y, or Y causes X. And frequently it could be the case that *neither* inference about causes is correct: Other factors may cause both X and Y.

To take another example, suppose a high positive correlation has been found between length of teachers' experience in a school and percentage of students from that school who go on to college. It might be thought that the relationship indicated that more experienced teachers were more effective at preparing students for college. Since going to college occurs *after* teachers have had their influence, doesn't this indicate the direction of cause and effect? Not necessarily. The presence of college-bound students in a school might cause the retention of experienced teachers. Alternatively—or maybe additionally, since there are usually multiple rather than single causes for anything—teachers may prefer to teach in wealthy neighborhoods for salary, status, or other reasons, and wealthy neighborhoods have higher proportions of students attending college. In this case, the relationship between the measures may occur because both are related to a third measure— neighborhood wealth.

The caution that finding a relationship does not establish causality has been so often repeated that it might as well be engraved in stone.

Example

Table A

Reported Adjustment to School of Children from Various Preschool Programs

Adjustment	Poorly adj. number	%	Well adj. number	%
State	40	40	60	60
Private	10	50	10	50
Parent-run	5	25	15	75
None	10	25	30	75
Not Known	15	25	45	75
	80	100.00	160	100.00

Obtained Chi-square = 8.25

Tabled Chi-Square = 7.79 for significance at the .10 level.

She noted that the relationship between the teachers' ratings of adjustment and the type of preschool attended was not statistically significant at the .05 level but was statistically significant if we used the more liberal .10 level. The pattern in the data was that two preschool experiences were associated with higher than "expected" numbers of pupils rated as "poorly adjusted": the state preschool and the private preschool.

The difference between the "poorly adjusted" proportions of pupils from these preschools and the proportions who had been to a parent-run preschool or no preschool were of sufficient magnitude to warrant further investigation. Qualitative observational studies would seem to be the approach to start with.

Notes for SPSSX Users

Correlation

To produce correlation coefficients, together with the number of cases used in the computation and the ONE-TAILED significance level, use the procedure PEARSON CORR. For example, if you had variables called "pretest," "posttest," "sex," and "absence," and if the values for each variable were recorded in numbers (not letters, such as F for female), the following command could be used:

```
PEARSON CORR pretest,  posttest,  sex,  absence
STATISTICS      1
```

The STATISTICS command causes means and standard deviations for each variable to be tabulated. A plot of the scores for two numeric variables can be obtained by

```
SCATTERGRAM pretest   posttest
STATISTICS      ALL
OPTIONS         7
```

which will provide you with the correlation coefficient and the standard error of estimate as well as a reasonable scatterplot.

Regression

The command to use if regression equations are needed is REGRESSION. The following commands would create a regression equation to predict "posttest" from "pretest" and would save the residuals for further analyses, saving them as a new variable that the user has named "zrespre" (standardized residuals from pretest as a predictor).

```
REGRESSION   VARIABLES = pretest, posttest
             /DEPENDENT = posttest
             /ENTER
             /RESIDUALS = OUTLIERS
             /SAVE ZRESID (zrespre)
```

The saved residuals could be used in the same run. For example, perhaps the evaluator wishes to look at the residuals from five different clinics from which pre- and posttest data were collected:

```
ONEWAY          zrespre BY clinic(1,5)
STATISTICS      ALL
```

Chi-Square

Contingency tables are produced for pairs of variables listed in the procedure CROSSTABS (from the word cross-tabulate), and the chi-square statistic is produced if you ask for statistic number 1. For example, if you had the variable "adjust," which contained a rating of adjustment to school, and a variable "presch," which indicated which preschool the child had attended, you could obtain a contingency table like the one in the worksheet with this command:

```
CROSSTABS =   presch BY adjust
STATISTICS    1
OPTIONS       3,4,16
```

Using options 3 and 4 gives row and column percentages in the contingency table, and option 16 produces standardized residuals so that you can see which cells have contributed most to the chi-square statistic.

We often think that once the data have been collected, statistics will come into play in analyzing the figures. But statistical methods are useful much earlier than that: in the phase of developing measurement instruments and analyzing pilot data. As we shall see, statistics can also give a rough answer to the often asked question, "How large a sample do I need?" For an evaluator of a large program this question is often vitally important since there are many kinds of data that could be collected and only limited resources of time and money. These resources must be used strategically, not wasted on a large sample where a small sample would be adequate.

Statistics also offers some guidance on how long tests should be, and on selecting items to go into the final version of a test. There are also procedures for developing subscales, sets of items that can be added up to give a score on a particular aspect. This development of sub-scales is particularly important in measuring attitudes.

This chapter presents these useful applications of statistics to the development and piloting of tests and questionnaires.

Reliability of a Test or Scale

If you tested a group one day and then again the next day only to find that the results were completely different, this would present problems. Which set of results should be used? Were students just guessing the answers? Was the test not suitable? We expect a certain amount of consistency in any measurement. The extent to which a measure is consistent is called its RELIABILITY.

When you use a ready-made, published test, the manual that accompanies the test will report various kinds of reliability using data the developers obtained from the norming groups. This section will help you to interpret those manuals. It is also important because the reliability of a test is not fixed. A test might be reliable for some groups or in some circumstances but not when used with other groups or in other circumstances. Consequently, you may wish to check at least the internal consistency reliability (explained below) of any test you use in your evaluation.

Three Kinds of Reliability

Test-retest reliability: STABILITY

If you give the test on one occasion and then again on a second occasion you could plot the results with the first occasion's results on the X axis and the second set of results on the Y axis. The correlation between the two sets of results would tell you the extent to which the rank orders stayed the same, the extent to which people who scored high on the first test scored high on the second test and vice versa, and the extent to which you could predict the second test results from the first test results. You will recall that the correlation coefficient does not indicate whether the *level* of the scores (e.g., the mean) has changed or not, or in what direction (see Chapter 4). The correlation between results from one administration of a test and another is called the test-retest reliability of the test. It is a measure of the test's STABILITY over time. Clearly, the correlation is likely to be weaker the longer the time between the two administrations, so that it is usual to report the time associated with the retesting, such as "the 3-month test-retest reliability was .69."

In an evaluation, tests are often used at the beginning of a program and then again at the end, or are administered each year for monitoring purposes. It is worthwhile to report the test-retest reliability *within each treatment group* from such data, simply by computing the correlation coefficient. You would not wish to mix up the experimental and control groups because there is the expectation that one group may do better than the other group and this would disturb the rank ordering and lower the correlation. Indeed, if there are subsets within either group that benefit particularly, this also will lower the test-retest correlation.

Alternate forms reliability: EQUIVALENCE

Sometimes published tests are available in two or more forms that are stated to be "equivalent forms." This means that any of the forms should yield about the same set of results. The correlation between the two tests should be high and they should yield the same mean and standard deviation of scores if given to the same or equivalent groups. It is convenient to use one form as a pretest and another form as a posttest.

There is another type of equivalence that can often be important in evaluations: the equivalence of raters, or inter-rater reliability. Many important measurements have to be made by human raters, by human judgment. For example, a clinical interview may enable ratings to be made on personality factors, adjustment to working conditions, fidelity to treatment regimens, attitude to a program, level of aspiration, and so on: judgments of complex dimensions that are considered important enough to try to assess. There is nothing necessarily unscientific about "subjective" judgments, but some care is needed in making them credible. For example, it is as well to be able to demonstrate that at least two people can *independently* come to fairly similar judgments.

If you have judgments to deal with in your evaluation, judgments based on interviews, on the coding of open-ended questionnaire responses, on observations and so on, you should get some, at least, of the judgments made by two independent raters and report the correlation between them (the INTER-RATER RELIABILITY) and also the extent of agreement and disagreement on levels of the ratings (as discussed in Chapter 4). Before the raters make their ratings, they should receive *written* instructions and *only* written instructions so that the criteria are explicit, recorded, replicable, and open to inspection. These characteristics of a measurement make it scientific, not whether or not it is a judgment rather than the results of a test. Of course, the most important aspect of using raters in the evaluation of programs is that, when conducting the ratings, the raters should not know whether they are dealing with a member of the experimental or the control group; that is, the raters should be "blind" to the treatment condition.

Split half reliability: INTERNAL CONSISTENCY

Suppose you split a test in half and computed, for each person, their score on each half of the test. You would then have two sets of scores, one for each half of the test, and you could compute a correlation between the two sets of scores. The correlation between these two halves of a test is called the SPLIT HALF RELIABILITY. It would be disturbing if the two halves did not correlate fairly well, say .60 at least. If the test is measuring ONE variable then whichever half of the test you look at should give results like the other half of the test. If this is the case, we say the test items are HOMOGENEOUS or the test shows high INTERNAL CONSISTENCY.

The concept of splitting the test in half is just a starting point for there are, of course, many ways of splitting a test in half. Using the idea of the items of a test being a sample from the population of items from which the test might have been composed, there is a statistic known as the KR20 formula (Kuder-Richardson formula 20), which is a widely used measure of internal consistency. It indicates how the test might be expected to correlate with other selections of similar items and its value is higher the stronger the inter-correlations among items of the test.

$$r_{tt} = \left(\frac{k}{k-1} \right) \left(1 - \frac{\Sigma \sigma_i^2}{\sigma_t^2} \right)$$

If the items of the test were not all measuring the same thing, then perhaps the test result shouldn't be reported as a single score from the test, but as several separate scores for the different things it is measuring. In other words, does the test need reporting in terms of sub-scales? Another aspect of this question is, "Are the items composing a subscale homogeneous, giving the subscale a reasonable reliability?"

The same question arises in another context: with respect to attitude measurements on questionnaires or on specially constructed attitude tests. A valuable approach in measuring attitudes is to construct a number of items that can be added up to give an index of an attitude. It is better to use a collection of items rather than just one item in case peculiarities of wording twist the results on any particular item. Consistent responses across a series of items that are all concerned with the same attitude give us more confidence in the measurement than if we have just one response to go on. Worksheet 5B illustrates how KR20 can be used to investigate the internal consistency of an attitude scale, and it should be noticed that the same kind of analysis could be applied to an achievement test or to the construction of profiles of achievement.

Steps	Example

Preview

$$KR20 = \left(\frac{k}{k-1}\right)\left(1 - \frac{\Sigma\sigma_i^2}{\sigma_t^2}\right)$$

where k = number of items

σ_i^2 = population variance of an item

σ_t^2 = population variance of total scores

1. Set out the data in a cases-by-items table

The items might be scored as 1 for correct or 0 for incorrect or they might be scored as so many points for each item.

1. Set out the data in a cases-by-items matrix

The table shows the scores of 6 patients on a diagnostic test. A 1 was recorded for success on a task and a 0 for failure.

				Test Items (tasks)							
Patient	1	2	3	4	5	6	7	8	9	10	Total
A	0	1	0	0	0	0	0	0	0	0	1
B	1	1	1	0	0	0	0	0	0	0	3
C	0	1	1	1	1	1	0	0	0	0	5
D	1	0	1	0	1	1	0	0	0	1	5
E	1	1	0	1	1	1	0	1	1	0	7
F	1	1	0	1	1	1	1	1	1	1	9
σ^2:	.222	.139	.250	.250	.222	.222	.139	.222	.222	.222	6.66
difficulty:	.3	.2	.5	.5	.3	.3	.2	.3	.3	.6	

2. Compute the variance for each item, writing it down at the bottom of the column for the item

Worksheet 2D showed how to compute the variance, which is the standard deviation squared. It is hoped you have a hand calculator to do this computation quickly and simply. Use the population variance, not the sample variance.

2. Compute the variance for each item

The *population* variance was computed with a handheld calculator and recorded on the row labeled σ^2 at the foot of the table.

3. Add up the variances of the items and record

Sum of item variances = [   ] = box A

3. Add up the item variances

Sum of the σ^2 values = [2.110] = box A

4. Add up the total score for each person and put this score in the final column of the cases-by-items table

4. Add up scores per person

The total scores were recorded in the last column in the table (see above).

Steps	Example

5. Compute the variance of the total scores

Variance of the total scores = | 46 | = box B

5. Compute the variance of the total scores

The population standard deviation was 2.582 = σ

σ_t^2 = variance of the total score = | 6.667 | = box B

6. Compute the ratio of the sum of item variances to the total variance

This ratio is box A divided by box B.

$$\text{ratio} = \frac{\boxed{\text{box A}}}{\boxed{\text{box B}}} = \boxed{} = \text{box C}$$

6. Compute the ratio $\Sigma\sigma_i^2/\sigma_t^2$

$$\frac{\Sigma\sigma_i^2}{\sigma_i^2} = \frac{\text{Box A}}{\text{Box B}} = \frac{2.110}{6.667} = \boxed{0.316} = \text{box C}$$

7. Compute k/(k – 1) where k = number of items on the test

$$k = (\quad)$$
$$k - 1 = (\quad)$$
$$\text{therefore } \frac{k}{k-1} = \boxed{} = \text{box D}$$

7. Compute k/(k – 1)

$$\left(\frac{k}{k-1}\right) = \left(\frac{10}{9}\right) = \boxed{1.111} = \text{box D}$$

8. Compute KR20

$$KR20 = (1 - \text{box C}) \times \text{box D}$$

8. Compute KR20

$$KR20 = r_u = (1 - 0.316) \times 1.111$$
$$= 0.759$$

You could include in your evaluation report the statement thát the internal consistency of the test, as indicated by KR20, was 0.76.

Note: If item 3 were removed the reliability would jump to 0.85. This suggests item 3 should not be included in the scale, particularly if it correlates negatively with total scores in a larger sample.

In general, examine the correlation of each item with the total. Weak positive correlations are fine—they add their contribution to the scale. But negative correlations mean the item is detracting from the homogeneity and therefore from the reliability of the scale.

Steps	Example

1. Create a selection of items

Create a set of statements with which respondents can agree or disagree. It is considered desirable that some of these statements be stated positively (so that agreement indicates a positive or favorable attitude) and others be stated negatively.

1. Create a selections of Items

In an evaluation of a new syllabus the attitudes that students held at the end of their course of study constituted one of the important variables. Some of the items in a scale to measure attitude to the subject were the following:

> Item 1: I found it hard to get down to work in this subject
> Item 2: I looked forward to lessons in this subject
> Item 3: I thought about this subject a lot even in my spare time
> Item 4: I worried about this subject
> Item 5: I regretted taking this subject
> Item 6: I preferred this subject to any of my other subjects

Students were asked to respond using this scale:

> 1 = not true of me at all
> 2 = not really true of me
> 3 = occasionally true of me
> 4 = this was fairly true of me
> 5 = this was very true of me

2. Pilot the items

That is, get responses from real people similar to those for whom the attitude scale is to be developed. Record their responses in a cases-by-items table.

2. Pilot the items

The responses made by 10 students, A to J, are shown in the cases-by-items table below.

Cases			Items			

	Items					
Cases	1	2	3	4	5	6
A	3	5	4	1	1	4
B	1	3	3	2	1	4
C	3	4	2	1	3	3
D	1	4	3	2	4	2
E	3	4	1	1	3	3
F	4	3	3	1	5	3
G	3	4	1	1	5	3
H	3	1	3	1	5	3
I	4	2	1	1	2	4
J	5	3	2	2	2	3

3. Reverse the scoring for negatively stated items; sum the scores per person

3. Reverse the scoring for negatively stated items; sum the scores by person

Each item had to be considered in turn. How would a student who had a positive attitude in the subject respond to the item. For item 1, it was guessed that a student with a positive attitude would answer with a 1 or a 2 rather than at the "very true of me" end of the scale. But we want *high* scores associated with positive attitudes

Steps	Example

Example

so we reverse the scoring and change 1 to 5; 2 to 4; 3 stays as 3; 4 becomes 2; and 5 becomes 1.

This reversed scoring is recorded in a new table (total scores per person and means have been added at the right-hand side):

Cases	1	2	Items 3	4	5	6	Total	Mean (scale score)
	3	5	4	5	5	4	26	4.33
	5	3	3	4	5	4	24	4.00
	3	4	2	5	3	3	20	3.33
	5	4	3	4	2	2	20	3.33
	3	4	1	5	3	3	19	3.17
	2	3	3	5	1	3	17	2.83
	3	4	1	5	1	3	17	2.83
	3	1	3	5	1	3	16	2.67
	2	2	1	5	2	4	16	2.67
	1	3	2	4	2	3	15	2.50

4. Compute KR20 for the entire set of items

4. Compute KR20 for the entire set of items

Following Worksheet 5A, KR20 was computed as

$$\left(\frac{6}{5}\right)\left(1 - \frac{6.24}{11.8}\right) = 0.56$$

5. Take steps to improve the scale if KR20 is not satisfactory

5. Take steps to improve the scale if KR20 is not satisfactory

There are three major points to consider if the scale has low reliability as measured by KR20.

An internal consistency of 0.56 was not considered quite high enough. The following steps were taken:

(a) Is the sample used for the pilot data too homogeneous? The scale will not appear to be reliable for a sample that all answer with much the same attitude. KR20 measures the extent to which the scale "sorts people out." To have a high value for KR20 you need people with differing attitudes in the sample. Try to obtain a sample that is as heterogeneous as possible whilst still being representative of the sample for whom the scale is being designed.

(a) *Sample.* The pilot sample showed a spread of attitudes but a larger sample would be helpful if possible.

(b) *"Poor" items.* Item 4 seemed poor because it correlated negatively with total score and because it showed little variance.

(b) Are some of the items "poor items"? One approach to locating poor items (such as item 3 in Worksheet 5A) is to compute KR20 leaving out each item in turn. (SPSSX RELIABILITY does this for you; see notes at the end of this chapter.) To do this by hand just keep repeating Worksheet 5A with one item omitted. The omission of one item will change the total score column and the sum of item variances.

KR20 was re-computed leaving out item 4 and adjusting the total scores accordingly. The result was, without item 4,

$$KR20 = \left(\frac{5}{4}\right)\left(1 - \frac{5.98}{12.41}\right) = 0.64.$$

Another way to locate poor items is to compute the correlation between an item and the total. If you wrote the cases-by-items table with the cases rank ordered by total score (as in the example), you will find you can often "see" a poorly correlated item by reading down the item column and total score column together. If it correlates, the numbers in the item column should go down along with the item totals.

This was some improvement over 0.56, and item 4 was dropped. Post hoc it was thought that worrying was more a function of personality than of attitude toward the subject. This thought was merely a speculation, of course, but it comforted the evaluators to have come up with an explanation.

Any item in which there is almost no variation in the answers (e.g., respondents all agreed or all disagreed) will be a poor item statistically, although you might want to include it for its information value.

(c) *More items?* The best remaining chance of improving the scale would be to add more items, it seemed. How many more would be needed to yield a reliability of .70? To answer this the Spearman-Brown formula was applied (see page 114)

(c) Is the scale long enough or does it need more items? Short scales are less reliable than long scales, other things being equal. There is help from statistics for this question. The Spearman-Brown "prophecy" formula prophesies what the reliability would

$$m = \frac{r_m(1 - r)}{r(1 - r_m)}$$

$$= \frac{.70(1 - .64)}{.64(1 - .70)} = \frac{0.252}{0.192}$$

$$= 1.31$$

Steps

be if you added more items (the Spearman-Brown formula is described later in this chapter and is applied in the example.)

6. Record a scale score for each person

Example

This suggested that the test needed to be made 1.3 times its present length; therefore, it needed about 0.3 more items. (0.3) * 6 = 2 more items were needed.

This seemed quite within reach, so 4 more items were written and tried out and finally a scale of 6 items was retained for use, with a reliability of well above .70.

6. Record a scale score for each person

Each student's attitude to the subject was expressed as a mean computed from summing the student's responses and dividing by the number of items. (The scale scores for the original 6-item scale were shown in the table.)

Item Analysis and Scale Construction

The worksheets have shown how internal consistency measures can assist you in developing measurement scales. There are some other procedures for examining items that apply to certain situations and some of these are described below. The situation in which these techniques apply is in the development of a test or attitude measure. Usually many items are written and a few are finally selected for use after piloting. How this selection is made will depend upon the purpose of the test, but there are some statistical effects that are worth knowing about.

Item difficulty

This concept applies, of course, to achievement or aptitude tests, in which there is a "right" answer. The difficulty of an item can be defined empirically by the proportion of persons taking the test who get the item wrong. Thus an item with a difficulty of .90 would be failed by 90%, or .90 of candidates—a difficult item. On your cases-by-items table you can record item difficulties along a row at the bottom (as in Worksheet 5A).

What use are item difficulties? One immediate use is to provide information on the parts of the test that students found difficult. This can have implications for instruction. Why were some items difficult? Had the work been covered? Had it been taught in a confusing way? Were some items inevitably difficult, or should an effort be made to improve scores on this part of the syllabus in the future? The item-by-item analysis of an achievement test can provide valuable information for the formative evaluation of instruction.

There is another less obvious use for item difficulties. The reliability of a test is related to its variance, and the variance of the test is composed of variances of its individual items. The larger the variance of the items the more reliable the test is likely to be. If p = proportion passing and q = proportion failing an item, the variance of the item is p × q. Playing around with a few figures (remembering that q must equal 1 – p) will convince you of something that can be proved with a little calculus: The variance of the item will be a maximum when p = .5. This implies that it might be wise to select items with difficulties closer to .5 rather than further away. Of course, such a statistical consideration cannot be the only consideration in developing a test. You might feel it is important to check students' knowledge of some important basic facts even if that means using a set of easy questions on which you expect very small proportions to fail. Nevertheless, it is as well to realize that the statistical properties of a test will improve with items near the .5 level of difficulty.

Another important consideration is that if the test is to be used to make decisions about students at the lower end of the distribution (say, for provision of remedial help) then it would be as well to include items that yield difficulties of .5 for the students scoring at the lower end of the scale. In general you want the items to have a difficulty of .5 over the range of scores for which you want the greatest precision. If you were selecting from the upper end of the scale then you would want to look at the difficulty levels (pass rates) of the items for the able pupils and choose items that yielded .5 difficulties for that subgroup. This would of course result in including more difficult items in a test to select more able students.

Analysis of Distractors

Multiple-choice items have a stem and then a number of possible answer from which the test-taker must select one. For example:

Newcastle Upon Tyne is in what part of England?

(a) north east
(b) north west
(c) south west
(d) south east
(e) middle

The incorrect alternatives are called distractors, and if they are performing their job well you would expect each distractor to receive some of the choices. Plotting distributions for each item gives a quick visual check. An example of a format that might be used to set out the results of a pilot study for consideration of the items is illustrated below:

```
 _____
|        Item          |   Results of Pilot  | DIFFICULTY |
|----------------------|---------------------|------------|
|1) Newcastle Upon Tyne is | x              |            |
|   in what part of England?| x             |            |
|   (a) north east     | x                   |            |
|   (b) north west     | x                   |    .60     |
|   (c) south east     | x  x                |            |
|   (d) south west     | x  x     x  x       |            |
|   (e) central        | x  x  x  x  x       |            |
|                      | ---------------     |            |
|                      | a  b  c  d  e       |            |
|                      | *                   |            |
|_____|_____|_____|
```

* = correct response

The number of items needed in a test

Decisions about the length of a test must balance at least two factors: The test must not be so long as to be too inconvenient to administer but it must also not be so short that it yields unreliable scores. The longer the test, other things being equal, the more reliable it is. There is some guidance available in the form of the Spearman-Brown formula:

```
--------------------------------------------
   The Spearman-Brown formula
--------------------------------------------

                    mr
      r   =     -------------
       m         1+(m-1)r
--------------------------------------------
```
where
r= reliability of the initial test

m= multiplication factor, the
   number of times the test is
   increased in length

r_m= reliability when the test
   length has been altered by
   a factor m
```
--------------------------------------------
```

The formula works on the assumption that the items to be added or subtracted to alter the length of the test are all "parallel" to the items already on the test. "Parallel" items are items with the same difficulty, intercorrelations, and content. This assumption might well be violated in practice, but the Spearman-Brown prophecy formula can provide some guidance, particularly when it is rearranged to provide a value for m and thus indicate how many more items will be needed. A little rearranging of the formula yields the following:

```
--------------------------------------------
The Spearman-Brown formula re-arranged
--------------------------------------------
          r  (1 - r)
           m
   m  =   -------------
          r (1 - r )
                   m
--------------------------------------------
     for an example of its use see
     worksheet 5B
--------------------------------------------
```

Confidence Intervals

Suppose you are trying to guess the numbers of peas in a jar. Person A might not have tried this task before and, feeling very uncertain, might say only that the number was probably somewhere between 200 and 500. Person B might have more confidence, having played the game before, and might feel better able to estimate the number, so might say "between 300 and 400." These guesses could be written in another way:

> Person A's rather uncertain guess could be written as 350 + 150 or 350 − 150 (350 plus or minus 150)

> Person B's more confident guess could be written as 350 + 50 or 350 − 50 (350 plus or minus 50)

This game can be used to introduce some terminology.

For Person A, 200 could be called the LOWER CONFIDENCE LIMIT and 500 the UPPER CONFIDENCE LIMIT. The range between 200 and 500 was the CONFIDENCE INTERVAL. The smaller confidence interval implied that the number had been more accurately estimated. The larger confidence interval suggests considerable uncertainty about the number.

We met confidence intervals previously in connection with estimating the population mean from a sample. To review, the smaller the sample, the less confidence we can have in the estimate. The quantity SE / $s\sqrt{n}$ is called the standard error of the mean and we expressed our estimate as

the mean plus or minus the standard error of the mean:

$$X + SE$$

The same kind of indication of accuracy should be made in reporting a test score. The test score is just one sample of a person's work on one sample of possible tests that could have been devised to test the work. We indicate the effect of the reliability of the test by putting a confidence interval on the test score. The standard error for a test score is called the standard error of measurement and is computed from the following equation.

```
--------------------------------------------
   The standard error of measurement
--------------------------------------------

     s        = s  √ 1 - r
      meas       t        tt
--------------------------------------------
```
where s_t = standard deviation
            of the test

      r_{tt} = reliability of the test
```
--------------------------------------------
```

The standard error of measurement serves as a warning against over-interpreting small differences on test scores. For an IQ test, for example, with s = 15 and a reliability of about .80 (for a group test, it would be higher than for an individually administered test) the SE of measurement can be expected to be about

$15 \times \sqrt{(1 - .80)}$ = approximately 7 points

When you report a confidence interval based on plus or minus one standard error (SE), this is called the 68% confidence interval. (Recall that 68% of scores lie within one standard deviation of the mean in a normal distribution.) It is more usual, though not necessarily more convenient or useful, to report the 95% confidence interval based on plus or minus 1.96 times the SE.

How Reliable Must a Test or Attitude Scale Be?

Some measurements do not need to be "reliable" at all. If what is being measured is expected to be unstable, such as mood swings or erratic pulses, then there is not much point in asking for there to be a large stable component. Reliability is an index of the proportion of a measurement that is *stable*. However, for most measurements we would want a reasonable level of reliability. What is reasonable? The answer to this question depends almost entirely on the purpose to which the measure is to be put. If important decisions about *individuals* rest on a measurement, then it should have very high reliability, say .90 or better. (Of course it should also have very high validity.) For the investigation of *group* differences, however, lower reliabilities are usually sufficient, say .60 upward.

It is sometimes thought that attitudes are more difficult to measure than cognitive variables such as achievement. However, as far as internal consistency goes, it is not difficult to achieve acceptable levels of internal consistency in attitude scales. Their validity might be more of a problem than the validity of cognitive measures, but the task is far from hopeless.

There is a major difference between attitude measurement and cognitive measurement: Respondents can *choose* how to answer attitude questions whereas on achievement items one cannot choose the correct answer without knowing it (or not consistently anyway). This brings us into the realm of the consideration of VALIDITY.

Validity

The validity of a test or questionnaire is the extent to which it measures what it purports to measure; whether it is valid for the purpose for which it is claimed to be valid. A test might be valid for one purpose but not for another. So, as with reliability, a figure for validity might be reported in the manual, but the figure needs to be checked in the particular circumstances under which the instrument is used.

Kinds of Validity

"Valid for what purpose?" we must ask, and validity measures can be divided into those concerned with the validity of the instrument as a measure of something and the validity of the instrument as a predictor of something.

The validity of an instrument as a measurement of something

Consider this situation. Evaluators propose to give a test to students in a special program designed to increase their knowledge of vocational and technical subjects. They write out a test and show it to a teacher in the program.

The teacher says, "You can't use that—it's not what I've been teaching at all. That's not what is meant by "technical and vocational education!" The teacher in this case is questioning the CONTENT VALIDITY of the test. Do the contents of the test appear to be measuring what you think the test should be measuring? It is a matter of judgment and definition, and statistics cannot help you particularly with this kind of validity. The evaluators, teachers, and administrators would need to confer to resolve this question of content validity, and come to some agreed definitions.

Another important kind of validity is called CONSTRUCT validity. Is the instrument measuring the construct it is claiming to measure? For example, is an instrument that is called a "self-concept" measure an adequate measure of this construct? Often this question about validity raises the whole issue of the nature of the construct: How is it defined, what evidence is there that it exists, and so on? Statistics can give some help with an approach called the multi-trait, multi-method approach (Campbell and Fiske, 1959). The idea is that if a construct exists it should be possible to measure it in more than one way. For example, self-concept might be measured with a paper and pencil self-report scale, a rating made by others and a projective test, or a clinical interview. The correlations among these different measures of the same thing should be strong and positive. (This approach is the quantitative parallel to the "triangulation" approach to validity in qualitative methods.) Moreover, if the same methods are applied to measure some other construct— for example, verbal ability—the results should *not* correlate highly with measures of self-concept. If they did, one would fear that self-concept and verbal ability were inextricably mixed up, calling into question one or both constructs, or at least the ways of measuring them.

The investigation of construct validity by the multi-trait, multi-method approach would be so time-consuming as to be beyond the purview of most evaluators. Suffice it to say, the approach requires the construction of a set of correlation coefficients derived from multiple instruments used to measure two or more "traits" (variables). Using the self-concept example, each r in the matrix below would need to be filled in with the relevant reliability coefficient, and each v with a correlation that would indicate validity (same trait measured by different methods). Correlations indicated by stars should be low.

Criterion-Related Validity

There are two purposes to which a test might be put that both involve correlating it with some other test, the "criterion." You might, for example, want to use test B rather than test A because test B is shorter, or cheaper, or more up-to-date. But you need to be assured that the

```
      Example of a multi-trait multi-method matrix
-------------------------------------------------------------
  TRAITS: ──────────────▶  Self              Verbal
                           concept           ability
            METHODS──▶     S   O   C         S   O   C
-------------------------------------------------------------
                   S |  r
  Self concept
                   O |  v   r
                   C |  v   v   r
-------------------------------------------------------------
  Verbal ability  S |  *               r
                   O |  *   *           v   r
                   C |  *   *   *       v   v   r
-------------------------------------------------------------
    NOTE:
    The methods were :
                         Self report     S
                         Report of others  O
                         Clinical interview  C
-------------------------------------------------------------
```

results will be as good as those previously obtained with test A. You would give both tests and see if they correlated highly. If they did, you might feel justified in using test B rather than test A. Test A is called the criterion test; it is the established test and you try to show that test B exhibits CONCURRENT VALIDITY in that results correlate highly with the criterion, given at the same time (concurrently).

Finally there is PREDICTIVE VALIDITY. This is the kind of validity you are concerned with if you are using a test to predict some future measurement. That is, you are concerned with the correlation between the test and a criterion test that will become available later. Chapter 4 dealt with prediction, and you will know from that chapter that along with the possibility of prediction goes the possibility of CONTROLLING for certain variables. In summary, four kinds of validity have been named, falling into two categories defined by the purpose behind the testing:

```
-------------------------------------------------------------
    Purpose                  |  Type of validity
-------------------------------------------------------------
    Obtaining a              |  CONTENT
    meaningful
    measurement              |  CONSTRUCT
-------------------------------------------------------------
    Prediction or            |  CONCURRENT }
    control                  |            } CRITERION-
                             |  PREDICTIVE } RELATED
-------------------------------------------------------------
```

The Standard Error of Estimate

One way to express the criterion-related validity of a test is to report the correlation between the test and the criterion, for some sample. Another way is to report how accurately a criterion score can be predicted from knowledge of the test score. As we have seen before with confidence limits on the mean and on a measurement, one can indicate how accurate a score is likely to be if one knows the standard error (SE). The SE for the prediction of a score on a criterion, say Y, from a knowledge of the score on some other test, say X, is given in the equation below and is called the STANDARD ERROR OF ESTIMATE.

    The Standard Error of Estimate

$$S.E._{est} = s_y \sqrt{1 - r^2}$$

----

where s_y = Standard deviation of the criterion (Y) scores

r = correlation between X and Y

How Large a Sample Do I Need?

The first point is that the size of your sample is not nearly as important as the adequacy of the design. Collecting large amounts of data from undefined sources is not to be recommended. If there is bias in the data, it is unlikely to go away as you collect more data. If you are conducting a survey rather than an experiment or quasi-experiment it is likewise more important to obtain a representative sample than a large sample. Identify the groups you need and put a good deal of effort into getting a high response rate (e.g., by phoning or sending reminders) rather than sending out huge numbers of questionnaires and letting a few undefined volunteers return them.

The second point to be made is that until you have some pilot data to go on, an answer to the question about sample size is difficult. Suppose you have collected some pilot data. You must then ask which is the smallest group for which you will be calculating a mean on the major dependent (outcome) variable Y. It might, for example, be grade 4 girls in the experimental group. Then ask yourself how accurate you need that mean to be. Plus or minus how much on the scale? Let this represent the SE of the mean. Once you have set that, and knowing from your pilot data what the standard deviation of the Y-scores is, you can find n, the number you need in that group because you know that

$$SE_{mean} = \frac{s_y}{\sqrt{n}}$$

From the size of your smallest group you can work out the total sample size you need for the kind of accuracy you chose.

These quantified instructions really only operationalize common sense. The size of sample you need depends upon two things: how accurate you want the summary data to be (if you want no sampling error at all for example you would need to measure each entire population) and how variable the data are. If you started measuring something and found that every measure was the same, you wouldn't go on very long repeating the measurements to increase your accuracy. On the other hand, the more the data vary, the more data you need to collect to get a reasonably accurate measure of the mean.

A third consideration is acceptability to participants and audiences. For example, in collecting the views of staff, it might not be acceptable to sample, even though a sample would appear to be statistically adequate. Every staff member might need to be heard so that no one feels left out and there is no suspicion of bias.

Sampling may also be unacceptable if it causes more disturbance than would measuring everybody. For example, it may disrupt a lesson more to withdraw six pupils than to test the entire class.

Finally some rules of thumb can be provided: Sample sizes over 30 have certain advantages statistically. Correlations are very unstable on samples smaller than 50 to 100. Often you will simply use the largest sample on which you can collect high quality data within the constraints of time and money available.

Notes for SPSSX Users

The procedure RELIABILITY is invaluable in the construction of tests and questionnaires. It will compute Cronbach's alpha (essentially the same as KR20) for the whole scale, and then compute it leaving out each item in turn. This is very valuable in locating "poor" items.

Developing Scales Composed of Items

The following procedure in SPSSX illustrates how eight items might be examined for their "behavior" (statistical properties) when they are used to form two scales, an attitude to school scale ("attsch") and an attitude to subject scale ("attsub"). Two items need their scoring reversed and this is done with a RECODE.

```
* * * * * * * * * * * * * * * * * * * *
  RECODE        Item 4, Item 5 (1 = 5) (2 = 4) (3 = 3) (4 = 2)
                (5 = 1) INTO Item 4R, Item5R
  RELIABILITY   VARIABLES = Item1 to Item3, Item4R,
                Item 5R, Item 6 to Item 8
                /SCALE(attsch) = Item1, Item5R to
                Item8
                /SCALE(attsub) = Item2, Item3,
                Item4r
  STATISTICS    1,3,4,9,10
* * * * * * * * * * * * * * * * * * * *
```

(1) The "item" variable must be previously defined variables in your SPSSX file. Some items have an R at the end of their name to indicate the coding has been reversed in order to get them ready to be added to the other items. The RECODE command accomplishes this for one or more items at a time. It is as well to save the recoded items as new items (e.g., Item3R) rather than recode under their original name (e.g., Item3) to avoid accidentally recoding twice on different runs with the result that the item gets un-recoded!

(2) The word in brackets after /SCALE is a label and can therefore be any word. Keep it under 8 characters because it will be convenient to use it later as a variable name. Use the label to remind yourself what the collection of items named to the right of the = sign is supposed to be measuring.

(3) In naming the variables to the right of the = sign, the TO convention applies to the order of variables listed after VARIABLES= on the RELIABILITY procedure line, NOT to the order in the original DATA LIST.

(4) If the scales yield satisfactory values of alpha use them as variables in subsequent analyses. Use, for example,

```
* * * * * * * * * * * * * * * * * * * *
  COMPUTE Attsch = Mean (Item1, Item5r, Item6 to Item8)
* * * * * * * * * * * * * * * * * * * *
```

Note that in the COMPUTE command, any list of variables using "TO" will refer to the items as they occurred in the DATA LIST for the file, not in the RELIABILITY list.

Chapter 6
Selecting Statistical Procedures

At the end of a course on statistics, it is quite common to find that one can compute a t-test and rattle off a chi-square and yet feel quite perplexed when confronted with a mass of real data. How does one go about selecting *when* to use a t-test? when to use a chi-square? That is the kind of problem addressed in this chapter.

Sometimes the analysis strategy is perfectly clear because the data were collected to test a specific hypothesis and the analysis follows directly from the design of the investigation. Thus if the data were collected from a pretest-posttest true-control-group design you would use a t-test to see if pretest means were equivalent (they should be with a true, i.e., randomly assigned, control group) and then use a t-test to examine posttest differences and compute effect sizes.

However, in many evaluation studies there is a certain amount of routine data collection and monitoring, particularly with formative evaluations, and you may well be confronted with a large body of data to explore. An approach to that exploration is set out below. Once again a worksheet format and step-by-step guide seem desirable for clarity. This format, however, forces a rather prescriptive tone on the writer, and that tone is not as appropriate to this chapter as to most of the other chapters. Data analysis is to some extent a creative effort, with something new in each new set of data. Moreover, the particular details of a set of data may dominate the entire analysis strategy. Nevertheless, some unequivocal clear guidance is good to have as a starting point—but it is only that: a starting point. Your best source of inspiration will be your own interest in the data, and that interest often grows from knowing the data well. Get up close to your data— examine instruments used to collect the data, participate in the data collection procedures, visit sites, listen and ask questions. When you are analyzing data that you care about, you will do a good job. (Of course, you must care about getting at the truth about the data more than about proving any particular point!)

Steps	Example

Background

A new style of Advanced Placement examination was to be introduced and, thanks to someone's unusual foresight, evaluators were requested to begin work a year or two before the new examination was used. The evaluators' task was to collect baseline data so that it would eventually be possible to make comparisons between the old and new examinations.

In a pilot study, six classes were asked to participate, these being randomly selected from lists of classes preparing for the examination. Teachers of the participating classes were interested in comparative data indicating how effective they were in obtaining advanced qualifications for their students.

The evaluator used the following model of achievement to guide data collection:

ACHIEVEMENT = f(ABILITY, OPPORTUNITY, EFFORT)

(Achievement in a subject is a function of—i.e., "is related to"—three factors: Ability, Opportunity to learn the subject, and the Effort made to learn the subject.)

Given limitations of time and resources, only two academic subjects were selected for the pilot study: mathematics and English. A measure of prior achievement in a wide variety of subjects was obtained to serve as an index of "ability" for academic work in general. A questionnaire was used to collect information from students on teaching methods used in the advanced course (part of the "opportunity" variable) and on the effort they made to learn the work. This effort-measure consisted of items about "working hard," "being one of the hardest workers in the class," and "getting work in on time."

In addition to these operationalizations of the factors in the model of achievement, it was felt important to include measures of home background since socioeconomic status is often related to achievement. Sex was also included since gender-related differences in schooling are widespread. Age was not included since a decision was made to investigate only students between the ages of 17 and 18 years.

When examination results became available these were added to the data from records of prior achievement and the questionnaire responses. (Because of the need to add examination results, the questionnaires could not be anonymous, but the names were replaced by code numbers before the data were permanently recorded.)

1. Set out the data in a cases-by-variables table

Put as much of your data as possible into something like a markbook or register: The cases are listed down the left-hand column, one case per row, and the columns are labeled to show what will be recorded in them, such as sex, personality test score, blood

1. Set out the data in a cases-by-variables table

The following cases-by-variables matrix (Table 5) represents the data from one of the six classrooms. The data for all six classrooms are reproduced in Appendix D. In Table 5, note how another way of grouping the variables is in terms of variables that

Steps	Example

pressure, and the like. Each column is a variable and each row contains the information for one case. For small sets of data you may draw up this table by hand, but for large sets of data you will plan to use a computer and you will therefore want to have the data entered into a computer file. This can be done quickly and accurately by professionals who can take it directly from questionnaires or test papers. Whether in a computer file or on a sheet of paper, your data will be referred to by the text that follows as residing on your data sheet or in your CASES-BY-VARIABLES table.

Most of this recording of data will be straightforward but there are three kinds of information that you may overlook and for which you may need to create special columns: grouping data, qualitative data, and constituent data.

Grouping data. The group or groups to which each case belongs must be indicated on the data sheet as a variable. For example, you may have three pages of data, one from each of three different sites. On each sheet, label one column 'site' and record either a 1, 2, or 3 to indicate which site. Of course, you could use letters or codes to indicate site; but whatever you use, site should be recorded *explicitly*. A grouping variable of particular importance is the designation of experimental or control group, if relevant.

Qualitative data. There may be some qualitative data that you want to code quantitatively in order to relate it to the quantitative data. The coding of qualitative data is described in *How to Assess Program Implementation* and *How to Use Qualitative Methods in Evaluation* (Volume 5 and Volume 4, respectively, in the *Program Evaluation Kit*). This is just a reminder to include it on your data sheet if it exists. If two or more raters have coded the qualitative data you might as well record their ratings on the data sheet and average them later, especially if the data are to be analyzed by computer.

Constituent data. You may have responses on a test, or a series of readings of blood pressure that have been averaged. Will you just record the total for the test or will you record the responses for each constituent item? Will you record average blood pressure or the series of readings from which the average was computed? It depends on your plans for the analysis, but it is a question that needs to be considered. For analyses conducted by hand you probably want to keep the data sheet as small as possible; but given the prospect of computer analysis you can afford to take the position of "Why throw away information?" and decide to record all the constituent data, not just means or sums of items. For tests or attitude measures you will need to record the constituent items if you plan to examine the internal consistency of the instrument.

describe the sample ("demographic data"), input variables (here represented as the prior achievement measure), process variables (those variables that represent events that might relate to the dependent variable), and output—the dependent variable. Sometimes the process variables cannot be obtained and we have simply an input-output model.

TABLE 5

Data for One Classroom

CASES					VARIABLES				
		DEMOGRAPHIC VARIABLES			INPUT	PROCESS VARIABLES			OUTPUT
student	SUBJ*	school	sex	SES	prior achiev-ement	classroom processes A B C D E	effort reports 1 2 3	advanced exam grade
001	1	2	2	14	5.55	5 3 1 2 2	4 4 3	4
002	1	2	1	8	5.75	4 3 3 2 2	4 4 3	4
003	1	2	2	15	5.90	5 2 2 2 2	4 4 4	5

```
                        etc., up to 16
                        --from appendix *
```

```
* SUBJECT 1 = taking ENGLISH
          2 = taking MATHEMATICS
          3 = taking both (ignored in this example)
```

Steps	Example

2. Describe each variable

Plot the distribution of each variable and examine each distribution. Is it reasonable? Are there outliers? When a computer is being used this step is vital to uncovering errors in data entry. Indeed the procedure of checking that the data have been accurately recorded is so important that it has earned a name: data cleaning. It is a procedure that can sometimes be surprisingly time-consuming.

If you had expected some variables to have a unimodal distribution but they in fact have a bimodal distribution, make a special note of this; the mean will not be a good representation of such a variable. You may wish to recode the variable, making it a dichotomous variable.

For questionnaires it is often convenient to record the distributions on a blank form of the questionnaire showing the numbers who responded in each category.

2. Describe each variable

The dependent variable, although representing a score, was available only as a 6-point scale, on which a 5 represents an A grade, a 4 = B grade, and so on. The distribution of grades for the six classrooms is displayed in Figure 57.

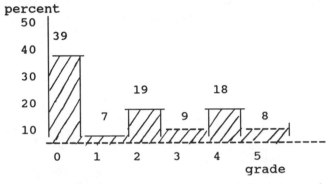

Figure 57. The distribution of grades on the Advanced Placement examination

On the prior achievement measure, the raw scores were available and the plot revealed the graphs in Figure 58.

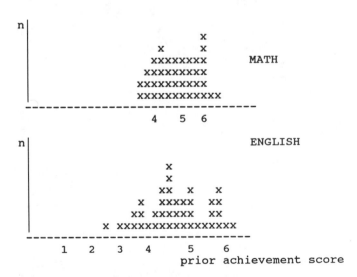

Figure 58. Distribution of prior achievement

Responses to the classroom process variables were recorded on a blank form of the questionnaire, indicating the percentages responding in each category and noting the number of missing responses. The distributions of other variables were similarly examined.

Steps	Example

3. Create scales if appropriate

Rather than setting out to analyze every single variable, there may well be sets of variables that should be summed to make a scale. These are variables that add up to one concept. For example, an index of deprivation might be the sum of a number of variables that classified income, living conditions, and so forth, on a scale from privileged to deprived. Ways of creating scales and analyzing their internal consistency were described in Chapter 5.

3. Create scales if appropriate

The "effort" variables were combined to form a scale that was found to have satisfactory internal consistency. The data from English and mathematics candidates were analyzed separately. Using all six classes, the reliabilities for the effort scale were as shown in Table 6.

TABLE 6
Reliabilities of the Effort Scale

	n	alpha
English	45	.78
Mathematics	50	.83

Since the scale had been found to have fairly satisfactory internal consistency as indicated by KR20 (alpha), scores on this summated scale were recorded as another variable on the data sheets.

The classroom process variables could also form a scale but it would not make sense to use KR20 in the way it was used for the effort scale. The effort variables related to each case, whereas the classroom process variables were not meant to be descriptive of the case: Rather, the case (i.e., the student) was serving as a RATER of the classroom. Each student provided a measure of the classroom in which that student was a member. One way to deal with this situation was to change the UNIT OF ANALYSIS.

4. Aggregate if appropriate

Suppose data were collected with students-as-cases, that is, with students as the "unit of analysis." In the cases-by-variables table,

4. Aggregate if appropriate

A new file was created with the class as the case (i.e., each class was a row). The classroom process variables were then investi-

Steps

each student is represented by a row of data. We could create another cases-by-variables table in which the *class* was the case, or in which the *school* was the case. Thus instead of a file of students, we might create a file of classrooms or schools. For variables that varied from student to student we could put down the average value. Thus each class would have an average prior achievement measure that was simply the average of the prior achievement measures of all the students in the class. Some variables, typical of the class rather than the student, might need to be added, such as class size.

Example

gated on this new file (call it the aggregated file) with KR20 and were found to yield reliable measures. For example, the data shown in Table 7 were responses to the following five questions:

Please indicate roughly how often you have studied in each of the following ways in mathematics (or English):

A. Class discussions led by the teacher
B. Discussions in groups
C. Working in pairs
D. Presenting your work to the class
E. Listening to another student present work to the class

Responses were made on the following 5-point scale:

1 = never
2 = occasionally
3 = sometimes
4 = often
5 = very often

The five items were designed to assess the amount of talking that students were encouraged to undertake in the classes. With the class as the unit of analysis, the AGGREGATED file was as shown in Table 7. Using this cases-by-variables data set, the reliability of a scale based on the above five questions was 0.95.

TABLE 7
The AGGREGATED File
(a file with the CLASS as the unit of analysis)

CASES				VARIABLES				
	DEMOGRAPHIC VARIABLES			INPUT	PROCESS VARIABLES	OUTPUT		
S U B J*	school	sex	SES	prior achiev- ement	classroom processes --------- A B C D E	advanced exam grade	effort mean	student talk
1	A	1.6	2.1	5.1	see detail graph below	2.7	3.4	2.8
1	C	1.9	2.1	4.9		2.4	3.0	3.6
1	D	1.6	1.6	3.9		.4	2.7	2.1
2	A	1.3	2.3	5.4		1.7	2.9	1.2
2	B	1.3	1.5	4.2		1.2	2.8	1.8
2	E	1.5	1.7	4.7		2.3	3.1	1.2

CLASSROOM PROCESSES				
A	B	C	D	E
4.6	2.7	2.3	2.3	2.2
3.8	3.5	3.5	3.4	3.5
3.7	2.4	1.9	1.0	1.2
1.2	1.0	1.4	1.0	1.0
2.7	1.8	1.7	1.2	1.4
1.3	1.0	1.3	1.0	1.0

Steps	Example

5. *Describe the sample*

Having explored each variable, created scales, and, possibly, thought of levels of aggregation, you are now ready to start producing tables to describe the data and examine relationships. You will draw up many more tables and graphs than you will finally use. Start by creating a table to describe what kind of sample you have.

Pick out those variables that describe your cases, sometimes called "demographic data," and use them to construct tables showing such characteristics of the sample as age, gender, socioeconomic status, and so on.

5. *Describe the sample*

The sample was described by creating Table 8.

TABLE 8

The Sample

ENGLISH CANDIDATES				
PERCENT MALE	PERCENT HIGH SES	PERCENT LOW SES	N	PERCENT OF TOTAL
SCHOOL				
A 38	12	25	16	35
C 14	7	14	14	30
D 38	44	6	16	35
TOTAL 31	22	15	15	100

MATHEMATICS CANDIDATES				
A 68	5	37	19	35
B 73	55	0	11	20
E 54	42	17	24	45
TOTAL 63	31	21	18	100

The six randomly selected classes contained 100 students located in five schools. Among English classes male students constituted only about 30% of the total, whereas they represented 63% of students in mathematics classes. Mean class size was approximately 17. Two classes were from the same school.

6. *Classify variables*

You will find it helpful to classify your variables under three headings:

- CATEGORICAL VARIABLES: variables that define groups rather than amounts. Usually they have only a few values.
- DICHOTOMOUS VARIABLES: variables that have just two values such as yes or no, present or absent, improved or got worse, experimental or control group.
- SCORES or "continuous variables": variables that can have many values, such as weight, test scores or the results of using summated scales.

In Step 2, you will probably have displayed the distribution of major score-type variables with box and whisker graphs or stem and leaf graphs. Important categorical variables may have been described with histograms.

6. *Classify variables*

A table was drawn up (for use in the analysis; this is not one of the tables to include in the report) classifying the variables as to their measurement type:

CATEGORICAL	DICHOTOMOUS	SCORES (continuous)
school	sex	prior achievement advanced grade student talk scale
SES (could be counted as a score)	subject	effort scale

Steps	Example

7. Relate pairs of variables

(1) Pairs of score-variables

Compute correlations and display in a table showing n, X̄, and s and the intercorrelations. A check for non-linear relationships might be necessary.

(2) Pairs of categorical or dichotomous variables

Compute chi-square to see if they are related. To indicate the strength of the relationship, discuss in terms of percentages emphasizing particularly those cells that contributed most to the chi-square value.

(3) Score-variables related to categorical or dichotomous variables

Categorical and dichotomous variables can be seen as ways of defining groups. Thus the dichotomous variable "sex" defines two groups: male and female. If you wanted to know if pulse rate was related to sex, you could compute the means and standard deviations for the pulse rates of each sex and compute an uncorrelated t-test to see if the difference between the means was statistically significant. You would also compute the effect size. In the same way, you could examine the relationship between any score variable and any dichotomous variable.

To relate a score variable to a categorical variable the procedure is similar: compute the means on the score variable for each value of the categorical variable. The statistical test for comparing several means (rather than just the two that the t-test compares) is the one-way analysis of variance (Worksheet 3B).

Summary

In short, an initial exploration of the data set can be made by examining pairs of variables, and the statistics you use are determined by the kind of variable being used: categorical (groups) or continuous (scores).

For each pair of variables related, you will want to report the statistical significance of the relationship and the nature of the relationship, for example its direction and strength. The statistical tests you use can be summarized as in Table 9:

TABLE 9

Statistical Test for Relationships Between Pairs of Variables

VARIABLE 1	VARIABLE 2 (OUTCOME VARIABLE)		
	DICHOTOMOUS	CATEGORICAL	SCORE
DICHOTOMOUS	r	chi square	t test
CATEGORICAL	chi square	chi square	ANOVA
SCORE	t-test or r	ANOVA	r

7. Relate pairs of variables

(1) Continuous ("score") variables

Table 10 was drawn up, including dichotomous variables along with score variables. The student was the unit of analysis.

TABLE 10

Summary Statistics and Inter-Correlations

VARIABLE		n	X	s	Inter-correlations (S)	(P)	(E)
E N G L I S H							
sex	(S)	46	1.7	.46			
prior achiev.	(P)	46	4.6	.94	.01		
effort index	(E)	46	3.1	.82	-.02	.43	
advanced gr.	(A)	46	1.8	1.76	-.01	.57	.38
M A T H E M A T I C S							
sex	(S)	54	1.4	.49			
prior achiev.	(P)	54	4.9	.85	.16		
effort index	(E)	54	2.9	.99	.06	.19	
advanced gr.	(A)	54	1.8	1.82	.00	.35	.47

In each subject, prior achievement/advanced grade correlations were computed separately for males and females, but there was no significant difference between the two correlations. For these 17- and 18-year-olds, gender differences seemed apparent only in the numbers taking English and mathematics. Within these groups, gender effects were negligible, with sex showing essentially no correlation with prior achievement, effort or advanced grade.

It was widely agreed that the Advanced Placement examination required hard work for success. Certainly students were frequently so admonished, and the correlations between effort and advanced grade seemed to confirm this: Higher reported effort was associated with higher grades. To understand the relationship better, further investigation would be needed to explore students' study methods. Interviews, essays, questionnaires, and student diaries might all be useful in such an investigation.

(2) Categorical variables

Schools and SES were cross-tabulated:

Steps

Example

Note that dichotomous variables can be related using the correlation coefficient. In a table of intercorrelations, it is sometimes useful to include not only score variables but also dichotomous variables.

TABLE 11

Schools and SES Levels

SES LEVEL:	low	med	high	TOTAL
	n (%)	n (%)	n (%)	n (%)
SCHOOL: A	3 (9)	21 (60)	11 (31)	35 (35)
B	6 (55)	5 (45)	0 (0)	11 (11)
C	1 (7)	11 (79)	2 (14)	14 (14)
D	7 (44)	8 (50)	1 (6)	16 (16)
E	10 (42)	10 (42)	4 (17)	24 (24)
	27 (27)	55 (55)	18 (18)	100 (100)

$$X^2 = 22.56, p = .004$$

A large chi-square value, statistically significant at better than the .01 level, indicated that schools and SES levels were not unrelated to each other: Schools differed in the distributions of pupils into SES categories. In particular, school A was the only school with a large proportion of students from high SES backgrounds (31%).

8. Look for moderator variables

Are there variables that might affect some of the relationships you have been examining? This question has to be asked whether or not you found substantial or statistically significant relationships. For example, if relationships were significant they might have been spurious, due to some relationship with a third variable; if they were nonsignificant, this might be because a third variable was masking a relationship that was really there. In other words, when a third variable is taken into account, it might either strengthen or weaken a relationship.

How does one take a third variable into account? This depends what kind of variable the third variable is.

Categorical-type third variables

The question you ask is whether a relationship you have found is true for all the groups of cases defined by the categorical variable. For example, does a relationship hold up if, instead of the whole group, you examine only males or only females? In this situation, you are asking if the relationship is different for the two sexes. If the relationship was determined as a correlation, you may need to use the test for the significance of differences between correlation coefficients (Chapter 4). If the relationship was examined with chi-square, compute chi-squares again, separately for each sex.

Score-type third variables

Suppose a relationship has been found between a locus-of-control measure and achievement. Before declaring this to be an important finding it would be necessary to take into account ability, which is always related to achievement. Does locus-of-control still relate to achievement once ability has been taken into account? To examine this question, you could compute residual scores for the regression of achievement on ability. Then, see if the residuals correlated with locus-of-control. If they did, it would

8. Look for moderator variables

An immediately obvious moderator variable was prior achievement, as a moderator for subsequent achievement. In general parlance, schools that obtain high grades on external examinations are often called "good schools." But perhaps, these schools only obtain these good grades because they enrolled many high ability students. A better question would be "Which schools obtained the best grades after taking ability into account?" ("CONTROLLING FOR" or "taking account of" a variable was introduced in Chapter 4. The technique is applied here.)

No "ability" measure was available, but prior achievement on a wide range of school subjects was taken as a good proxy. Using the student file and treating English and mathematics separately, A-grade and prior achievement were correlated and residual scores computed as in Worksheet 4C. These residual scores were added to the cases-by-variables matrix. Table 12 shows the addition of the residuals. (Process variables have been omitted to save space.)

TABLE 12

Showing the Addition of Computed Variables

CASE	SUBJECT	SCHOOL	AGRADE	EFFORT	ERESID	MRESID
1	1	A	4	3.67	1.19412	.
2	1	A	4	3.67	.97661	.
3	1	A	5	4	1.81710	.
4	1	A	4	3.33	1.65601	.
5	1	A	2	3	.19952	.
6	1	A	3	2.33	.41969	.
7	1	A	4	4	.44491	.
8	1	A	0	3.67	-1.74248	.
9	1	A	0	3.67	-1.26878	.
10	1	A	1	3.67	-1.93477	.
11	1	A	5	3	1.71076	.
12	1	A	4	4	.82892	.
13	1	A	5	4.67	3.06418	.
14	1	A	0	2.67	-1.48146	.
15	1	A	0	2.67	-.67908	.

Steps

show that even after the variability of scores due to prior achievement had been taken into account (by the regression) there was still some variability left that related to locus-of-control. If on the other hand the residuals did not correlate with the locus-of-control measure, then one would report that although locus-of-control was correlated with achievement, this relationship disappeared once ability was controlled for.

The effects of moderator variables

As you may be beginning to surmise, this question of a third variable opens up a can of worms. Why not a fourth variable and a fifth? We may end up concluding that everything affects everything else so that every statement needs qualifying with another statement about the conditions under which the statement is true. We might, for example, end up modifying a finding with the statement "but this only applies if the cases are male and employed and have varicose veins."

There are two principal defenses against endless complications: a design with major variables controlled by random assignment (See *How to Design a Program Evaluation*, Volume 3 of the *Program Evaluation Kit*) and/or a good theory to guide the analysis. Theory often specifies the important variables and how they are expected to interact. There is much truth in the statement "There is nothing so practical as a good theory." Unfortunately, social science theories are not used any too frequently in evaluation work. Whether this is due to the inadequacies of the existing theories, our inadequacies as evaluators, or the constraints of the situations in which evaluators find themselves is not clear, but the greater application of theory is a goal to strive toward. (A short article titled "Theory-Based Evaluation" [Fitz-Gibbon and Morris, 1975] commended this approach; a shortened version of this article is included here as Appendix B.)

More sophisticated data analysis approaches

To examine the effects of many variables at once it becomes necessary to learn to use multi-factor (n-way) ANOVA and/or multiple regression techniques. These extend the ideas introduced in Worksheets 3B and 4C to more variables. Learn to use a statistical package on a computer before embarking on these analysis strategies.

One over-arching concept (a meta concept or organizing principle, if you will) is perhaps worth mentioning: that is the concept of "EXPLAINED VARIATION." Data analysis can be conceived of as an attempt to carve out more and more "explained" variation from the observed total variation. The explained variation is sometimes called the systematic variation; it is the variation in a dependent variable that can be attributed to variation in other measured variables. The *unexplained* variation is quite often larger than the explained variation and is attributable to the inherent variation in cases (e.g., individual differences in responses to treatment, in abilities, attitudes, etc.) to errors of measurement, and to variables not included in the analysis either because they are things we haven't thought of or because their measurement was not possible.

Example

16	1	A	2	3	1.10341	.
17	1	C	3	3	.24246	.
18	1	C	4	3.33	2.30586	.
19	1	C	5	4	3.62488	.
20	1	C	2	3	.30586	.
21	1	C	2	2	-1.04384	.
22	1	C	1	2	-1.11950	.
23	1	C	2	4	-.81662	.
24	1	C	2	2	-.99922	.
25	1	C	3	2.67	1.48309	.
26	1	C	3	3.33	1.09318	.
27	1	C	2	3.33	.12863	.
28	1	C	1	3.33	-.69414	.
29	1	C	4	3.33	.82892	.
30	1	C	0	3	-1.39875	.
31	1	D	0	2.67	-.09904	.
32	1	D	0	3.67	-2.22584	.
33	1	D	0	3.33	-2.09291	.
34	1	D	0	3.50	-2.22584	.
35	1	D	0	2	-.45351	.
36	1	D	2	3	1.65556	.
37	1	D	0	3	.66053	.
38	1	D	0	4.67	-2.22584	.
39	1	D	1	3.67	-.56121	.
40	1	D	0	2.67	-2.10768	.
41	1	D	2	1	1.05024	.
42	1	D	0	1.67	730	.
43	1	D	0	1.33	-.94976	.
44	1	D	0	1.67	-.55478	.
45	1	D	2	3.33	.45087	.
46	1	D	0	2.33	-.57757	.
47	2	A	0	1	.	-2.22572
48	2	A	3	2.33	.	-.111
49	2	A	2	3	.	.42044
50	2	A	2	3	.	-.06876
51	2	A	0	3	.	-2.49779
52	2	A	4	4.33	.	1.16213
53	2	A	0	3.67	.	-2.79536
54	2	A	1	3	.	-.64191
55	2	A	0	2.67	.	-1.81762
56	2	A	0	2	.	-2.15770
57	2	A	0	2	.	-1.40952
58	2	A	2	2	.	-.78497
59	2	A	2	3.67	.	-.78497
60	2	A	4	3.67	.	2.16145
61	2	A	4	4.67	.	1.29816
62	2	A	0	1.33	.	-1.70426
63	2	A	4	4.33	.	2.04635
64	2	A	3	3.67	.	.29816
65	2	A	1	2.67	.	-1.36931
66	2	B	0	2.33	.	-1.47753
67	2	B	0	2	.	-.72935
68	2	B	0	2	.	-1.20546
69	2	B	5	3.33	.	3.68765
70	2	B	0	3.33	.	-1.66589
71	2	B	0	2.67	.	-.51963
72	2	B	2	2	.	.98158
73	2	B	1	3.67	.	-1.32775
74	2	B	0	2.67	.	-1.36579
75	2	B	5	3.33	.	2.85930
76	2	B	0	3	.	-1.20546
77	2	E	4	5	.	2.71140
78	2	E	5	1	.	3.45445
79	2	E	0	2	.	-1.72920
80	2	E	2	4	.	.49526
81	2	E	4	3	.	2.72652
82	2	E	3	2.67	.	.71382
83	2	E	3	3.33	.	.44780
84	2	E	2	2	.	.54514
85	2	E	5	3.33	.	2.52262
86	2	E	4	4.33	.	1.29816
87	2	E	4	4.50	.	1.96322
88	2	E	2	3.67	.	-.42977
89	2	E	4	4.67	.	2.20667
90	2	E	4	3.67	.	1.44780
91	2	E	0	3	.	-1.01842
92	2	E	0	3.67	.	-1.14312
93	2	E	4	2.33	.	1.67225
94	2	E	0	1.67	.	-1.08077
95	2	E	3	4	.	2.11519
96	2	E	0	4	.	-.70667
97	2	E	0	1.67	.	-2.02847
98	2	E	0	2	.	-1.78739
99	2	E	2	2.33	.	-1.78739
100	2	E	2	1.67	.	-.07835

The proportion of variance in advanced grades explained by the prior achievement scores was only .32 for English and .12 for mathematics (computed by squaring the correlation coefficients). This could be due partly to the fact that the evaluator was dealing with a restricted range of prior achievement (those entering for the difficult advanced tests). Although the prior achievement test

Steps	Example

was clearly not a strong predictor, to have it was far better than having no prior cognitive measure to "control" for differences in intakes to the various schools.

Correlations were computed between the residuals and several other variables to see if these latter were related to advanced grades once prior achievement had been "controlled for" (Table 13).

For each school, a mean residual score was computed. This served as an index of how good the Advanced Placement grades were, considering the prior achievement level of the students being entered.

TABLE 13
The Aggregated File

subject	school	MEANS: sex	SES	prior achievement	advanced exam grade	Eff.	* Engl. residual	Math. residual
1	A		2.1	5.1	2.7	3.4	.39	
1	C		2.1	4.9	2.4	3.0	.28	
1	D		1.6	3.9	.4	2.7	-.64	
2	A		2.3	5.4	1.7	2.9		-.57
2	B		1.5	4.2	1.2	2.8		-.18
2	E		1.7	4.7	2.3	3.1		.54

*residual from the regression of Advanced grade on prior achievement

School A was seen, from Table 13, to have obtained better than expected grades in English (mean residual 0.39) and worse than expected grades in mathematics (-.57). Although no weight should be placed on this small set of results in which school A was compared with different schools in English than in mathematics, these pilot data did lend some support to the decision to treat each academic subject separately.

9. Ruminate

Thinking is the principal task of the evaluator. Ask yourself, "What is going on here?" Sometimes you perceive a new question (called "progressive focusing" in qualitative analysis). Sometimes you need to invent an "index" of something that is indicative of a process and this index might need a new term. Do not forget to review the way constructs have been operationalized, that is, the procedures used to obtain the numbers for each variable.

On the whole, it is very difficult to suggest how you might go about thinking, but if you have become closely involved with the data, and have kept an ear open to what people say, you will find plenty to ruminate about.

9. Ruminate

The distribution of the dependent variable, the Advanced level grade, was strongly positively skewed (i.e., there were large numbers of low grades awarded; see Figure 57). It seemed necessary to investigate this distribution, if only because it raised the question of whether unsuitable candidates were being entered for the examination. Teachers, candidates, and administrators were questioned and the feeling was unanimous that the candidates entered for the examination had benefited from studying the course material and that there was no other advanced syllabus that would meet the needs of these candidates. It was just seen as unfortunate that so many failed. The evaluator seemed forced to the conclusion that the assigning of grades in the examination needed investigation: There were strong indications that the high failure rate was inappropriate and made it look as though schools were wasting candidates' time, when in fact teachers and candidates did not see this as the case at all. In mathematics, in particular, it was not difficult to demonstrate quite objectively that even candidates who failed had learned a great deal in the course. Such learning should receive the recognition of certification.

Ruminating over Table 8 and considering the current national alarm over a shortage of mathematics teachers, it seemed

Steps	Example

important to ask questions about how many and which students opted for advanced mathematics. The extent to which a school attracted students into mathematics as opposed to English was labeled its "pulling power," and an index of pulling power was defined as follows: number taking maths./number taking English. When data on a larger sample of schools had been collected it would then be possible to ask several questions about pulling power. Was it associated with certain teaching methods? Were the residual gains higher in schools with high pulling power, suggesting that the teaching was particularly good? Were the extra numbers taking mathematics made up primarily of females, indicating that enrollments in mathematics could be improved by making the subject more appealing to females? These questions were posed for subsequent years and indicated the need not only for an expanded sample but also for one that would have both mathematics and English classes from the same school. Interview data would also be useful in further exploration of this question. The impact of the new examination system on the mathematics course-taking might be an important question for policy analysis.

10. Summarize critically

When you have completed your analyses (or, more usually, when you have run out of time and must call a halt to exploring your data), then write up a report. You have to find ways to make it clear and easy to read. One way is to pose a series of questions and show how the data analysis gives the answers to each of these questions in turn. *How to Communicate Evaluation Findings* (Volume 9 of the *Program Evaluation Kit*), particularly Chapter 2 offers a number of suggestions for effective reporting.

However you choose to structure your report, it will be important to distinguish clearly between relationships that have simply been found in the data and *cannot* be taken as causal relationships ("correlation is not causation") and those relationships that have been found under controlled design conditions in which one or more variables have been *manipulated* and the evidence for causal relationships is strong.

It is worth stressing here the need to include in your report a section titled "Limitations of the Present Study." You must make the limitations of your study clear. Points to consider are the adequacy of the sample, of the measurements (reliability and validity, problems in administration of the instruments, data coding disagreements), design problems, and data analysis issues. In summary, include any necessary caveats with regard to

- the sample
- the measurements
- the analysis
- the design

The most important distinction to be made (it bears saying again and again) is the distinction between experimental studies as opposed to observational (or epidemiological) studies. Correlation and co-variation must not be taken as evidence of causation.

Evaluation studies often present particular difficulties because they lie uneasily between controlled experiments and passive

10. Summarize critically

The evaluator wrote a progress report that included the following comments:

There were two major aims in the current phase of the evaluation: (1) to develop ways of predicting Advanced grades so that these PREDICTION EQUATIONS could be used later to provide comparisons with the new examinations and (2) to compare the effectiveness of the participating schools.

Prediction. Using the prior achievement measure, the correlations with the advanced grade were $r = .35$ for math, $r = .57$ for English. The raw score regression equations were:

```
ENGLISH:
-----------------------------------
AGRADE = 1.06 (PRIOR ACH.) -3.09
-----------------------------------

MATHEMATICS:
-----------------------------------
AGRADE = 0.75 (PRIOR ACH.) -1.78
-----------------------------------
```

Steps	Example

observational studies. There has been an intervention (the program being evaluated) but often it has not been given to randomly assigned groups. Conclusions about its effects must often be tentative. C'est la vie.

School effectiveness. On the basis of the residual scores, schools could be rank ordered as follows:

SCHOOL	N	MEAN RESIDUAL *
English		
A	16	.39
C	14	.28
D	16	-.64
Math		
E	24	.54
B	11	-.18
A	19	-.57

* A positive residual meant that the advanced grades achieved were better than expected on the basis of the prior achievement of candidates and the general pattern of results in the sample. A negative residual indicated lower than expected advanced grades.

Limitations of the Present Study, and Recommendations for Improvement

The sample

The sample of schools was small but served to provide a first look at the data and guide subsequent data collection. At least the sample was somewhat representative due to its having been selected by random sampling.

Only two academic subjects were studied in this pilot work. Extension to other advanced subjects would be desirable. However, even in this limited data there were indications that it would be wise to analyze the academic subjects separately.

Some students declined to answer questions on socioeconomic status (e.g., father's job, if employed, etc.) and it would seem desirable to offer more reassurance regarding confidentiality and to explain that names were needed only to record the advanced grades when they became available. Of course, students, as others, have every right to decline to participate in surveys and data collection exercises.

The measurements

Process variables were to some extent unsatisfactory. The effort measure relied exclusively on self-report by students, as did the classroom process variables. Both these sources of information need some corroboration. The time spent could possibly be checked by the use of random checks on the time spent the night before on homework (less subject to memory distortion than an estimate of the amount of time "usually" spent). The classroom process variables need to be enhanced with reports from teachers and classroom observations.

The analysis

Even though the approach chosen is widely used in studies of school effects, the analyses of residuals presents some problems

Steps	Example
	[see Chapter 4]. The adequacy of the controlling variable must be considered.

The design

These figures must be considered with caution. Pupils were not randomly assigned to schools and the statistical control provided by the prior achievement measure may not be adequate. The inclusion of an ability measure that would be less affected by earlier schooling would be an improvement. It will be important to see if the residuals show the same pattern in the next few years. If they are consistent in schools in which practices and personnel do not change, then we might be more justified in interpreting the residuals as indicating the effects of schools on students' performance in the Advanced examinations.

On the whole we have tried to keep references to the literature to an absolute minimum in this book, partly to increase readability and partly, perhaps, because we believe you will learn more by doing than by reading: how-to-do-it is more important than where-to-read-about-it. In the chapter on meta analysis, however, it has seemed necessary to reference more heavily. This is partly because the technique is fairly new and debates about its details continue so you might wish to follow up the topic in the professional literature.

Meta Analysis and Evaluation

The data obtained directly from one study are called PRIMARY DATA, and much of this book has been about the analysis and interpretation of primary data. At some point, however, an attempt has to be made to make sense of not just what one study tells us but of what many studies can tell us. We need to analyze and synthesize the results of many studies. Systematic and quantitative methods for summarizing findings from many studies have developed under several titles but especially under the title META ANALYSIS (Glass, McGaw, & Smith, 1981).

> Meta analysis is a set of techniques for summarizing the findings of several studies.

How does meta analysis relate to the work of an evaluator? You will find that someone has conducted a meta analysis in almost any literature you undertake to study, and for this reason alone you will want to be familiar with the technique in order to interpret the literature. You may also find it directly useful for the following reasons. Many evaluations involve several replications of an intervention. A new program may be implemented not only at several sites, such as schools or hospitals, but also within each site with several different groups (e.g., classes, age groups, or therapist groups). Meta analysis techniques provide clear and simple ways of summarizing the data from the different sites and groups. Moreover, because education, health treatments, therapies, and other human-service interventions are often administered to *small numbers* of persons, statistical significance testing at the traditional .05 level tends to be discouraging. Results have to be very strong to show up as statistically significant if the sample size is small. Meta analysis avoids confounding the results with the sample size and therefore lets substantial effects show up clearly even in small samples. It seems likely that effect sizes conform more closely with the judgments of experienced practitioners than do the often discouraging results of tests of statistical significance *with small sample size*.

The kind of meta analysis that will be considered here is the kind that summarizes the results of studies in which there was some kind of control or comparison group so that an EFFECT SIZE can be calculated for each study. This kind of meta analysis is particularly important because it focuses attention on the question to which people want an answer:

> How much difference does an intervention make?

Before meta analysis, the question answered was generally

> If the null hypothesis were true, how likely is it that these results would arise by random sampling?

which was not the question hot on people's lips. Indeed, the widespread and almost exclusive focus on statistical significance testing has confused people so much that Carver (1978) called it "a corrupt form of the scientific method" and was at pains to show how widely it was misunderstood, over-interpreted, and misused. In statistical terms, the advent of meta analysis has meant a shift of emphasis toward parameter estimation—how much difference does the intervention make?—and away from hypothesis testing—is the null hypothesis acceptable? (Fitz-Gibbon, 1984).

Chapter 3 introduced the concept of an EFFECT SIZE, and it is the effect size (ES) that we need to estimate in order to answer the major question of interest: How much difference does an intervention make? In this chapter, rather than considering meta analysis for the synthesis of data extracted from the literature, we consider the use of meta analysis for providing a clear summary of the results of an intervention that has been applied at several sites, a situation that may well occur in large-scale evaluations. In a situation in which the intervention has been used at a number of sites and with a number of different groups, we need to ask the following questions:

A. For different sites and different groups, what were the ESs?
B. Did the intervention seem to have a consistent effect?
C. Can we identify subsets of the sites or groups in which the effects were different from the average effect?

The answers to these questions will be important for summative or formative evaluation. In particular, the analyses of ESs by groups may provide some clues as to where the intervention is working well and where it is not working well, that is, it may provide valuable information for formative evaluation. Ways in which questions A, B, and C are addressed are presented in the worksheet for this chapter.

There are other statistical techniques that can be used in a multi-site evaluation when you have access to the primary data, and if you are comfortable with the analysis of variance (ANOVA) you may wish to use it on primary data from all sites. Results could be compared with those from the meta analysis approach. You will, however, be well advised to summarize the findings in terms of effect sizes. Not only will these be enlightening for the interpretation of your own data but they will facilitate use of your findings by researchers in the future and therefore contribute toward making social science cumulative.

The steps presented for the worksheets have been extracted primarily from Hedges and Olkin (1985), a text you may wish to consult for details and advanced techniques.

Steps	Example

Background

An exploratory study of the use of cross-age tutoring in mathematics was conducted at four sites. The aims of this pilot study were to see if cross-age tutoring was as effective as normal classroom instruction and to generate hypotheses about implementation variables. As is often the case in evaluation studies, the intervention could not be applied in exactly the same way at each site; but in this case there was a control group of one kind or another at each site, and variations in implementation might cast light on how best to run the projects. After the project, teachers raised the issue of how tutees should be assigned to tutors: On what basis, if any, should tutors and tutees be matched?

1. Identify the effect size that is to be investigated

The concept of an EFFECT SIZE implies that there is a "true" or population value for the effect of something and each time we run an experiment we obtain one sample of this effect. We can expect the obtained ESs to fluctuate around the population value just as sample means fluctuate around the 'true' mean. In order to apply this concept there must be some reason to suspect a *SINGLE* effect size—in other words, a single outcome that a program is to affect. When you have decided what this single ES is, you can measure it by the equation given below. Y stands for the outcome measure that is affected by the program or the 'treatment' received by the experimental group (E-group). Whether the control group (C-group) receives a competing treatment or no treatment can be expected to affect the ES, so it will be as important to record what has happened to the C-groups as well as to the E-groups.

1. Identify the effect size that is to be investigated

In this study there were at least two ESs: the ES for tutors and the ES for tutees. Each should be investigated, but this meta analysis concentrated on the ES for tutors because projects had been started largely to increase the achievement of the tutors.

Definition of Effect Size

$$ES = \frac{(\text{mean } Y \text{ for E-group}) - (\text{mean } Y \text{ for C-group})}{\text{SD of } Y}$$

$$ES = \frac{(\bar{Y} \text{ for Tutors}) - (\bar{Y} \text{ for Control Group})}{\text{SD of } Y}$$

Where $\bar{Y}$ was the mean on any outcome variable that measured achievement in math, specifically fractions.

Note: In early meta analyses the SD used was that of the control group alone but it is now considered best to used the POOLED standard deviation of Y. This should give a more precise estimate and it is often the only one that can be retrieved.

2. Develop coding sheets

Coding sheets describe the conditions under which each intervention was implemented. They are like questionnaires to be answered about each site.

2. Develop coding sheets

Coding sheets were developed including such variables as school, SES index, the time allocated to tutoring, the actual length of the tutoring sessions (20, 30, or 40 minutes), the instruction received by C-groups and so on.

Steps	Example

Ideally two persons who have the site reports or who know the project well should independently complete the coding sheets. Measures of INTER-RATER RELIABILITY can then be made.

The coding sheets should be designed by someone who knows the projects well and can pick out, from the hundreds of variables that might be recorded, some that seem likely to have influenced the ESs. As the coding sheets are being drawn up and completed, a descriptive and analytic essay should be written to put flesh on the statistical bones. The procedures of meta analysis are not a substitute for analyses of the complexity of each project (Slavin, 1985).

What should be included in the coding sheets? Facts about each site (e.g., size of school, locality, the status of the person running the project, how the project had been introduced to the site), assessments of the design for that site (e.g., the nature of control groups—how they were assigned and the instruction they received); costs in terms of time, money, and personnel for the E- and the C-group; details of the implementation of the project that might affect the ES (e.g., type of treatment, duration and intensity of treatment, percentage female in the E- and C-groups, and other sample characteristics)—these are the kinds of information coded on coding sheets.

3. Extract effect sizes

In an evaluation with multi-site field trials you will most likely have access to data that will enable you to calculate the ESs from each site directly. If, however, the data have already been processed and t-values calculated you might as well use these. In meta analyses of studies for which you only have reports that give summary data, you may have to work out effect sizes from t-tests or correlation coefficients. This is not difficult using the following equations:

FROM t:

$$ES = \sqrt{\frac{1}{n_E} + \frac{1}{n_C}} \times t$$

where n_E = number in the experimental group
n_C = number in the control group

This way of transforming the t-value to yield an effect size follows directly from the equation given for t in Chapter 3.

Notice that the quantity

$$(1/n_E + 1/n_C)$$

3. Extract effect sizes

From reports of the original data, t-test data were collected and tabulated below. The last column, the ES, was computed from each t-test.

Because of the concern over matching, an effort was made to separate out from each site those students who had been well matched and those who had been poorly matched and to compute separate ESs for them, comparing their posttest scores with those of the control groups. (Space for these data is indicated in the table but the data are not reported in order to keep the worksheet simple.)

Steps	Example

is used. It will be called "n tilde" (written $\tilde{n}$) for the remainder of this worksheet, for convenience because n is easier to write than

$$(1/n_E + 1/n_C) = \tilde{n}$$

FROM r, the ES is given approximately by:

$$ES = \frac{2r}{\sqrt{1 - r^2}}$$

where r = correlation between Y and group-membership

1	2	3	4	5	6
Group	n_E	n_C	$\frac{1}{n_E} + \frac{1}{n_C}$	t	ES
Site 1 Well matched Poorly matched					
All students	8	12	.208	1.84	.839
Site 2 Well matched Poorly matched					
All students	8	8	.25	1.47	.735
Site 3 Well matched Poorly matched					
All students	7	12	.226	4.02	1.912
Site 4 Well matched Poorly matched					
All students	14	5	.271	1.13	.589

Figure 59. Data from tutoring experiments at four sites

4. Compute standard errors

The standard error is a measure of how accurately the ES has probably been measured. The smaller the error, the more accurate the measurement.

Standard error for ES

$$\text{SE for ES} = \sqrt{\frac{d^2}{2(n_E + n_C)} + \tilde{n}}$$
$$= \sqrt{v}$$
$$= e$$

4. Compute standard errors

Steps

This equation is easily worked out using the table below: Compute ES squared, divide by the number in column 3, getting the result of this and then adding the number in column 4 (n). This is the error variance and should be entered in column 5. The square root of this result can then be entered in column 6 as the error.

1	2	3	4	5	6	7	8
SITE	ES	$2(n_E + n_C)$	$\tilde{n}$	v	error	d − e	d + e
1	2	3	4	5	6	7	8

Example

1	2	3	4	5	6	7	8
Site	ES = d	$2(n_E + n_C)$	$\tilde{n}$	v	$\sqrt{v}$ = error = e	d − e	d + e
1	.839	40	.208	.226	.475	.36	1.31
2	.735	32	.250	.267	.517	.22	1.25
3	1.912	38	.226	.322	.567	1.34	2.48
4	.589	38	.271	.281	.530	.06	1.12

Figure 60. Standard error for ES

5. Graph and ruminate

Worksheet 2E demonstrated graphs to display summary data from several groups. Similar graphical displays can be presented for ESs at this step. The graphical display is probably the most valuable piece of information for generating hypotheses about what might be influencing the ES.

The 68% confidence limits can be plotted using the following:

ES + e and ES − e from column 7 and 8 above.

Or the 95 percent limits using:

ES + 1.96 × e and ES − 1.96 × e

5. Graph and ruminate

ES + e and ES − e were used to graph ESs per site.

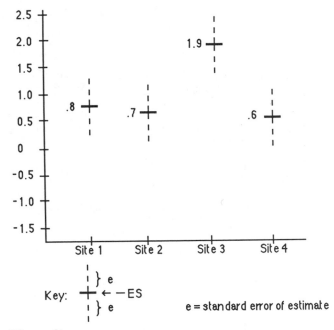

Figure 61

6. Compute a mean ES

This can simply be the mean computed by adding up the ESs and dividing by the number of them. However, if the ESs come from sites with very different sizes of project, it is reasonable to weight

6. Compute a mean ES

The unweighted mean ES was 1.02, computed by adding up the ESs and dividing by the number of them. Weighting d, the ES, gave values for w and wd shown in the table, and yielded a mean effect size of 0.977.

Steps

the larger projects more heavily than the smaller projects. This is done with the following equation:

Weighting d, the ES.

$$\dot{\bar{d}} = \frac{\Sigma wd}{\Sigma w}$$

1	2	3	4	5
SITE	ES = d	v	weight w = 1/v	w X ES = w d
SUM =			Σw	Σwd

The mean ES, weighted to take account of different sample sizes, is obtained by dividing the sum of column 5 by the sum of column 4. This weighted mean will be called "d bar," that is, $\bar{d}$.

7. Test for homogeneity of the effect sizes

As was remarked earlier, the search for synthesis of results implies that there is a single ES. At this step we ask whether the obtained ESs look as though they were random samples estimating a single ES (i.e., whether they look homogeneous) or whether they appear to come from different populations, (i.e., appear heterogeneous).

Homogeneity Statistic

$$H = \Sigma(d - \bar{d})^2 \times w$$

1	2	3	4	5
site	ES d	weight w	$(d - \bar{d})$	$(d - \bar{d})^2 \times w$
		SUM =		$\Sigma(d - \bar{d})^2 \times w$ Homogeneity Statistic

Example

1	2	3	4	5
Site	ES = d	v	weight $w = \frac{1}{v}$	w•ES = wd
1	.839	.226	4.424	3.712
2	.735	.267	3.745	2.753
3	1.912	.322	3.106	5.939
4	.589	.281	3.550	2.091
			14.833	14.495

$$\bar{d} = \frac{\Sigma wd}{\Sigma w} = \frac{14.495}{14.833} = 0.977$$

Figure 62

7. Test for homogeneity of the effect sizes

The value of .977 was used for $\bar{d}$

Homogeneity statistic
$H = \Sigma(d - \bar{d})^2 • w$

1	2	3	4	5
Site	ES = d	weight = w	$(d - \bar{d})$	$w•(d-\bar{d})^2$
1	0.839	4.424	-0.138	0.084
2	0.735	3.745	-0.242	0.219
3	1.912	3.106	0.935	2.715
4	0.589	3.550	-0.388	0.534
			Thus, H =	3.552

Figure 63

Steps

The homogeneity statistic is the sum of the values in column 5. This must be compared with a chi-square for df = k – 1, where k is the number of sites. If the value is *larger* than the critical value in the chi-square table, this suggests there was significant *heterogeneity*; the ESs did not appear to estimate a single population value.

This computation of the homogeneity statistic provides an answer to question B: Did the intervention seem to have a consistent effect? This statistic may be used in conjunction with information about each site to cast more light on the situation. Just as KR20 was used to locate a set of items that were homogeneous, this statistic H could be used to examine the homogeneity of ESs for various groups of sites, or for various types of replication.

Example

There were 4 studies, so the critical value for the homogeneity statistic could be found from the chi-square Table C.9 to be 7.81 at the .05 level.

This computation of the homogeneity statistic provided an answer to question B: Did the intervention seem to have a consistent effect? Of course, it was hardly necessary or appropriate with just four sites, but with larger numbers of sites (or, more generally, with larger numbers of independent replications) this statistic may cast more light on the situation.

Just as it is appropriate to test at the .25 level when seeking to establish the equivalence of pretest means (see Chapter 3), it would be appropriate to test at the .25 level when seeking to establish the homogeneity of ESs. At this level, the critical chi-square is 3.11, a value that is exceeded by the obtained value, indicating heterogeneity. Clearly the study that contributed most to this heterogeneity was study 3. Without study 3 the mean ES was 0.73.

8. Relate the ES findings to the data on the coding sheets

The aim here is to answer question C:

C. Can we identify subsets of the sites or groups in which the effects were different from the average effect?

This question can be broken down into three separate questions:

(a) Were there characteristics of the intervention (the independent variable or IV) that related to the ESs?
(b) Were there characteristics of the outcome measure (the dependent variable, or DV,) that related to the ESs (if various different outcome measures were used)?
(c) Were there contextual variables related to ESs?

8. Relate the ES findings to the data on the coding sheets

Were there subsets of the sites or groups in which the effects were different from the average effect?

Three aspects of this question will be discussed here for illustration.

Question C(a): Were there characteristics of the intervention (the independent variable or IV) that related to the ESs?

Yes. The strongest ES was at site 3 where inquiry revealed that the "control" group students, although randomly selected (thus forming a "true" control group) were not specifically taught the same topic, nor did they use the same materials as was the case at all the other sites. Although the topic (fractions) was in their syllabus and although they would have been taught it previously, they were more like a NO TREATMENT CONTROL GROUP, whereas other groups were COMPETING TREATMENT CONTROL GROUPS. This information explained the heterogeneity located by Step 8 and suggested by the graph in Step 6.

The matching, as rated post hoc by teachers, did not show strong effect sizes (data are not given here) but in qualitative observations concern was expressed about one or two tutors whose tutees seemed quicker-witted than the tutors, a situation that appeared to have bad effects on the tutors in some cases.

Question C(b): Were there characteristics of the outcome measure (the dependent variable, or DV) that related to the ESs?

Yes. There were two methods used to test the mathematics learned: One was a speed test—simple problems to be done as fast as possible. Another was an untimed test including more difficult problems. (It is the results of the latter that have been shown above.) The ESs associated with the speed test were about 0.03, essentially zero. It seemed that the intervention improved student's capacity to do the math, but not to do it quickly. Thus the

Steps	Example

effects were strong on one kind of outcome variable but weak on another.

Question C(c): Were there contextual variables related to ESs?

Contextual variables are variables that were constant at any one site but may have varied from site to site. In this case the tutoring sessions were held in the mornings at sites 1, 2, and 3, and after lunch at site 4. Additionally the time allowed for the tutoring was longer at site 4 so any effect of this must be considered confounded with a time of day effect, if such an effect exists. Other possible contextual effects would be the SES levels if the sites were in very different kinds of areas. With only four sites, the effects of contextual variables could not be examined adequately.

9. Interpret the size of the effect by reference to other information

9. Interpret the size of the effect by reference to other information

The best estimate of the effect of being a tutor on the tutor's own learning, in contrast with learning the topic in ordinary classroom conditions, appears from this study to be about 0.73 standard units if we exclude study 3. Below, this finding is interpreted from a variety of perspectives.

General expectation

Have there been previous meta-analyses with which the findings of this study can be compared? Cohen (1977) has suggested that ESs of about 0.20 are small, 0.50 are medium, and ESs of 0.80 are large.

General expectation

An effect size of about 0.70 is generally regarded as a medium effect (Cohen, 1977) and is slightly above the median value reported by Bloom (1984) in a list of ESs for various interventions to raise achievement.

Expectations from the specific literature

At the time of the study what is in the literature about this intervention?

Expectations from the specific literature

At the time of the study there were few controlled experiments in tutoring available in the literature and very few concerned with the effects on *the tutors*. (Since then Cohen, Kulik, & Kulik, 1982, conducted a meta analysis of 64 studies that yielded a value of .60 for the effects of tutoring in mathematics on tutors—a good fit with the results obtained here.)

Original metric

The outcome measure Y should be interpreted directly whenever possible. What test or measurement was Y exactly? If it was several different tests, then examine each separately. What did the mean difference imply in terms of number of items correct or in terms of shift in attitude (i.e., what was the meaning of the ES in the metric used)?

The difference made should be discussed in terms of the length and cost of the program.

Original metric

The test consisted of 65 items on fractions and the experimental group mean represented 56% of these items correct as opposed to only 34% in the control group. Thus the ES of .73 here indicated a difference of 22% of the marks on the posttest or 14 items that the E-group, on average, answered correctly but the C-group, on average, did not. Both groups made gains from the pretest but whereas the C-group gained only about 15 items the E-group gained about 29 items on average. This difference was not enormous, but it had arisen from a small three-week program. If the same difference in learning continued over many weeks, and was cumulative, the difference could be substantial.

Familiar metrics

Since an ES is a standardized mean difference, it might help to compare it directly with other standardized scales, such as

(1) the IQ scale to give the ES in terms of ABILITY EQUIV-ALENT UNITS
(2) GRADE EQUIVALENT UNITS: One standard deviation for

Familiar metrics

Ability Equivalent Units. If an ES of .73 is translated into the familiar IQ scale, and if the control group is regarded as average (mean IQ 100), then the experimental group behaved as though their IQ was 111. As a difference in *group* means this is substantial, as experienced teachers might have noticed.

| Steps | Example |

a Grade Equivalent score represents 10 months of instruction (as noted in Chapter 2).

Grade Equivalent Units. In terms of Grade Equivalent Units the ES of .73 would represent about 7 months of instruction. Thus it could be argued that if the difference held up across the entire syllabus and throughout the school year, the experimental group would be 7 months ahead of the control group at the end of the year. Of course, these are large assumptions: Not every part of the syllabus might lend itself as well to tutoring as the topic chosen here (fractions), and if tutoring were continued for a longer period some of the initial enthusiasm might wane. Nevertheless the translation into a Grade Equivalent Score provides a flag that says, "This was possibly an important effect."

Percentiles

If we assume normal distributions, then the E-group mean can be expressed as a percentile point in the C-group distribution.

Without making any assumptions, this percentile can be reported from the raw data if they are available. Count the number in the C-group with scores below the mean score for the E-group.

Percentiles

If we assume normal distributions, then an ES of 0.73 represents a percentile score of 77. The implication is that the average E-group student scored above 77% of the C-group.

Two More Adjustments That May Be Important

Throughout this book the emphasis is on the practical use of statistics. Complications that are of little practical import have been avoided. It is highly unlikely in the human sciences that *precision* of the measurements or statistics in any one study will be vitally important or informative. What is needed is the accumulation of many studies on the same topic, so that we get a sense of the stability and generalizability of the results we are getting. So it is with apology that two more complications are presented below. The first is included because small samples need to be encouraged. Waiting for studies with large samples may mean too long a wait and too few studies to indicate conditions under which the results replicate. If we are to encourage the use of small samples in well-controlled studies, we perhaps need the corrections for small sample sizes that Hedges and Olkin provided (1985). The second complication is included because it can have a potentially large effect and, if the problem is not recognized, we may all be misled about the sizes of effects or about their homogeneity.

These two complications are described with equations only. By now, readers will be able to set up their own spreadsheets to implement formulas.

Correction for small samples

For small samples the ES calculated from the sample data slightly over-estimates the population value. The estimate will be more accurate if reduced by a correction factor c.

Correction factor for small samples

$$c = 1 - \left[\frac{3}{4(n_E + n_C) - 9} \right]$$

Correction for small samples

The correction for small samples applied to the three homogeneous effect sizes was made by extracting data from Figure 56:

Site	NETNC	C	ES	Corrected ES
1	20	.958	.839	.804
2	16	.945	.735	.695
4	19	.955	.589	.563

Unweighted mean ES corrected for small samples = 0.687

As can be seen, the correction factor was not far from 1.00 (no correction) so that ES were not changed by large amounts.

Steps	Example

For samples smaller than 10 in the E-group or in the C-group you may wish to apply this correction factor at the end of Step 3, before recording effect sizes.

Correction for restricted ranges

In education, particularly, the situation of restricted ranges is likely to arise frequently. If an intervention is aimed at low achieving students, then the standard deviation of any outcome measure can be expected to be smaller than it would be if a full range of attainment were represented. The smaller standard deviation will inflate the ES. To make a correction we need to adjust the obtained standard deviation (the restricted SD) and use a value that would be the standard deviation in an unrestricted group.

$$\frac{\sigma^2_{rest}}{\sigma^2} = 1 + \frac{z_B H_B - z_A H_A}{1 - B - A} - \frac{(H_B - H_A)^2}{(1 - B - A)^2}$$

It seems appropriate to end with the well-loved normal curve.

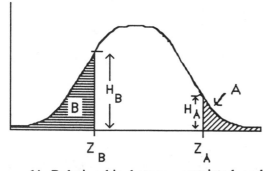

Figure 64. Relationship between restricted and unrestricted standard deviations

Correction for restricted ranges

The experimental and control groups had been drawn from the lower half of the ability range at each site but did not include students below 70 IQ (Z = –2.00). Thus the appropriate diagram was as follows:

The areas and ordinates were obtained from Table C.1.

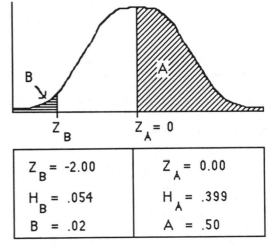

$Z_B = -2.00$	$Z_A = 0.00$
$H_B = .054$	$H_A = .399$
$B = .02$	$A = .50$

Figure 65

$$\frac{\sigma^2_{rest}}{\sigma^2} = 1 + \frac{(-2.00)(.054) - (0)(.399)}{1 - .02 - .50} - \frac{(.054 - .399)^2}{(1 - .02 - .50)^2}$$

$$= 1 + \frac{(-.108 - 0)}{.48} - \left(\frac{.119}{.23}\right)$$

$$= 1 + (-.225) - .517$$

Thus

$$\frac{\sigma^2_{rest}}{\sigma^2} = 0.258$$

so

$$\frac{\sigma_{rest}}{\sigma^2} = \sqrt{0.258} = 0.508$$

The value of σ we might wish to use would

thus be $\sigma = \dfrac{\sigma_{rest}}{0.508}$

By almost doubling the standard deviation, the ESs would be almost halved. The practice of correcting for restricted ranges did not appear widespread in the existing literature so it was decided to report ESs without this correction but to note on coding sheets the extent of restriction of range in the data.

Notes for SPSSX Users

Run 1 for Meta Analysis

```
DATA LIST / SITE 2, NEXPT 4-6 NCONT 8-10   T 12-15
    TREATCAT 20
BEGIN DATA INPUT
    1   8  12  1.84   1
    2   8   8  1.47   1
    3   7  12  4.02   2
    4  14   5  1.13   1
END DATA INPUT
VARIABLE LABELS  NEXPT 'no.in exptal.gp'
                 / NCONT 'no. in control gp.'
                 / T 'obtained t value'
```

COMMENT   compute d from the given t values

COMPUTE $D = T * SQRT((1/NEXPT)+(1/NCONT))$

COMMENT

    ******* to apply the correction for small samples

    *******use the commands on the next three lines:

    COMPUTE C = 1– (3/4*(NEXPT+ NCONT–2) –1))

    COMPUTE D=C*D

    VARIABLE LABELS D 'D corrected for small sample'

COMMENT   Compute the variance for each D

COMPUTE $V = ((NEXPT+NCONT)/(NEXPT*NCONT))+D**2/(2*(NEXPT+NCONT))$

COMMENT   Compute upper and lower 0.68 percent confidence limits for each D:

COMPUTE   LLIMDS=D–(SQRT(V))

COMPUTE   ULIMDS=D+(SQRT(V))

VARIABLE LABELS   ULIMDS 'upper CL, 68 percent'

VARIABLE LABELS   LLIMDS 'lower CL, 68 percent'

COMMENT   Next compute, for each affect size, quantities that will be needed for weighted averages

COMPUTE   W=1/V

COMPUTE   WD=D/V

COMPUTE   WDD=D**2/V

COMMENT   Have data printed out to 4 decimal places, for checking, not interpreting:

PRINT FORMATS   V,D,W,WD,WDD,LLIMDS, ULIMDS(F7.4)

COMMENT   If the range from LLIMDS to ULIMDS included 0 then that effect size was not significantly different from 0 at the 0.32 level.

COMPUTE case=\$CASENUM

LIST CASES   VARIABLES=case, NEXPT,NCONT, D,V,LLIMDS,ULIMDS, W,WD,WDD

COMMENT   Create a grouping variable that defines the entire data set as one group and then aggregate for the entire group. Also have LIST CASES to check that data have been read in correctly:

COMPUTE   WHOLEGP=1

FILE HANDLE   HMETASP1 /NAME='HMETASP1'

AGGREGATE   OUTFILE=HMETASP1
     / BREAK= WHOLEGP
     /SUMWD'weighted sum of Ds' = SUM(WD)
     /SUMW 'Sum of weights' = SUM(W)
     /SUMWDD 'Sum of W * D-squared' = SUM(WDD)

COMMENT   If the range from LLIMD to ULIMD includes 0 then that effect size was not significantly different from 0 at the 0.05 level, of course.

FILE HANDLE   'HMETASPS /NAME=HMETASPS'

SAVE OUTFILE=HMETASPS

FINISH

\$ENDFILE

\$SIGNOFF

Some Output From Run 1

CASE	NEXPT	NCONT	D	V	LLIMDS	ULIMDS	W	WD	WDD
1.00	8	12	.8398	.2260	.3645	1.3152	4.4254	3.7167	3.1214
2.00	8	8	.7350	.2669	.2184	1.2516	3.7470	2.7540	2.0242
3.00	7	12	1.9119	.3224	1.3441	2.4797	3.1019	5.9305	11.3385
4.00	14	5	.5887	.2805	.0590	1.1184	3.5644	2.0984	1.2354

NUMBER OF CASES READ = 4   NUMBER OF CASES LISTED = 4

A SYSTEM FILE HAS BEEN WRITTEN TO THE FILE DESIGNATED BY 'HMETASP1'.
IT CONTAINS 4 VARIABLES AND 1 CASE.

Run 2 for Meta Analysis

FILE HANDLE HMETASP1 /NAME='HMETASP1'

GET FILE   HMETASP1

COMMENT   Compute DDOT=D. the best estimate of delta, the population effect size, based on the whole group of ESs:

COMPUTE   DDOD=SUMWD/SUMW

COMMENT   compute the confidence limits on DDOT:

COMPUTE   SIGMA=SQRT(1/SUMW)

```
COMPUTE          LLDDOT=DDOT-1.96*SIGMA
COMPUTE          ULDDOT=DDOT+1.96*SIGMA
COMMENT:   Compute HTOT1=the homogeneity sta-
           tistic for the whole set:
                HTOT1=SUMWDD-
                ((SUMWD**2)/SUMW)
PRINT FORMATS  DDOT,ULDDOT,LLDDOT,
               HTOT1(F7.4)
LIST CASES     CASES=/VARIABLES=ALL
```

COMMENT   The larger the homogeneity statistic the more HETEROGENEOUS the set of effect sizes. Test for significant heterogeneity (i.e. lack of consistency among ESs) by noting that HTOT is distributed as chi-square with df=k–1 where k is the number of ESs.

```
FINISH
$ENDFILE
$SIGNOFF
```

Some Output From Run 2

```
FILE:       AGGREGATED FILE

WHOLEGP  SUMWD   SUMW  SUMWDD   DDOT SIGMA  LLDDOT  ULDDOT  HTOT1

  1.00   14.50  14.84   17.72  .9771   .26   .4683  1.4860 3.5512
```

References

Bloom, B.S. (1984) *The 2 sigma problem: The search for methods of group instruction as effective as one-to-one tutoring.* Educational Researcher.

Campbell, D. T. & Fisk, D. W. (1950) Convergent and discriminant validation by the multivariant-multimethod matrix. *Psychological Bulletin, 56*(2): 81-105.

Carver, R. P. (1978) The case against statistical significance testing. *Harvard Educational Review, 48*(3): 378-399.

Cohen, J. (1977) *Statistical power analysis for the behavioral sciences.* New York: Academic Press.

Cohen, P.A., Kulik, J.A., & Kulik, C.L. (1982) Educational outcomes of tutoring: A meta-analysis of findings. *American Educational Research Journal, 19*(2): 237-248.

Fisher, R.A. (1921) *On the probable error of a coefficient of correlation deduced from a small sample.* Metron Part 4.

Fitz-Gibbon, C. T. & Morris, L. L. (1975) Theory-based evaluation. *Evaluation Comment, 5*(1): 1-4.

Fitz-Gibbon, C.T. (1984) Meta-analysis: An explication. *British Educational Research Journal, 10*(2): 135-144.

Glass, G. V, McGaw, B. & Smith, M.L. (1981) *Meta-analysis in social research.* Newbury Park, CA: Sage.

Hedges, L.V. & Olkin, I. (1985) *Statistical methods for meta-analysis.* New York: Academic Press.

Hotelling, H. (1940) The selection of variates for use in prediction with some comments on the general problem of nuisance parameters. *Annals of Mathematical Statistics, 11*: 271-283.

Newton, J.S. (1987) Terse Reports 1: Three methods of history teaching. *Evaluation Research in Education, 1*(1): 39-41.

Pearson, E.S. & Hartley, H.D. (1970) *Biometrika tables for statisticians.* Cambridge: Cambridge University Press.

Slavin, R.E. (1984) Meta-analysis in education: How has it been used? *Educational Researcher, 13*(8): 6-15, 24-27.

Tukey, J.W. (1977) *Exploratory data analysis.* London: Addison-Wesley.

We call it simply "a five".
If the young woman on the left of the illustration has an empty
bag into which she puts ten of these chips, what is the
probability that, when the young man on the right pulls out a
chip from the bag, it will be a five?

-> Probability = ____

Since there are only "fives" in the bag, it is a certainty that
the chip pulled will be a five. Thus the probability is 1.00 or
100%. (Remember that 100 _percent_ means 100 /100 = 1.00)

Suppose the young woman empties the bag then places into it ten
"fives" and ten "threes". Now what is the probability that the
young man will, without looking, select a five?

-> Probability of drawing a five from n = 10 fives and n = 10
   threes is ____

You are correct if you think he has an even chance this time,
fifty-fifty. The probability is 0.50 or 50%. To put it in a
general form, the chance of getting a particular result is given
by the proportion:

```
       No. of ways of getting the particular result
       ------------------------------------------------
              Total no. of results possible
```

In the last case the number of ways of getting a five (the
"particular result") was 10 and the total number of possible
results was 20.

We could illustrate the distribution of fives and threes in the
bag as follows:

```
                      x     x
                      x     x
                      x     x
                      x     x
                      x     x
               --------------------
                1  2  3  4  5  6
```

Each x stands for a chip.

Here is another distribution of chips in the bag:

Distribution A

```
                   x  x  x  x  x
                   x  x  x  x  x
               --------------------------------
                1  2  3  4  5  6  7  8  9  10
```

-> How many chips are there in the bag? ____
-> How many fives are there? ____
-> What is the probability, this time, that the young man will
   draw a five? ____

== The number of chips in distribution A was n = 10, made up of two
   threes, two fours, two fives, two sixes and two sevens.

== There were thus n = 2 fives.

== The probability of the "particular result," drawing a 5, is
   given as follows:

```
    no. of ways of getting
    the particular result                No. of ways of getting 5
  ------------------------------   =    -------------------------------
  total no. of possible results         total no. of possible results

                                     = 2/10
                                     = 0.20
```

The chance of drawing a 5 was 1/5th, 0.20 or 20 percent.

Try a few more examples. For each distribution state the
probability of drawing a five.

Distribution B

```
                x              x
                x              x
                x  x  x  x     x  x
               --------------------------------
                1  2  3  4  5  6  7  8  9  10
```

-> Probability of drawing a five from distribution B = ____

== 1/10 = 0.10

Figure A.1

This is a "chip" with the number "5" on it.

Figure A.2

Distribution C

```
                    x
                    x
                x   x   x   x   x
        ------------------------------
        1   2   3   4   5   6   7   8   9   10
```

-> Probability of drawing a five from distribution C = ___

== 4/8 = 0.50

Distribution D

```
                x
            x   x   x
        x   x   x   x   x   x
        ------------------------------
        1   2   3   4   5   6   7   8   9   10
```

-> Probability of drawing a five from distribution D = ___

== 1/10 = 0.10

Now the young lady has some chips marked with a negative number
e.g.

Figure A.3

Suppose she puts into the bag the following distribution of chips

```
                x   x   x   x   x   x   x   x
            x   x   x   x   x   x   x   x   x   x   x   x
        ----------------------------------------------------
        -10 -9  -8  -7  -6  -5  -4  -3  -2  -1  0   1   2   3   4   5   6   7
```

-> What is the probability of drawing out +5? ___

== 1/20 = 0.05

-> What is the probability of drawing out -5? ___

== 1/20 = 0.05

-> What is the probability of drawing out any kind of 5? ___

== 2/20 = 0.10

Here are a couple more examples: In these examples we'll call the
value of the chip "z" and use the notation Pr(A) for "the
probability of A".

Distribution E

```
                            x
                            x
                x       x   x   x               x
        x   x   x   x   x   x   x   x   x   x   x   x   x
        ------------------------------------------------
        -6  -5  -4  -3  -2  -1  0   1   2   3   4   5   6
```

-> What is the probability of drawing a +5 chip, i.e. what is
    Pr(z = 5)? ___

== 2/20 = 0.10

-> What is Pr(z = -5)? ___

== 2/20 = 0.10

-> What is Pr(|z| = 5)? ___

== 2/20 = 0.20 (|z| = "mod" z = value of z ignoring the sign
                       = "absolute value of z")

Distribution F

```
                            x
                    x       x   x
        x   x   x   x   x   x   x   x   x   x   x
        ----------------------------------------
        -5  -4  -3  -2  -1  0   1   2   3   4   5
```

-> Pr(z = 5) = ___

== 1/15 ~ 0.0667

-> Pr(z = -5) = ___

== 1/15 ~ 0.0667

-> Pr(|z| = 5) = ___

== 2/15 ~ 0.133

We will now look at the probability of getting any one of a range
of scores rather than just any one score.

What is the probability, given distribution F, that the young man
will draw either a +3, a +4 or a +5? Stating the question another
way, what is the probability that z ⩾ or = 3, i.e. z is greater than
or equal to 3?

-> Pr(z ⩾ 3) = ___

In this case the "particular result of interest is "a 3 or a 4 or a
5". The probability is given by:

$$\frac{\text{no. of ways of getting the particular result}}{\text{total no. of results possible}} = \frac{3}{15} = \frac{1}{5} = 0.20$$

-> What is Pr(|z| ⩾ 3) in distribution F? ___

== 6/15 = 0.40

Revision Questions

Referring back to the distribution named, report the
probabilities named in the following ten questions.

1. Distribution A Pr (x = 3)   = ____

2. Distribution B Pr (z ⩾ 7)   = ____

3.   "   Pr (z ⩽ 6)   = ____

4. Distribution C Pr (z ⩾ 5)   = ____

5. Distribution D Pr (z ⩽ 3)   = ____

6. Distribution E Pr (|z| ⩾ 6) = ____

7.   "   E Pr (|z| ⩾ 3) = ____

8. Distribution F Pr (z ⩾ 4)   = ____

9.   "   F Pr (z ⩽ -4) = ____

10.   "   F Pr (|z| ⩾ 4) = ____

Now consider this distribution of "chips" which could be scores
on a test:

Distribution G

(There are 100 "X"s)

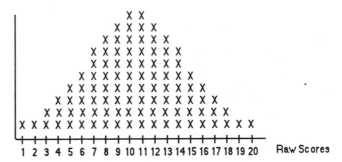

Figure A.4

Below is "distribution N". It has 100 "X"s as distribution G had.
The only difference is that the horizontal axis has been assigned
a different set of numbers. For each of the following statements
about distribution N, indicate if the statement is true or false.

Distribution N

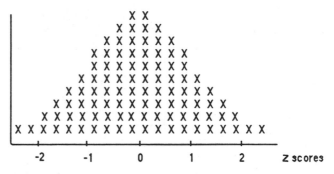

Figure A.5

_____ 1.   The probability of an observation larger than 1, i.e.
           Pr (z > 1) is 16 or 16%.

_____ 2.   The probability of an observation larger than 2,
           regardless of sign, is 0.04 or 4%.

_____ 3.   In general for this shape of a distribution, the
           further the value of z is from the centre of the
           distribution, the smaller the associated probability of
           obtaining that value on one observation.

_____ 4.   The chance of obtaining a chip (an observation) with
           absolute values smaller that 1 is 0.34 or 34% ("absolute
           value" of z = mod z = |z| = value of z without the
           sign).

_____ 5.   The chance of obtaining an observation with absolute
           values less than 2 is 96%.

Answers: 1. True 2. True 3. True 4. False, 68% 5. True

The distribution last looked at, distribution N, is roughly
equivalent to a "normal" distribution, the one that Lady Luck is
most likely to put in the bag when her selection of chips is the
result of random events.

Now look at this way of representing the probability associated
with the value of the chips:

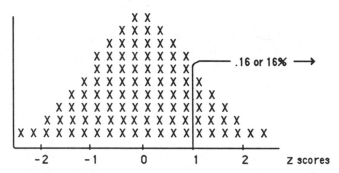

Figure A.6

The CRITICAL VALUE z = 1.0 cuts off the top of 16% of the
distribution. That is the critical value 1.0 has an associated
probability of .16. How many "X"s are there, therefore, between
0 and 1.0? Since there must be 50 "X"s to the right of the 0,
and there are 16 beyond 1.0, there must be 34 between 0 and 1.0.
You can check this by counting on the figure. Note also that
with 16 "x"s above z = 1, there must be 84 "x"s below z = 1.

Now examine the table "The Normal Distribution" which is in
Appendix B. Find the z value 1.00. The proportion associated
with it in the table is .84 (correct to two decimal places).
This is, the probability of obtaining such an observation or one
smaller than it from a normal distribution (i.e. from a bag in
which Lady Luck has arranged a distribution with the
characteristics of a normal curve).

Now let's move from considering discrete Xs to considering a
"continuous" distribution shown by a curve.

To compare the continuous normal curve with the discrete
distribution, fill in the correct numbers on the following two
diagrams. Fill in one value on the left by counting "X"s, then
fill in the value on the right by reference to the table of the
Normal Distribution.

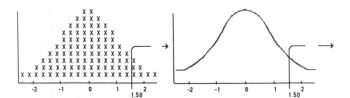

Figure A.7

The answer to the last question is given below. The shaded area
under the curve in the "upper tail" of the distribution is the
probability of z larger than 1.5. You read .93 from the table
and subtract it from 1.00 to obtain the area in the upper tail of
the distribution.

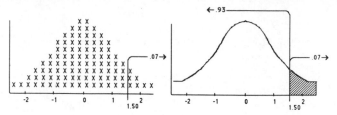

Figure A.8

Here is another example: Look up in the table, again, z = 1.00
and examine the figure below.

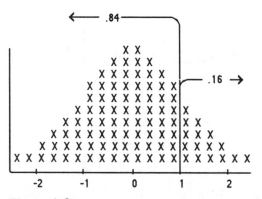

Figure A.9

The critical value z = 1.0 divides the distribution so that 84%
(that is 50 + 34) of the observations fall below z = 1 and 16%
fall above it. There are 84 "chips" below z = 1 in the
distribution and 16 "chips" (represented by "X"s) above z = 1.

To summarize: the normal distribution of 100 discrete chips can
be replaced by a continuous curve representing the distribution
of a set of observations.

The Normal Curve

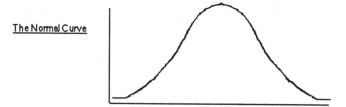

Figure A.10

Instead of counting "X"s, we can think of the area under the
curve as representing the probability. For example to find the
probability of getting an observation with a value as large or
larger than 2.00 look up z = 2.00 in the table. The associated
area is 0.977 which rounds to 0.98. Thus the area above 2.00 on
the normal curve is 0.02 or 2%, approximately.

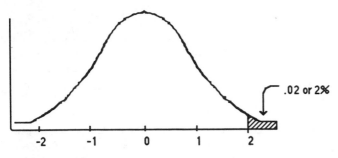

Figure A.11

Using the table for the Normal Distribution, fill out the probabilities associate with the z values on the next pair of diagrams.

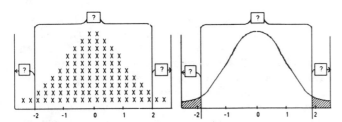

Figure A.12

ANSWERS: For the diagram on the left the probability of drawing a chip <u>larger than 2</u> is .02 or 2% and the probability of an observation <u>less than -2</u> is also .02 or 2%. The middle box for the <u>left</u> diagram, (the diagram showing a distribution of one hundred discrete "observations") is to represent the probability of a score falling within the range of values between -2 and 2. This probability is 96% or .96. The figure .96 can be found by counting the Xs or by subtracting the 4 Xs in the two tails of the distribution from 100, since there are 100 Xs in all.

For the right hand diagram we find from the normal distribution table the entry" 1.96 ... 0.975. The value 1.96 was chosen because it is a very commonly used cut-off score.)

$$1.00 - 0.975 = 0.025$$

Thus the probability of an observation larger than z = 1.96 is .025 or 2.5%. The probability of an observation smaller than z = 1.96 is .025 or 2.5%. What therefore is the probability of a score more extreme than 1.96? (i.e. What is the probability that |z| >= 1.96 ___)

ANS: .025 + .025 = .05 or 5%

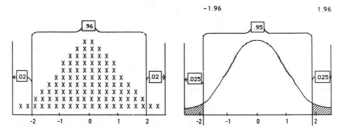

Figure A.13

The probability of an observation or score <u>larger than</u>, say, 1.96 is called a <u>one-tail</u> probability, because it represents the probability of scores in one tail (the upper tail) of the distribution. Similarly the probability of an observation or score <u>less than</u> -1.96 is also a one-tail probability.

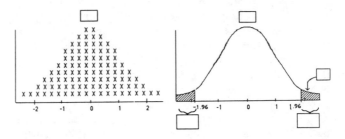

Figure A.14

The probability that a score will be <u>either larger than or smaller than</u> this value is called a <u>two-tail</u> probability, because it represents the probability of scores in <u>either tail</u> of the distribution.

You have now reached a point at which you can see where some of the numbers used in statistical hypothesis testing come from.

Appendix B

A Shortened Version of "Theory-Based Evaluation"

Which originally appeared in *Evaluation Comment*
by Carol Taylor Fitz-Gibbon
and Lynn Lyons Morris

What do we mean by theory-based evaluation? A theory-based evaluation of a program is one in which the selection of program features is determined by an explicit conceptualization of the program in terms of a theory, a theory which attempts to explain how the program produces the desired effects. The theory might be psychological, such as a theory of child development (e.g., Piaget's) or a theory of learning (e.g., S → R theory), or social psychological (e.g., attitude change theories; organization theories) or philosophical (e.g., the "Summerhill" philosophy). The essential characteristic is that the theory points out a causal relationship between a process A and an outcome B. A → B; that is, A leads to, or causes, B. (A, of course, may consist of many necessary components or stages—the whole process deemed necessary, by the theory, to produce B.) Thus, by a "theory-based" evaluation, we do not mean an evaluation based on a theory about evaluation. We mean rather, one based on a theory about how a program operates. Perhaps the inclusion of philosophies as theories needs some justification, especially as we shall subsume "models" under the same rubric. We justify the inclusion by defining a philosophy as a set of attitudes. There has been extensive consideration of the nature of attitudes in the literature of social psychology. In the affect-cognition model (Rosenberg, 1960), Rosenberg postulates that a person's attitude toward X is a function of the expectation (subjective probability) that X leads to Y and an emotional response to Y.

$$\text{Attitude to } X = f \begin{pmatrix} \text{subjective} & \text{emotion} \\ \text{probability,} & \text{associated} \\ X \to Y & \text{with } Y \end{pmatrix}$$

In the cognitive component, there is a postulated causal relationship: the perceived probability that X → Y. Attitudes involve theories, therefore, since they postulate causal relationships. For this reason, philosophies, like theories, suggest variables to study and imply that certain outcomes are likely to occur from certain processes.

The term "theory-based" evaluation, then, means an evaluation based on a model, theory, or philosophy about how the program works; a model, theory, or philosophy which indicates the causal relationships supposedly operating in the program.

How does theory-based evaluation differ from the kind of evaluations currently produced?

As indicated by the preceding definition of theory-based evaluation, the major impact of choosing a theory-based mode of evaluation occurs at that very early stage of evaluation, when a selection is made of the program features or variables which will be studied. One cannot measure or observe or report on everything about a program; inevitably, one selects. Does one choose to measure atomistic variables such as positive words per minute uttered by the teacher, concrete "variables" such as materials used, cognitive variables such as reading difficulty of materials, molar variables such as teacher "directiveness," monetary variables such as cost per child, social-psychological variables such as peer acceptance and roles enacted, sociological variables such as socioeconomic status of teachers and students, or such a prosaic but perhaps powerful variable as hours spent on instruction? The possibilities are endless.

Stake (1967, p. 536) suggested that deciding which variables to study is an "essentially subjective commitment" in evaluation. Such a contention has the effect of closing discussion on the matter, relegating the problem to some intractable region of pure opinion. We do not agree with this position. The choice of variables to study need not remain a matter of opinion. Eventually, we will want to study those variables which explain the most variance in the outcomes of interest. Hopefully some of these variables will be manipulable and yield powerful positive results in improving educational practice. Discovering what these variables are is a major task for educational research, and not one that we can assume has already been accomplished.

When a theory-based evaluation is planned, the variables selected for study are those which a theory (this might be, but does not necessarily have to be, the theory on which the program itself is based) indicates are crucial in producing the desired program outcomes. The theory chosen is stated and the degree of its operationalization within the program is documented. The methods of theory-based evaluation would resemble, then, those traditionally used to measure degree of program implementation: questionnaires and interviews, examination of records and classroom observation.

An example of a theory-based evaluation

Skager's evaluation of the Los Angeles Alternative School (Skager, Morehouse, Russock, & Schumacher, 1973) struck us as a qualitatively different kind of evaluation, an approach to evaluation meriting a term of its own to describe its methodology. Skager and his associates were confronted with the task of evaluating an "alternative school" which was in its first year of operation. What variables were chosen for study? Skager based the selection of variables on a model and a philosophy. The model was Carroll's (1963) model of the school learning process from which Skager deduced, for example, the need to contrast the instruction provided to students who were high and low in "perseverance." The philosophy which informed the selection of variables was Neill's (1969) Summerhill philosophy, a cornerstone of which was understood to be that the student should choose freely what and when he studies, if indeed he studies at all. Working from these "theories" (Carroll's model and Neill's philosophy), Skager and his co-workers selected the variables which the evaluation would measure. Using Carroll's model, the extent to which low and high persevering students were treated differently in the school was assessed and taken as one indication of the quality of instruction. Selecting a crucial variable from Neill's philosophy, the manner in which students selected their activities was investigated, permitting a well-supported statement to be made that "the notion of freedom of choice for the individual child [was] a reality" (Skager et al., 1973, p. 42). This indicated a successful operationalization of Neill's philosophy.

We can note immediately several reasons why this theory-based evaluation was highly appropriate: (a) The program being evaluated was based to some extent on Neill's philosophy. In a sense, the theory-based evaluation was necessary as a check on program implementation, if for no other reason. (b) The audience for the evaluation report wanted to know if the philosophy had been operationalized. Many parents may have wanted the philosophy to be implemented out of a here-and-now quality-of-life concern, being willing to trust that the ultimate outcomes would be desirable, as predicted by the philosophy. (c) Many of the outcomes of greatest concern were not precisely measurable. One may find evaluators who will agree to measure creativity, mental health, and self-esteem, but one should not place great trust in such measurements. The existence and measurability of some variables have yet to be established. (d) Many important desired outcomes were of the nature of long-term consequences rather than immediately measurable outcomes. That is to say, even if over the long term some measures of mental health and vigor could be obtained, this does not mean that beneficial effects of a program could be detected at the end of one year.

When should theory-based evaluation be used?

We shall now attempt to typify situations in which theory-based evaluations appear to be a desirable, perhaps necessary manner of operation. Briefly, these are situations in which evaluation of process (A, in the A φ B conceptualization described earlier) must be assessed either because we are evaluating an instructional program that is itself based on theory or because the client asks questions to which only theory-based answers are now possible. Each situation is discussed below.

Theory-based evaluation should be done when the program to be evaluated is itself based upon a theory, model, or philosophy. If school personnel plan a program in which teaching is structured to conform to models which rest on theories or philosophies about people and schools, an evaluator should identify the operational components of the model and develop ways to measure these.

Theory-based evaluation, in this case, expands the evaluator's job to assessing "goodness of fit" of at least three factors:

- the fit between the theoretical interpretation of the model by program personnel and the evaluator's interpretation (which should represent an informed one)
- the fit between each of these interpretations and the operationalization of the program
- the fit between outcomes predicted by the model and observed outcomes (if the model indeed predicts outcomes that are measurable)

Theory-based evaluation should be employed where an instructional program aims toward distant or intangible outcomes. Outcomes might be unobservable at a given point in time if they involve some slow change, such as character development,

attitude change, or the development of complex problem-solving competencies. Such outcomes not only present enormous problems for measurement, but they also cannot be expected to reach a measurable magnitude in a year or two. They are outcomes that are intangible or so remote in future time that their effects might not be observable within the short time span of most evaluations.

Remoteness and inconcreteness of objectives seem, in fact, to be particularly characteristic of the humanistic trend in education. It seems that it will be good practice for the educational evaluator to adapt to this. After all, schools cannot and should not be forbidden to concern themselves with such complex, but important concepts as a child's self-esteem, and yet evaluation of a program might be required before such outcomes become evident or measurable. The evaluator should therefore expand his or her repertoire to include not only evaluation based on the measurement of immediate outcomes, but also theory-based evaluation, evaluation which recognizes and holds the program staff accountable for implementing the theory adopted for the instructional program. When the outcome B is postulated, by a theory, to follow from a certain process, A, then the process can be evaluated prior to the time when outcomes might possibly be measured. In these cases, the job of the evaluator, it seems, alters in focus: The evaluation question becomes

> Have the variables which theory indicates are crucial to the program actually been operationalized?

Perhaps the social sciences do not currently provide us with theories that are as reliable as those in the natural sciences, but there seems to be enough theoretical richness in psychology and sociology, for instance, to supply the evaluator with at least a place to begin.

A couple of cautions

One caution which needs to be advanced regarding theory-based evaluations is that citing unproven theory might inadvertently become an "appeal to authority" when included in reports to lay audiences. When evaluations of the kind we are discussing are performed, their theory-based nature should be carefully explained; the evaluator must stress the "if this theory is correct" basis of his or her conclusions. A second problem we foresee is that theory-based evaluation will require quite broadly educated and informed evaluators. The conceptualizations and operationalizations demanded will require greater familiarity with diverse theories and greater flexibility in designing the evaluation than a simple input/output analysis.

What advantages can be derived from conducting theory-based evaluations?

Exposure of assumptions. At present, evaluations are preponderantly atheoretical (Alkin, Kosecoff, Fitz-Gibbon, & Seligman, 1974). Rarely does the evaluator present any rational for the choice of variables (a sin of omission almost certainly attributable to tradition rather than to deliberate negligence). A hallmark of theory-based evaluation would be the presentation of a rational for the choice of variables to study. Of course, demanding that this rational be explicit exposes the evaluator to criticism which might otherwise be avoided had he or she stuck to tradition and slurred over this step. The selection of variables does occur, however, whether it be by subjective hunches, by simple adherence to tradition, or by theory-guided considerations. The requirement to spell out assumptions, while irksome, is frequently salutory in its effects.

Advancing knowledge. One value of a theory is its power to predict. Who among us can predict student learning, for example, solely from observation of the process of schooling? The literature is replete with prediction studies, but (apart from teacher effectiveness studies) they largely concern the prediction of student achievement from prior measurements of students. It would be an interesting challenge to competing theories of the process of learning to have several evaluators perform theory-based evaluations of several different programs, with each evaluator basing the evaluation on a particular theory of learning or instruction. How much evidence could be mustered from these theories which would accurately predict differences in the learning outcomes of the various programs? If a theory—when used to examine process in the way we have been advocating—could consistently discriminate between effective and ineffective programs, it would provide a solid foundation on which to base both the planning and evaluation of programs.

Cronbach (1963) in his highly influential article urging formative evaluation, expressed a similar hope (he used the term "course" where we have been using the term "program"):

In so far as possible, evaluation should be used to understand how the course produces its effects and what parameters influence its effectiveness. . . . Hopefully, evaluation studies will go beyond reporting on this or that course and help us understand educational learning. (p. 675)

References

Alkin, M. C., Kosecoff, J., Fitz-Gibbon, C. T., & Seligman, R. (1974). *Evaluation and decision making: The Title VII experience* (CSE Monograph Series in Evaluation, No. 4). Los Angeles: Center for the Study of Evaluation, University of California.

Carroll, J. B. (1963). A model of school learning. *Teachers College Record, 64*(8), 723-733.

Cronbach, L. J. (1963) Course improvement through evaluation. *Teachers College Record, 64*(8), 672-683.

Neill, A. S. (1969). Summerhill. New York: Hart Publishing Co.

Rosenberg, M. J. (1960). Cognitive reorganization in response to the hypnotic reversal of attitudinal affect. *Journal of Personality, 28*(1), 39-63. Quoted in Jones, E. E., & Gerard, H. B. (1967). *Foundations of social psychology.* New York: John Wiley.

Skager, R. Morehouse, K., Russock, R., & Schumacher, E. (1973). *Evaluation of the Los Angeles Alternative School: A report to the Board of Education of the Los Angeles Unified School District.* Los Angeles: Center for the Study of Evaluation, University of California.

Stake, R. E. (1967). The countenance of educational evaluation. *Teachers College Record, 68*(7), 523-540.

Appendix C
Tables

TABLE C.1
The Normal Curve

The table shows p, the proportion of a normal distribution which lies below a given z-score. The associated Y value is also shown.

Illustration:

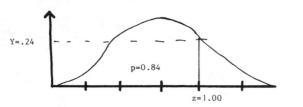

z	p	Y	z	p	Y	z	p	Y
1.50	.933	.129	2.00	.977	.053	2.50	.993	.017
1.51	.934	.127	2.01	.977	.052	2.51	.993	.017
1.52	.935	.125	2.02	.978	.051	2.52	.994	.016
1.53	.936	.123	2.03	.978	.050	2.53	.994	.016
1.54	.938	.121	2.04	.979	.049	2.54	.994	.105
1.55	.939	.120	2.05	.979	.048	2.55	.994	.015
1.56	.940	.118	2.06	.980	.047	2.56	.994	.015
1.57	.941	.116	2.07	.980	.046	2.57	.994	.014
1.58	.942	.114	2.08	.981	.045	2.58	.995	.014
1.59	.944	.112	2.09	.981	.044	2.59	.995	.013
1.60	.945	.110	2.10	.982	.043	2.60	.995	.013
1.61	.946	.109	2.11	.982	.043	2.61	.995	.013
1.62	.947	.107	2.12	.982	.042	2.62	.995	.012
1.63	.948	.105	2.13	.983	.041	2.63	.995	.012
1.64	.949	.103	2.14	.983	.040	2.64	.995	.012
1.65	.950	.102	2.15	.984	.039	2.65	.995	.011
1.66	.951	.100	2.16	.984	.038	2.66	.996	.011
1.67	.952	.098	2.17	.984	.037	2.67	.996	.011
1.68	.953	.097	2.18	.985	.037	2.68	.996	.010
1.69	.954	.095	2.19	.985	.036	2.69	.996	.010
1.70	.955	.094	2.20	.986	.035	2.70	.996	.010

z	p	Y	z	p	Y	z	p	Y
1.71	.956	.092	2.21	.986	.034	2.71	.996	.010
1.72	.957	.090	2.22	.986	.033	2.72	.996	.009
1.73	.958	.089	2.23	.987	.033	2.73	.996	.009
1.74	.959	.087	2.24	.987	.032	2.74	.996	.009
1.75	.959	.086	2.25	.987	.031	2.75	.997	.009
1.76	.960	.084	2.26	.988	.031	2.76	.997	.008
1.77	.961	.083	2.27	.988	.030	2.77	.997	.008
1.78	.962	.081	2.28	.988	.029	2.78	.997	.008
1.79	.963	.080	2.29	.988	.028	2.79	.997	.008
1.80	.964	.078	2.30	.989	.028	2.80	.997	.007
1.81	.964	.077	2.31	.989	.027	2.81	.997	.007
1.82	.965	.076	2.32	.989	.027	2.82	.997	.007
1.83	.966	.074	2.33	.990	.026	2.83	.997	.007
1.84	.967	.073	2.34	.990	.025	2.84	.997	.007
1.85	.967	.072	2.35	.990	.025	2.85	.997	.006
1.86	.968	.070	2.36	.990	.024	2.86	.997	.006
1.87	.969	.069	2.37	.991	.024	2.87	.997	.006
1.88	.969	.068	2.38	.991	.023	2.88	.998	.006
1.89	.970	.066	2.39	.991	.022	2.89	.998	.006
1.90	.971	.065	2.40	.991	.022	2.90	.998	.005
1.91	.971	.064	2.41	.992	.021	2.91	.998	.005
1.92	.972	.063	2.42	.992	.021	2.92	.998	.005
1.93	.973	.061	2.43	.992	.020	2.93	.998	.005
1.94	.973	.060	2.44	.992	.020	2.94	.998	.005
1.95	.974	.059	2.45	.992	.019	2.95	.998	.005
1.96	.975	.058	2.46	.993	.019	2.96	.998	.004
1.97	.975	.057	2.47	.993	.018	2.97	.998	.004
1.98	.976	.056	2.48	.993	.018	2.98	.998	.004
1.99	.976	.055	2.49	.993	.017	2.99	.998	.004
2.00	.977	.053	2.50	.993	.017	3.00	.998	.004

z	p	Y	z	p	Y	z	p	Y
.00	.500	.398	.50	.691	.352	1.00	.841	.241
.01	.503	.398	.51	.694	.350	1.01	.843	.239
.02	.507	.398	.52	.698	.348	1.02	.846	.237
.03	.511	.398	.53	.701	.346	1.03	.848	.234
.04	.515	.398	.54	.705	.344	1.04	.850	.232
.05	.519	.398	.55	.708	.342	1.05	.853	.229
.06	.523	.398	.56	.712	.341	1.06	.855	.227
.07	.527	.397	.57	.715	.339	1.07	.857	.225
.08	.531	.397	.58	.719	.337	1.08	.859	.222
.09	.535	.397	.59	.722	.335	1.09	.862	.220
.10	.539	.396	.60	.725	.333	1.10	.864	.217
.11	.543	.396	.61	.729	.331	1.11	.866	.215
.12	.547	.396	.62	.732	.329	1.12	.868	.213
.13	.551	.395	.63	.735	.327	1.13	.870	.210
.14	.555	.395	.64	.738	.325	1.14	.872	.208
.15	.559	.394	.65	.742	.322	1.15	.874	.205
.16	.563	.393	.66	.745	.320	1.16	.876	.203
.17	.567	.393	.67	.748	.318	1.17	.878	.201
.18	.571	.392	.68	.751	.316	1.18	.880	.198
.19	.575	.391	.69	.754	.314	1.19	.882	.196
.20	.579	.391	.70	.758	.312	1.20	.884	.194
.21	.583	.390	.71	.761	.310	1.21	.886	.191
.22	.587	.389	.72	.764	.307	1.22	.888	.189
.23	.590	.388	.73	.767	.305	1.23	.890	.187
.24	.594	.387	.74	.770	.303	1.24	.892	.184
.25	.598	.386	.75	.773	.301	1.25	.894	.182
.26	.602	.385	.76	.776	.298	1.26	.896	.180
.27	.606	.384	.77	.779	.296	1.27	.897	.178
.28	.610	.383	.78	.782	.294	1.28	.899	.175
.29	.614	.382	.79	.785	.292	1.29	.901	.173
.30	.617	.381	.80	.788	.289	1.30	.903	.171

z	p	Y	z	p	Y	z	p	Y
.31	.621	.380	.81	.791	.287	1.31	.904	.169
.32	.625	.379	.82	.793	.285	1.32	.906	.166
.33	.629	.377	.83	.796	.282	1.33	.908	.164
.34	.633	.376	.84	.799	.280	1.34	.909	.162
.35	.636	.375	.85	.802	.277	1.35	.911	.160
.36	.640	.373	.86	.805	.275	1.36	.913	.158
.37	.644	.372	.87	.807	.273	1.37	.914	.156
.38	.648	.371	.88	.810	.270	1.38	.916	.153
.39	.651	.369	.89	.813	.268	1.39	.917	.151
.40	.655	.368	.90	.815	.266	1.40	.919	.149
.41	.659	.366	.91	.818	.263	1.41	.920	.147
.42	.662	.365	.92	.821	.261	1.42	.923	.145
.43	.666	.363	.93	.823	.258	1.43	.923	.143
.44	.670	.362	.94	.826	.256	1.44	.925	.141
.45	.673	.360	.95	.828	.254	1.45	.926	.139
.46	.677	.358	.96	.831	.251	1.46	.927	.137
.47	.680	.357	.97	.833	.249	1.47	.929	.135
.48	.684	.355	.98	.836	.246	1.48	.930	.133
.49	.687	.353	.99	.838	.244	1.49	.931	.131
.50	.691	.352	1.00	.841	.241	1.50	.933	.129

TABLE C.2

Critical Values of z

The table shows the "level of significance" associated with a selection of z-scores. Read the level from the top line of the table for a two tail test or from the bottom line for a one tail test.

Illustration:

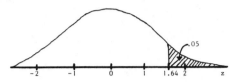

If z = 1.64 the level of significance using a two tail test was .10. For a one tail test the level of significance was .05.

Level for two tail test:	.50	.20	.10	.05	.02	.01	.001
z	.67	1.28	1.64	1.96	2.33	2.58	3.29
Level for one tail test:	.25	.10	.05	.025	.01	.005	.0005

TABLE C.3

Critical Values of t

Illustration:

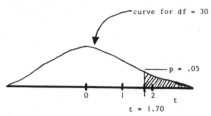

Level for two tail test:	.50	.20	.10	.05	.02	.01	.001
df							
1	1.00	3.07	6.31	12.70	31.82	63.65	636.62
2	.81	1.88	2.92	4.30	6.96	9.92	31.59
3	.76	1.63	2.35	3.18	4.54	5.84	12.92
4	.74	1.53	2.13	2.77	3.74	4.60	8.61
5	.72	1.47	2.01	2.57	3.36	4.03	6.86
6	.71	1.44	1.94	2.44	3.14	3.70	5.95
7	.71	1.41	1.89	2.36	2.99	3.49	5.40
8	.70	1.39	1.86	2.30	2.89	3.35	5.04
9	.70	1.38	1.83	2.26	2.82	3.25	4.78
10	.70	1.37	1.81	2.22	2.76	3.16	4.58
11	.69	1.36	1.79	2.20	2.71	3.10	4.43
12	.69	1.35	1.78	2.17	2.68	3.05	4.31
13	.69	1.35	1.77	2.16	2.65	3.01	4.22
14	.69	1.34	1.76	2.14	2.62	2.97	4.14
15	.69	1.34	1.75	2.13	2.60	2.94	4.07
16	.69	1.33	1.74	2.12	2.58	2.92	4.01
17	.68	1.33	1.74	2.11	2.56	2.89	3.96
18	.68	1.33	1.73	2.10	2.55	2.87	3.92
19	.68	1.32	1.72	2.09	2.53	2.86	3.88
20	.68	1.32	1.72	2.08	2.52	2.84	3.85
21	.68	1.32	1.72	2.08	2.51	2.83	3.81
22	.68	1.32	1.71	2.07	2.50	2.81	3.79
23	.68	1.31	1.71	2.06	2.50	2.80	3.76
24	.68	1.31	1.71	2.06	2.49	2.79	3.74
25	.68	1.31	1.70	2.06	2.48	2.78	3.72
26	.68	1.31	1.70	2.05	2.47	2.77	3.70
27	.68	1.31	1.70	2.05	2.47	2.77	3.69
28	.68	1.31	1.70	2.04	2.46	2.76	3.67
29	.68	1.31	1.69	2.04	2.46	2.75	3.65
30	.68	1.31	1.69	2.04	2.45	2.75	3.64
40	.68	1.30	1.68	2.02	2.42	2.70	3.55
60	.67	1.29	1.67	2.00	2.39	2.66	3.46
120	.67	1.28	1.65	1.98	2.35	2.61	3.37
	.67	1.28	1.64	1.96	2.32	2.57	3.29

120: For df larger than 200 treat t as z.

Level for one tail test:	.25	.10	.05	.025	.01	.005	.0005

Note: For independent t-test, df = $n_e + n_c - 2$

For paired data t-test, df = N-1 where N = no. of pairs

TABLE C.4
Critical Values of F

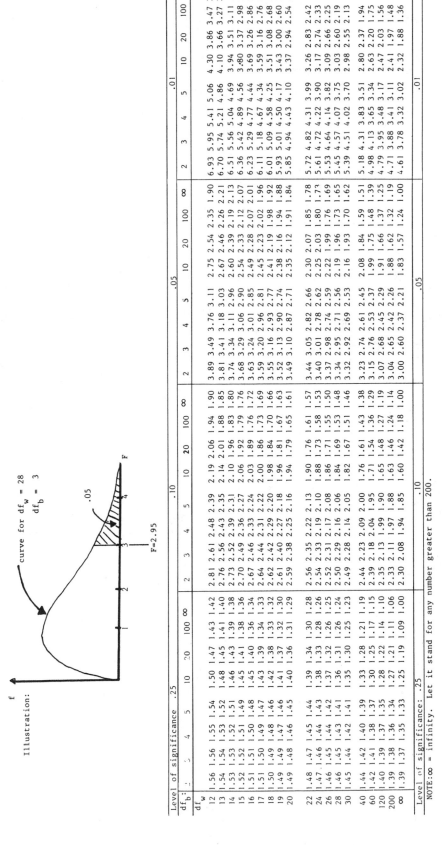

Illustration:

curve for $df_w = 28$
$df_b = 3$

.05

F=2.95

Level of significance

df_w	.25 df_b=2	3	4	5	10	20	100	∞	.10 df_b=2	3	4	5	10	20	100	∞
12	1.56	1.56	1.55	1.54	1.50	1.47	1.43	1.42	2.81	2.61	2.48	2.39	2.19	2.06	1.94	1.90
13	1.54	1.54	1.53	1.52	1.48	1.45	1.41	1.40	2.76	2.56	2.43	2.35	2.14	2.01	1.88	1.85
14	1.53	1.53	1.52	1.51	1.46	1.43	1.39	1.38	2.73	2.52	2.39	2.31	2.10	1.96	1.83	1.80
15	1.52	1.52	1.51	1.49	1.45	1.41	1.38	1.36	2.70	2.49	2.36	2.27	2.06	1.92	1.79	1.76
16	1.51	1.51	1.50	1.48	1.45	1.40	1.36	1.34	2.67	2.46	2.33	2.24	2.03	1.89	1.76	1.72
17	1.51	1.51	1.49	1.47	1.43	1.39	1.34	1.33	2.64	2.44	2.31	2.22	2.00	1.86	1.73	1.69
18	1.50	1.50	1.49	1.46	1.42	1.38	1.33	1.32	2.62	2.42	2.29	2.20	1.98	1.84	1.70	1.66
19	1.49	1.49	1.47	1.46	1.41	1.37	1.32	1.30	2.61	2.40	2.27	2.18	1.96	1.81	1.67	1.63
20	1.49	1.48	1.48	1.45	1.40	1.36	1.31	1.29	2.59	2.38	2.25	2.16	1.94	1.79	1.65	1.61
22	1.48	1.47	1.45	1.44	1.39	1.34	1.30	1.28	2.56	2.35	2.22	2.13	1.90	1.76	1.61	1.57
24	1.47	1.46	1.44	1.43	1.38	1.33	1.28	1.26	2.54	2.33	2.19	2.10	1.88	1.73	1.58	1.53
26	1.46	1.45	1.44	1.42	1.37	1.32	1.26	1.25	2.52	2.31	2.17	2.08	1.86	1.71	1.55	1.50
28	1.46	1.45	1.43	1.41	1.36	1.31	1.26	1.24	2.50	2.29	2.16	2.06	1.84	1.69	1.53	1.48
30	1.45	1.44	1.42	1.41	1.35	1.30	1.25	1.23	2.49	2.28	2.14	2.05	1.82	1.67	1.51	1.46
40	1.44	1.42	1.40	1.39	1.33	1.28	1.21	1.19	2.44	2.23	2.09	2.00	1.76	1.61	1.43	1.38
60	1.42	1.41	1.38	1.37	1.30	1.25	1.17	1.15	2.39	2.18	2.04	1.95	1.71	1.54	1.36	1.29
120	1.40	1.40	1.37	1.35	1.28	1.22	1.14	1.10	2.35	2.13	1.99	1.90	1.65	1.48	1.27	1.19
200	1.39	1.38	1.36	1.34	1.27	1.21	1.11	1.06	2.33	2.11	1.97	1.88	1.63	1.46	1.24	1.14
∞	1.39	1.37	1.35	1.33	1.25	1.19	1.09	1.00	2.30	2.08	1.94	1.85	1.60	1.42	1.18	1.00

Level of significance: .25 ... .10

df_w	.05 df_b=2	3	4	5	10	20	100	∞	.01 df_b=2	3	4	5	10	20	100	∞
12	3.89	3.49	3.26	3.11	2.75	2.54	2.35	1.90	6.93	5.95	5.41	5.06	4.30	3.86	3.47	3.36
13	3.81	3.41	3.18	3.03	2.67	2.46	2.26	2.21	6.70	5.74	5.21	4.86	4.10	3.66	3.27	3.17
14	3.74	3.34	3.11	2.96	2.60	2.39	2.19	2.13	6.51	5.56	5.04	4.69	3.94	3.51	3.11	3.00
15	3.68	3.29	3.06	2.90	2.54	2.33	2.12	2.07	6.36	5.42	4.89	4.56	3.80	3.37	2.98	2.87
16	3.63	3.24	3.01	2.85	2.49	2.28	2.07	2.01	6.23	5.29	4.77	4.44	3.69	3.26	2.86	2.75
17	3.59	3.20	2.96	2.81	2.45	2.23	2.02	1.96	6.11	5.18	4.67	4.34	3.59	3.16	2.76	2.65
18	3.55	3.16	2.93	2.77	2.41	2.19	1.98	1.92	6.01	5.09	4.58	4.25	3.51	3.08	2.68	2.57
19	3.52	3.13	2.90	2.74	2.38	2.16	1.94	1.88	5.93	5.01	4.50	4.17	3.43	3.00	2.60	2.49
20	3.49	3.10	2.87	2.71	2.35	2.12	1.91	1.84	5.85	4.94	4.43	4.10	3.37	2.94	2.54	2.42
22	3.44	3.05	2.82	2.66	2.30	2.07	1.85	1.78	5.72	4.82	4.31	3.99	3.26	2.83	2.42	2.31
24	3.40	3.01	2.78	2.62	2.25	2.03	1.80	1.73	5.61	4.72	4.22	3.90	3.17	2.74	2.33	2.21
26	3.37	2.98	2.74	2.59	2.22	1.99	1.76	1.69	5.53	4.64	4.14	3.82	3.09	2.66	2.25	2.13
28	3.34	2.95	2.71	2.56	2.19	1.96	1.73	1.65	5.45	4.57	4.07	3.75	3.03	2.60	2.19	2.06
30	3.32	2.92	2.69	2.53	2.16	1.93	1.70	1.62	5.39	4.51	4.02	3.70	2.98	2.55	2.13	2.01
40	3.23	2.74	2.61	2.45	2.08	1.84	1.59	1.51	5.18	4.31	3.83	3.51	2.80	2.37	1.94	1.80
60	3.15	2.76	2.53	2.37	1.99	1.75	1.48	1.39	4.98	4.13	3.65	3.34	2.63	2.20	1.75	1.60
120	3.07	2.68	2.45	2.29	1.91	1.66	1.37	1.25	4.79	3.95	3.48	3.17	2.47	2.03	1.56	1.38
200	3.04	2.65	2.42	2.26	1.88	1.62	1.32	1.19	4.71	3.88	3.41	3.11	2.41	1.97	1.48	1.28
∞	3.00	2.60	2.37	2.21	1.83	1.57	1.24	1.00	4.61	3.78	3.32	3.02	2.32	1.88	1.36	1.00

Level of significance: .05 ... .01

NOTE: ∞ = infinity. Let it stand for any number greater than 200.

TABLE C.5
Critical Values of Fmax

Level of significance (always one-tailed)		.05						.01			
k:	2	3	4	5	6		2	3	4	5	6
n-1											
5	7.15	10.8	13.7	16.3	18.7	5	14.9	22	28	33	38
6	5.82	8.38	10.4	12.1	13.7	6	11.1	15.5	19.1	22	25
7	4.99	6.94	8.44	9.70	10.8	7	8.89	12.1	14.5	16.5	18.4
8	4.43	6.00	7.18	8.12	9.03	8	7.50	9.9	11.7	13.2	14.5
9	4.03	5.34	6.31	7.11	7.80	9	6.54	8.5	9.9	11.1	12.1
10	3.72	4.85	5.67	6.34	6.92	10	5.85	7.4	8.6	9.6	10.4
12	3.28	4.16	4.79	5.30	5.72	12	4.91	6.1	6.9	7.6	8.2
15	2.86	3.54	4.01	4.37	4.68	15	4.07	4.9	5.5	6.0	6.4
20	2.46	2.95	3.29	3.54	3.76	20	3.32	3.8	4.3	4.6	4.9
30	2.07	2.40	2.61	2.78	2.91	30	2.63	3.0	3.3	3.4	3.6
60	1.67	1.85	1.96	2.04	2.11	60	1.96	2.2	2.3	2.4	2.4
∞	1.00	1.00	1.00	1.00	1.00	∞	1.00	1.0	1.0	1.0	1.0
Level of significance			.05						.01		

TABLE C.6
Critical Values of q

NOTE: q is used to compare pairs of means from a set of k groups of means. It may be used following a significant F value in ANOVA. The independent groups t-test could be used for such pairwise comparisons but results would have to be treated with caution as the t-test is based on the assumption of only two random samples. The q test keeps the type I error rate to the indicated level "EXPERIMENTWISE". The experimentwise type I error rate is the probability of making one or more false claims in an experiment, if H_0 is true.

$$q = \frac{\overline{x}_1 - \overline{x}_2}{\sqrt{\frac{MS_{within}}{n}}}$$

If group sizes are unequal, use $\dfrac{k}{(\frac{1}{n_1} + \frac{1}{n_2})}$ in place of n.

Level for two tail test:		.10					.05					.01			
k:	2	3	4	5	6	2	3	4	5	6	2	3	4	5	6
df within															
5	2.85	3.72	4.26	4.66	4.98	3.64	4.60	5.22	5.67	6.03	5.70	6.98	7.80	8.42	8.91
6	2.75	3.56	4.07	4.44	4.73	3.46	4.34	4.90	5.30	5.63	5.24	6.33	7.03	7.56	7.97
7	2.68	3.45	3.93	4.28	4.55	3.34	4.16	4.68	5.06	5.36	4.95	5.92	6.54	7.01	7.37
8	2.63	3.37	3.83	4.17	4.43	3.26	4.04	4.53	4.89	5.17	4.75	5.64	6.20	6.62	6.96
9	2.59	3.32	3.76	4.08	4.34	3.20	3.95	4.41	4.76	5.02	4.60	5.43	5.96	6.35	6.66
10	2.56	3.27	3.70	4.02	4.26	3.15	3.88	4.33	4.65	4.91	4.48	5.27	5.77	6.14	6.43
11	2.54	3.23	3.66	3.96	4.20	3.11	3.82	4.26	4.57	4.82	4.39	5.15	5.62	5.97	6.25
12	2.52	3.20	3.62	3.92	4.16	3.08	3.77	4.20	4.51	4.75	4.32	5.05	5.50	5.84	6.10
13	2.50	3.18	3.59	3.88	4.12	3.06	3.73	4.15	4.45	4.69	4.26	4.96	5.40	5.73	5.98
14	2.49	3.16	3.56	3.85	4.08	3.03	3.70	4.11	4.41	4.64	4.21	4.89	5.32	5.63	5.88
15	2.48	3.14	3.54	3.83	4.05	3.01	3.67	4.08	4.37	4.59	4.17	4.84	5.25	5.56	5.80
16	2.47	3.12	3.52	3.80	4.03	3.00	3.65	4.05	4.33	4.56	4.13	4.79	5.19	5.49	5.72
17	2.46	3.11	3.50	3.78	4.00	2.98	3.63	4.02	4.30	4.52	4.10	4.74	5.14	5.43	5.66
18	2.45	3.10	3.49	3.77	3.98	2.97	3.61	4.00	4.28	4.49	4.07	4.70	5.09	5.38	5.60
19	2.45	3.09	3.47	3.75	3.97	2.96	3.59	3.98	4.25	4.47	4.05	4.67	5.05	5.33	5.55
20	2.44	3.08	3.46	3.74	3.95	2.95	3.58	3.96	4.23	4.45	4.02	4.64	5.02	5.29	5.51
24	2.42	3.05	3.42	3.69	3.90	2.92	3.53	3.90	4.17	4.37	3.96	4.55	4.91	5.17	5.37
30	2.40	3.02	3.39	3.65	3.85	2.89	3.49	3.85	4.10	4.30	3.89	4.45	4.80	5.05	5.24
40	2.38	2.99	3.35	3.60	3.80	2.86	3.44	3.79	4.04	4.23	3.82	4.37	4.70	4.93	5.11
60	2.36	2.96	3.31	3.56	3.75	2.83	3.40	3.74	3.98	4.16	3.76	4.28	4.59	4.82	4.99
120	2.34	2.93	3.28	3.52	3.71	2.80	3.36	3.68	3.92	4.10	3.70	4.20	4.50	4.71	4.87
∞	2.33	2.90	3.24	3.48	3.66	2.77	3.31	3.63	3.86	4.03	3.64	4.12	4.40	4.60	4.76

NOTE: For more than 6 groups, consult Pearson and Hartley (1970) Table 29.

TABLE C.7
Critical Values of r

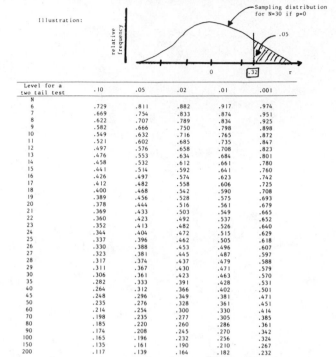

Level for a two tail test	.10	.05	.02	.01	.001
N					
6	.729	.811	.882	.917	.974
7	.669	.754	.833	.874	.951
8	.622	.707	.789	.834	.925
9	.582	.666	.750	.798	.898
10	.549	.632	.716	.765	.872
11	.521	.602	.685	.735	.847
12	.497	.576	.658	.708	.823
13	.476	.553	.634	.684	.801
14	.458	.532	.612	.661	.780
15	.441	.514	.592	.641	.760
16	.426	.497	.574	.623	.742
17	.412	.482	.558	.606	.725
18	.400	.468	.542	.590	.708
19	.389	.456	.528	.575	.693
20	.378	.444	.516	.561	.679
21	.369	.433	.503	.549	.665
22	.360	.423	.492	.537	.652
23	.352	.413	.482	.526	.640
24	.344	.404	.472	.515	.629
25	.337	.396	.462	.505	.618
26	.330	.388	.453	.496	.607
27	.323	.381	.445	.487	.597
28	.317	.374	.437	.479	.588
29	.311	.367	.430	.471	.579
30	.306	.361	.423	.463	.570
35	.282	.333	.391	.428	.531
40	.264	.312	.366	.402	.501
45	.248	.296	.349	.381	.471
50	.235	.276	.328	.361	.451
60	.214	.254	.300	.330	.414
70	.198	.235	.277	.305	.385
80	.185	.220	.260	.286	.361
90	.174	.208	.245	.270	.342
100	.165	.196	.232	.256	.324
150	.135	.161	.190	.210	.267
200	.117	.139	.164	.182	.232
Level for a one tail test:	.05	.025	.01	.005	.0005

NOTE: Critical values of r can be computed directly by looking up t for df = N-2 and then computing:

$$r = \frac{t}{\sqrt{t^2 + N-2}}$$

TABLE C.8
Changing r to Fisher's Z

r	Z	r	Z	r	Z	r	Z	r	Z
.000	.000	.200	.203	.400	.424	.600	.693	.800	1.099
.005	.005	.205	.208	.405	.430	.605	.701	.805	1.113
.010	.010	.210	.213	.410	.436	.610	.709	.810	1.127
.015	.015	.215	.218	.415	.442	.615	.717	.815	1.142
.020	.020	.220	.224	.420	.448	.620	.725	.820	1.157
.025	.025	.225	.229	.425	.454	.625	.733	.825	1.172
.030	.030	.230	.234	.430	.460	.630	.741	.830	1.188
.035	.035	.235	.239	.435	.466	.635	.750	.835	1.204
.040	.040	.240	.245	.440	.472	.640	.758	.840	1.221
.045	.045	.245	.250	.445	.478	.645	.767	.845	1.238
.050	.050	.250	.255	.450	.485	.650	.775	.850	1.256
.055	.055	.255	.261	.455	.491	.655	.784	.855	1.274
.060	.060	.260	.266	.460	.497	.660	.793	.860	1.293
.065	.065	.265	.271	.465	.504	.665	.802	.865	1.313
.070	.070	.270	.277	.470	.510	.670	.811	.870	1.333
.075	.075	.275	.282	.475	.517	.675	.820	.875	1.354
.080	.080	.280	.288	.480	.523	.680	.829	.880	1.376
.085	.085	.285	.293	.485	.530	.685	.838	.885	1.398
.090	.090	.290	.299	.490	.536	.690	.848	.890	1.422
.095	.095	.295	.304	.495	.543	.695	.858	.895	1.447
.100	.100	.300	.310	.500	.549	.700	.867	.900	1.472
.105	.105	.305	.315	.505	.556	.705	.877	.905	1.499
.110	.110	.310	.321	.510	.563	.710	.887	.910	1.528
.115	.116	.315	.326	.515	.570	.715	.897	.915	1.557
.120	.121	.320	.332	.520	.576	.720	.908	.920	1.589
.125	.126	.325	.337	.525	.583	.725	.918	.925	1.623
.130	.131	.330	.343	.530	.590	.730	.929	.930	1.658
.135	.136	.335	.348	.535	.597	.735	.940	.935	1.697
.140	.141	.340	.354	.540	.604	.740	.950	.940	1.738
.145	.146	.345	.360	.545	.611	.745	.962	.945	1.783
.150	.151	.350	.365	.550	.618	.750	.973	.950	1.832
.155	.156	.355	.371	.555	.626	.755	.984	.955	1.886
.160	.161	.360	.377	.560	.633	.760	.996	.960	1.946
.165	.167	.365	.383	.565	.640	.765	1.008	.965	2.014
.170	.172	.370	.388	.570	.648	.770	1.020	.970	2.092
.175	.177	.375	.394	.575	.655	.775	1.033	.975	2.185
.180	.182	.380	.400	.580	.662	.780	1.045	.980	2.298
.185	.187	.385	.406	.585	.670	.785	1.058	.985	2.443
.190	.192	.390	.412	.590	.678	.790	1.071	.990	2.647
.195	.198	.395	.418	.595	.685	.795	1.085	.995	2.994

TABLE C.9
Critical Values of chi-squares

Illustration:

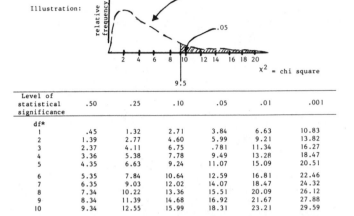

Level of statistical significance	.50	.25	.10	.05	.01	.001
df*						
1	.45	1.32	2.71	3.84	6.63	10.83
2	1.39	2.77	4.60	5.99	9.21	13.82
3	2.37	4.11	6.75	.781	11.34	16.27
4	3.36	5.38	7.78	9.49	13.28	18.47
5	4.35	6.63	9.24	11.07	15.09	20.51
6	5.35	7.84	10.64	12.59	16.81	22.46
7	6.35	9.03	12.02	14.07	18.47	24.32
8	7.34	10.22	13.36	15.51	20.09	26.12
9	8.34	11.39	14.68	16.92	21.67	27.88
10	9.34	12.55	15.99	18.31	23.21	29.59
11	10.34	13.70	17.27	19.67	24.72	31.26
12	11.34	14.84	18.55	21.03	26.22	32.91
13	12.34	15.98	19.81	22.36	27.69	34.53
14	13.34	17.11	21.06	23.68	29.14	36.12
15	14.34	18.24	22.31	24.99	30.58	37.70

NOTE: For an approximate value of x^2 if the df value is larger than 15, compute $x^2 = \frac{1}{2}(\sqrt{(df)*2-1} + z)^2$ using the z value below for the level of significance indicated at the top of the table.

z	0.00	0.67	1.28	1.96	2.33	3.09

*df = (r-1)(c-1) where r = number of rows
c = number of columns

CASE	SUBJECT	SCHOOLA	SEX	SES	AVOC	DISCUSS	DGROUPS	PAIRS	PRESENT	LISTEN	HARD	HARDEST	ONTIME	AGRADEN
1	1	A	2	3	5.55	5	3	1	2	2	4	3	4	4
2	1	A	1	1	5.75	4	3	3	2	2	4	3	4	4
3	1	A	2	3	5.90	5	2	2	2	2	4	4	4	5
4	1	A	1	2	5.11	5	4	5	5	5	4	2	4	4
5	1	A	1	2	4.60	4	2	2	2	2	3	2	4	2
6	1	A	2	3	5.33	4	3	3	2	2	3	2	2	3
7	1	A	2	3	6.25	5	3	1	1	1	4	3	5	4
8	1	A	2	2	4.55	5	3	1	2	2	4	3	4	0
9	1	A	2	2	4.10	5	3	3	2	2	3	3	5	0
10	1	A	2	1	5.67	5	2	1	1	1	4	3	4	1
11	1	A	1	2	6.00	5	3	2	3	3	3	2	4	5
12	1	A	2	2	5.89	3	2	3	2	2	4	4	4	4
13	1	A	2	2	4.73	5	2	3	3	2	5	5	4	5
14	1	A	1	2	4.30	5	3	2	3	3	2	2	4	0
15	1	A	2	2	3.55	4	4	3	3	3	3	1	4	0
16	1	A	1	2	3.75	5	2	2	2	2	3	2	4	2
17	1	C	2	3	5.50	4	4	3	4	4	3	2	4	3
18	1	C	2	2	4.50	3	3	2	2	2	4	1	5	4
19	1	C	1	2	4.20	4	3	3	3	3	4	4	4	5
20	1	C	2	2	4.50	3	4	4	4	4	3	2	4	2
21	1	C	2	2	5.77	5	5	5	4	4	3	1	2	2
22	1	C	2	2	4.90	3	3	3	3	3	2	2	2	1
23	1	C	2	2	5.56	3	4	3	3	3	4	3	5	2
24	1	C	2	2	5.73	4	3	4	4	4	1	1	4	2
25	1	C	2	2	4.33	4	3	4	2	2	2	2	4	3
26	1	C	2	3	4.70	5	5	4	4	5	3	3	4	3
27	1	C	2	1	4.67	5	2	4	4	4	4	2	4	2
28	1	C	2	2	4.50	5	5	4	5	5	4	2	4	1
29	1	C	2	2	5.89	3	4	3	3	3	4	2	4	4
30	1	C	1	2	4.22	3	2	3	3	3	3	2	4	0
31	1	D	2	2	3.00	5	1	1	1	1	3	2	3	0
32	1	D	2	1	5.00	3	3	3	1	1	4	3	4	0
33	1	D	2	2	4.88	5	2	2	1	1	4	2	4	0
34	1	D	1	3	5.00	5	4	4	1	1	4	.	3	0
35	1	D	2	1	3.33	4	2	1	1	1	3	1	2	0
36	1	D	2	2	3.23	4	2	1	1	1	3	2	4	2
37	1	D	2	1	2.29	1	1	1	1	1	3	2	4	0
38	1	D	1	1	5.00	4	3	2	1	4	4	5	5	0
39	1	D	2	2	4.38	5	4	4	1	1	4	3	4	1
40	1	D	1	2	4.89	3	3	2	1	1	3	2	3	0
41	1	D	1	2	3.80	2	2	2	1	1	1	1	1	2
42	1	D	2	1	2.90	5	2	2	1	1	3	1	1	0
43	1	D	2	1	3.80	5	3	2	1	1	2	1	1	0
44	1	D	2	2	3.43	4	2	1	1	1	1	1	3	0

45	1	D	1	2	4.36	3	2	2	1	1	3	3	4	2
46	1	D	1	1	3.45	2	3	1	1	2	3	2	2	0
47	2	A	1	3	5.36	1	1	1	1	1	1	1	1	0
48	2	A	2	3	6.40	1	1	1	1	1	2	1	4	3
49	2	A	1	2	4.50	1	1	1	1	1	3	2	4	2
50	2	A	1	2	5.15	1	1	1	1	1	3	2	4	2
51	2	A	2	2	5.73	2	1	1	1	1	3	2	4	0
52	2	A	1	3	6.18	1	1	4	1	1	5	3	5	4
53	2	A	2	2	6.13	2	1	2	1	1	4	3	4	0
54	2	A	1	2	4.58	1	1	1	1	1	3	2	4	1
55	2	A	1	3	4.82	1	1	1	1	1	3	1	4	0
56	2	A	1	3	5.27	1	1	1	1	1	2	2	2	0
57	2	A	1	2	4.27	1	1	1	1	1	1	1	4	0
58	2	A	2	3	6.11	1	1	1	1	1	1	1	4	2
59	2	A	2	2	6.11	2	1	2	1	1	4	3	4	2
60	2	A	1	3	4.85	1	1	4	1	1	4	3	4	4
61	2	A	1	2	6.00	1	1	1	1	1	5	4	5	4
62	2	A	1	2	4.67	1	1	1	2	1	1	1	2	0
63	2	A	2	2	5.00	1	1	1	1	1	4	4	5	4
64	2	A	1	1	6.00	3	1	1	1	1	3	3	5	3
65	2	A	1	2	5.56	1	1	1	1	1	3	2	3	1
66	2	B	1	2	4.36	1	1	2	1	1	2	1	4	0
67	2	B	2	2	3.36	3	2	1	1	1	1	2	3	0
68	2	B	2	2	4.00	3	2	2	1	1	2	1	3	0
69	2	B	1	1	4.14	3	3	1	1	1	3	3	4	5
70	2	B	1	1	4.62	2	2	2	2	2	3	3	4	0
71	2	B	1	2	3.08	2	1	2	1	1	2	2	4	0
72	2	B	2	1	3.75	4	2	1	1	2	1	1	4	2
73	2	B	1	1	5.50	2	2	3	2	2	3	4	4	1
74	2	B	1	1	4.21	2	2	2	2	.	2	2	4	0
75	2	B	1	2	5.25	4	2	2	1	1	4	2	4	5
76	2	B	1	1	4.00	4	1	1	1	2	3	2	4	0
77	2	E	2	1	4.11	1	1	1	1	1	5	.	5	4
78	2	E	1	1	4.45	1	1	1	1	1	1	1	1	5
79	2	E	2	1	4.70	1	1	1	1	1	1	1	4	0
80	2	E	2	2	4.40	2	1	2	1	1	4	.	4	2
81	2	E	1	1	4.09	1	1	1	1	1	2	3	4	4
82	2	E	1	3	5.44	1	1	1	1	1	3	1	4	3
83	2	E	1	2	5.80	1	1	1	1	1	4	2	4	3
84	2	E	1	1	4.33	1	2	3	1	1	2	1	3	2
85	2	E	1	3	5.70	3	1	1	1	1	4	3	3	5
86	2	E	2	2	6.00	1	1	1	1	1	4	4	5	4
87	2	E	2	2	5.11	2	1	2	1	1	4	.	5	4
88	2	E	1	1	5.64	2	1	1	1	1	4	2	5	2
89	2	E	2	2	4.79	1	1	1	1	1	5	4	5	4
90	2	E	2	3	5.80	1	1	1	1	1	4	3	4	4
91	2	E	1	2	3.75	3	1	1	1	1	3	2	4	0
92	2	E	1	2	3.92	1	1	2	1	1	4	3	4	0
93	2	E	1	1	5.50	1	1	1	1	1	2	1	4	4
94	2	E	1	2	3.83	1	1	1	1	1	2	1	2	0
95	2	E	1	1	3.57	1	1	1	1	1	5	3	4	3
96	2	E	1	1	3.33	1	1	1	1	1	4	4	4	0
97	2	E	2	2	5.10	1	1	1	1	1	2	1	2	0
98	2	E	2	2	4.36	1	1	1	1	1	2	1	3	0
99	2	E	2	3	4.78	2	1	3	1	1	1	2	4	0
100	2	E	2	1	5.17	2	1	3	1	1	2	1	2	2

Index

NOTES

NOTES

NOTES

NOTES